D1716732

Rule-based Programming with OPS5

Rule-based Programming with OPS5

Thomas Cooper and Nancy Wogrin

Digital Equipment Corporation

Foreword by John McDermott

Morgan Kaufmann Publishers, Inc.
San Mateo, California

Editor and President *Michael B. Morgan*
Production Manager *Shirley Jowell*
Book Design *Beverly Kennon-Kelley*
Cover Designer *Irene Imfeld*
Composition *Arthur Ogawa*
Illustrations *Marian E. Goldeen*
Copy Editor *Lyn Dupré*
Proofreader *Linda Medoff*

With grateful thanks to Harold Cohen for the illustration used on the front cover, and to Becky Cohen who photographed the illustration.

Library of Congress Cataloging-in-Publication Data is available

88-21519
ISBN 0-934613-51-6

Morgan Kaufmann Publishers, Inc.
2929 Campus Drive, Suite 260
San Mateo, CA 94403

Printed in the United States of America

ISBN: 0-934613-51-6

93 92 91 90 89 5 4 3 2 1

Foreword

IT IS A PLEASURE TO INTRODUCE this book because it provides significant insight into a very powerful, but as yet, poorly understood programming paradigm. OPS5 is about 10 years old. Although it has been used to develop several large, knowledge-based systems in use in industry, its use, at this point, is not very widespread. It is a low-level AI language in the sense that it does not supply mechanisms for performing particular kinds of search. Instead (unlike most other rule-based programming languages), it provides a powerful pattern-description capability that can be used to define precisely the situations within which a piece of knowledge will be relevent. This capability has shown itself to be effective in two types of tasks: (1) tasks in which many task features have significance for what to do next, but where only a small fraction of the possible combinations of features ever occur, and (2) tasks in which the order that actions need to be performed is highly variable. OPS5's pattern-matching capability satisfies the central problem-solving requirement for such tasks—the capability of effectively indexing into a large body of knowledge on the basis of a set of interrelated features.

OPS5 is a simple language; easy to learn to use, but also easy to misuse. The hard part about learning to be an effective OPS5 programmer is learning how to impose control in a way that will make the continued development of the program, the never-ending modification of the knowledge base, as straightforward as possible.

Novice programmers typically make two kinds of mistakes:

> They fail to identify explicitly the control knowledge in their programs (presumably because they have learned to program using languages such as COBOL or PASCAL, in which much of the control knowledge is carried in the sequence of instructions and is thus implicit).
>
> They over-control by imposing an ordering on subsets of instructions when the task does not demand an ordering (again presumably because in languages like COBOL or PASCAL the programmer is required to position each instruction with respect to the others).

This book is designed to help the would-be OPS5 programmer learn how to avoid such misuse of the language, presenting the collective wisdom of experienced OPS5 programmers in a well-organized fashion. The use of numerous examples of OPS5 programs makes it easy to make contact with the ideas.

I believe we are just beginning to appreciate how to exploit the power of languages like OPS5 and, as our understanding grows, we will discover a programming paradigm that can radically simplify our thinking about the computational requirements of certain classes of tasks. A programming language is valuable when it gives a programmer precisely the tools necessary to describe some problem-solving process, but it does not require the programmer to elaborate on parts of the process that are either irrelevant or repetitive. A programming language is also valuable when the set of tasks for which the language is appropriate is large. For some of the tasks OPS5 has been used to automate, the descriptive power of the language has turned out to fit very well with the needs of the programmer. As OPS5 is used more widely, we will understand just how broad its scope is.

This book provides a solid introduction to OPS5, and is also an ideal foundation on which to build an understanding of what higher-level control strategies are and how they can be integrated with OPS5. The authors offer practical advice based on what is being used to build successsful systems today, and give pointers to the current research being done in the area of higher-level control strategies. Wogrin and Cooper have not relied just on their own extensive experience with OPS5, but have spent a great deal of time interacting with other experienced OPS5 programmers and have thus ended up with strongly grounded guidelines for how to use OPS5 effectively. The book presents those guidelines clearly and concretely. Anyone who assimilates the programming insights presented in this book will be ready to engineer robust OPS5 applications now, and explore the use of higher-level control strategies as such strategies become better defined in the future.

John McDermott
Digital Equipment Corporation
Carnegie Mellon University

Preface

THE SURGE OF INTEREST in the field of artificial intelligence in the late 1970s and early 1980s motivated the development of a plethora of new programming languages, tools, and environments. The programmer that embarks on learning how to use one of these programs has no trouble finding out what each feature in the language is and does, but is usually left with the question: *How do I use it?*

OPS5 is a modest language with a small set of features and limited syntax. It was developed at Carnegie Mellon University by Charles Forgy, John McDermott, Allen Newell, and Mike Rychener during the late 1970s and early 1980s, motivated by the development of a very fast pattern-matching algorithm, called RETE. The original implementation of the language was in FRANZ LISP, which, along with implementations in several other LISP dialects, is available and in the public domain today.

There is no rule-based language to date that has been put to more rigorous use than has been OPS5. In addition to many small- and medium-sized applications, OPS5 is the implementation language of Digital Equipment Corporation's (DEC's) expert systems XCON (R1) and XSEL, which contain thousands of rules and are used daily for completing DEC™ orders and configuring DEC computers. The experience building and maintaining these systems resulted in a great deal of expertise using OPS5 for real-world systems—expertise that answered the question, *how do I use it?* Since such extensive, practical experience was rare and valuable, we decided to try to capture the techniques and methodology in a practical guide for OPS5 developers.

The capabilities of OPS5 do not differ significantly among implementations, and we have tried to remain as independent of specific implementations as possible. Most of the code in this book should run in any OPS5 implementation. Where there are distinctions between implementations, we usually draw on examples from a COMMON LISP OPS5 implementation to represent LISP-based OPS5s, and from VAX OPS5™, DEC's OPS5 product, to represent non-LISP implementations. Appendix A catalogs the differences between these implementations. When we refer to features that are specific to VAX OPS5, we say so explicitly in the text.

We assume that the reader is familiar with the fundamentals of software engineering, such as data structures, data abstraction, and structured design. Experience with another programming language is helpful, particularly to understand and use the material in Chapter 8, *External Routines*; users of a LISP-based OPS5 will find LISP programming skills extremely useful. We do not assume that the reader has had experience with rule-based programming, expert systems, or artificial intelligence, although the programming methodology we present is motivated by expert-system domains.

Acknowledgments

The expertise that went into writing this book comes from many sources, the most important being the Intelligent Systems Technologies group at Digital Equipment Corporation. Thanks to our "team" of internal reviewers: Mike Kiskiel, Edmund Orciuch, Judy Bachant, and especially John Frost, our most persistent and timely reviewer. There are many people we have to thank for sharing their expertise on specific topics: Bill Barabash, Bob Breau, Robin Downs, Alan Ewald, Michelle Fineblum, Ken Gilbert, Mike Grimes, Keith Jensen, Robin Krumholz, Lisa Spielman, Tom Stones, and Bill Yerazunis. We want to thank John McDermott for his critical reviews.

A special thanks to Mike Kiskiel for his enthusiasm and help in getting us started, and to Dennis O'Connor, Frank Lynch, and Sandra S. Mills for helping us do this project with DEC's blessing. Thanks to Jeff Clanon for giving us the opportunity to test material on the students of the Intelligent Systems Technology Training Program. The feedback from the students and from other instructors who used the material has greatly improved this book.

The thorough comments from the reviewers outside of DEC were extremely helpful in checking our biases. We hope that Donald Rosenthal, Paul Birkel, Gregg Vesonder and Wayne Homren find enough of their comments incorporated in the final text to meet their standards.

Finally, we could not have made it through these last 3 years without the support, encouragement, and understanding of our families. We would like to dedicate this book to them. Nancy dedicates this book to Tom Gruber. Tom dedicates this book to his wife Sue.

Tom Cooper
Marlboro, Massachusetts

Nancy Wogrin
Palo Alto, California

March 1988

Contents

CHAPTER 1

An Introduction to Rule-based Systems and OPS5

OPS5 BELONGS TO a class of programming languages that are based on the general computational strategy called a rule-based system, or production system.* The strategy is straightforward; as the basis of a programming language, it is both simple and powerful.

This chapter covers background material on rule-based languages, and provides the motivation for using a rule-based language as a computer-programming language. It introduces the underlying problem-solving logic of rule-based languages without using terms specific to OPS5. It answers questions frequently asked by new users, and lists characteristics of the problem domains for which OPS5 is appropriate.

There is much related material that this chapter intentionally touches on only lightly or omits. We believe that this material has been covered adequately in other sources and is not central to the task of programming in OPS5. For readers who want more information on important topics, Section 1.6 suggests sources for further reading.

1.1 An Overview of Rule-based Systems

The first use of a rule-based system is attributed to the mathematician E. Post in 1943 [Post 1943]. He called his system a *production system*. Production

---

*A distinction can be made between rule-based systems and production systems [Waterman 1978]; for our purposes, we use the terms synonymously.

systems represent the solution to a problem as a set of rules that specify "how some string of symbols may be transformed into other strings of symbols" [Minsky 1967]. Variations of this idea have since been applied in several other contexts, including algorithms (Markov algorithms [Markov 1954]), linguistics (Chomsky's "rewrite rules" [Chomsky 1957]), psychology (Newell and Simon's studies of human problem-solving behavior [Newell 1972]), and as in this book, a general computer-programming language.

Most people are familiar with applications of production systems. An example familiar to most elementary school students is the rules of English grammar. A grammar rule transforms one part of speech into its component parts or into words in the language. For example, a sentence (`S`) can be transformed into a noun phrase (`NP`) and verb phrase (`VP`), or the part of speech `determiner` can be transformed into the word *the*. Figure 1.1 lists a few simple grammar rules of this type.

If we start with the symbol `S`, we can use these rules to generate a grammatical English sentence. There is only one rule (numbered 1) that transforms `S`; when we apply that rule we are left with the two symbols `NP` and `VP`. When we try to transform further the symbols `NP` and `VP`, we see that both can be transformed by more than one rule. For now, we arbitrarily choose which of these rules to use. Figure 1.2 shows the process of using one rule at a time to transform `S` into a complete sentence.

Let's look more closely at the steps we used to apply each rule in Figure 1.2. We started with one or more symbols. We matched the symbols we had with the left-hand side of the rules (the part before the arrow). This is a simple form of *pattern matching*. Pattern matching can become quite complicated in rule-based systems, and has to be implemented efficiently if the rule-based language is to be useable.

---

1. `S` ⟶ `NP VP`
2. `NP` ⟶ `Det Adj Noun`
3. `NP` ⟶ `Det Noun`
4. `NP` ⟶ `Noun`
5. `VP` ⟶ `Verb`
6. `VP` ⟶ `Verb NP`
7. `Det` ⟶ the
8. `Noun` ⟶ cat
9. `Noun` ⟶ river
10. `Noun` ⟶ south
11. `Verb` ⟶ swam
12. `Verb` ⟶ flew
13. `Adj` ⟶ hesitant
14. `Adj` ⟶ chilly

Key: `S` — sentence
`NP` — noun phrase
`VP` — verb phrase
`Det` — determiner
`Adj` — adjective

Figure 1.1 Production rules for a subset of English grammar.

Rule Applied	Resulting Expression
	S
S ⟶ NP VP	NP VP
NP ⟶ Det Adj Noun	Det Adj Noun VP
Det ⟶ the	The Adj Noun VP
Adj ⟶ hesitant	The hesitant Noun VP
Noun ⟶ cat	The hesitant cat VP
VP ⟶ Verb NP	The hesitant cat Verb NP
Verb ⟶ swam	The hesitant cat swam NP
NP ⟶ Det Noun	The hesitant cat swam Det Noun
Det ⟶ the	The hesitant cat swam the Noun
Noun ⟶ river	The hesitant cat swam the river.

Figure 1.2 Using the grammar rules shown in Figure 1.1.

When there was more than one rule that matched our current pattern, we took the extra step of deciding which rule to use. In Figure 1.2, we decided which rule to apply at each step, deliberately choosing rules so that the resulting sentence had meaning. Notice that we could have chosen different rules and ended up with a different sentence; we also could have used the same rules but in a different order, yielding the same sentence. The point here is that the result of using the rules depends on which and in what order those rules are applied. Rule-based computer languages have to institute strategies for making these decisions, or have to implement a set of strategies from which the programmer can choose.

When we chose the rule to use, we applied the rule by replacing our pattern with the pattern on the right-hand side of the rule. In rule-based languages, the relationship between the left- and right-hand sides of the rule may represent something other than a replacement. The right-hand side may assert a new, related statement, or may contain a set of actions to perform. The transformation of one pattern to another in a rule-based language is understood to represent an IF–THEN implication. Rules can express associations between concepts:

IF
  this is rain
  and we're in Spain
THEN
  we must be on the plain

or operations to be performed:

IF
  block A is on block B
  and A has nothing on top of it

THEN
  take block A off block B

The computer implementation of a rule-based system distinguishes among three components (Figure 1.3): the rule base, the working memory, and the rule interpreter.

The set of rules, like those in Figure 1.1, is called the *rule base*. The rule base is analogous to the "program" of other computer languages.

The data that represent the state of problem-solving at any time (the patterns) are held in a separate storage area called *working memory*. The data are matched to and transformed by rules when the program runs.

Finally, the computer language has to have the machinery, usually called a *rule interpreter*, or inference engine, that runs the program. The interpreter does the matching between the data and the rules and chooses the rule to apply at each step.

1.2 Forward and Backward Chaining

The previous section covered only one of the possible uses of rules. We made the assumption that the current pattern is matched to the left-hand side of the rule and is transformed into the new pattern on the right-hand side. But what would happen if our initial data were the sentence

```
The chilly bird flew south
```

and we wanted to find out whether the sentence was grammatically correct?

To answer this question, we can use the same set of rules that we used to generate grammatical sentences. One way to do this is to start generating all possible grammatical sentences from the symbol S until we have generated the sentence in question. Or, we can imagine the arrow in the rules pointing

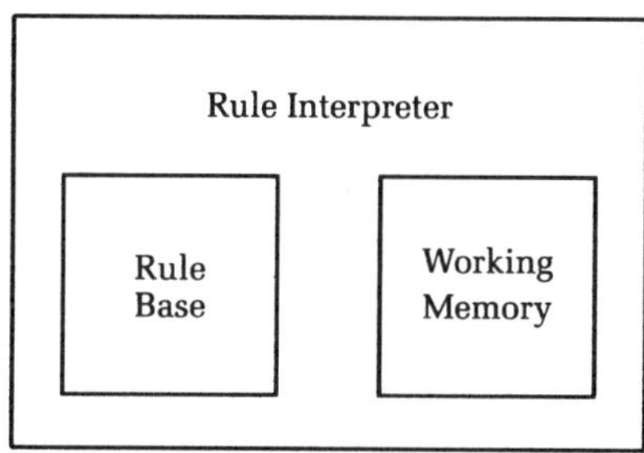

Figure 1.3 The components of a rule-based language.

in the opposite direction, and thus make the reverse implications to reduce the sentence first to grammatical structures such as `Noun` and `Adj`, and finally to the symbol `S`. Figure 1.4 shows the process of proving the sentence to be grammatically correct by using the rules in the "opposite direction."

The way we have used the grammar rules from left to right to generate a sentence, and from right to left to prove the correctness of a sentence, are simple examples of *forward* and *backward chaining.* "Forward" and "backward" here refers to the direction we travel in the steps we use to solve a problem; we can move forward from some current state to a goal state, or backward from a desired goal to a state that confirms the goal.

Forward-chaining problems usually have a large number of data in their initial state from which a solution must be constructed. Typically, there is neither a single nor an optimal goal state—there is only a set of constraints to which the goal must conform. At each step in a forward-chaining process the question is, "What is the next step to take to move closer to the goal?"

Scheduling problems can usually be solved by forward-chaining rules. A scheduling task starts with the events or objects to be scheduled and the constraints on putting the parts together. The final schedule is generated by heuristics (rules of thumb) that satisfy the constraints.

Backward-chaining problems start with a hypothesis or goal, and derive the substantiating evidence for that conclusion. At each step in a backward-chaining process the question is, "What must be true in order for the current state to be true?" Backward-chaining problems are those for which a set of solutions is known and for which the current case must be classified as one of the known solutions. Diagnostic problems are the most common examples of backward-chaining problems.

One way to tell whether a problem should be solved by forward or backward chaining is to look at its initial and goal states. If the initial state contains many facts that must be synthesized into a solution, then forward chaining is appropriate. If there is a description of a current state that must be analyzed to

Rule Applied	**Resulting Expression**
	The chilly bird flew south
Det ← the	Det chilly bird flew south
Adj ← chilly	Det Adj bird flew south
Noun ← bird	Det Adj Noun flew south
Verb ← flew	Det Adj Noun Verb south
Noun ← south	Det Adj Noun Verb Noun
NP ← Det Adj Noun	NP Verb Noun
VP ← Verb Noun	NP VP
S ← NP VP	S

Figure 1.4 Using the grammar rules in the opposite direction.

find the facts in the database that support that state, then backward chaining is more suitable. Some problems are best solved using a combination of backward and forward chaining: Forward chaining produces results that must be confirmed by backward chaining.

OPS5 executes rules in a forward-chaining fashion. It is most often used to *construct* solutions. Although the rule interpreter is inherently forward-chaining, OPS5 can also be programmed for backward-chaining problem solving. An OPS5 program can create data that represent a hypotheses or goal (forward chaining) and can then determine whether that goal can be confirmed (backward chaining).

1.3 Problem Domains for Rule-based Languages and OPS5

Rule-based systems have been used for many types of problems, such as scheduling, configuration, and monitoring. Rather than producing an exhaustive list of problem types, however, we identify some of the characteristics of problems that can be solved with rule-based programming, and specifically with OPS5. Not all of these characteristics must be true for a problem to be suitable for a rule-based solution.

- *Symbolic manipulation is required.* Some problems can be solved only by manipulation of symbols rather than by numeric calculation. Rule-based languages manipulate symbols by pattern matching between data and rules. The OPS5 rule interpreter is based on an efficient pattern-matching algorithm.

- *The problem is difficult or impractical to formulate as an algorithm.* An algorithm is a powerful tool to have for solving a problem. It provides a verifiable, step-by-step problem-solving strategy that is adequate for defined input data. Sequential languages have the control constructs necessary for implementing algorithms. Rule-based languages, on the other hand, are best at implementing heuristics, which are reliable but not guaranteed methods for reaching a solution. In these problems, the amount and complexity of the knowledge used to solve the problem is such that there is no general solution for all cases, so exception cases are treated individually. Sometimes, a problem is programmed in a rule-based language because the algorithm is not yet known. The process of encoding it in rules may elucidate the algorithmic portions.

- *An optimal solution is not required.* Because a rule-based system implements heuristics, it is important that the problems it solves do not require a mathematically optimal solution.

- *The problem requires a growing or changing knowledge base.* Rules are modular nuggets of information that are not explicitly directed by control statements in the program. In some rule bases, it is possible to add or remove rules without changing the overall structure of the program or the information about the program's flow of control. If a program is based on a large amount of constantly changing information, the capability to change the information easily may be crucial.

- *The solution to the problem is naturally expressed in IF–THEN rules.* The first rule-based systems were used for expert systems.* One of the reasons cited for this use is that it is more common and natural for people to express what they know as IF–THEN associations, rather than as algorithms or all-inclusive theories [Barr 1981] [Newell 1972]. When an OPS5 program is based on human problem solving that has not been encoded previously in any computer representation, it is important that the process be expressed in IF–THEN rules.

1.4 Questions Frequently Asked About OPS5

No matter how well-suited a problem is for a rule-based solution, there are myriad practical considerations that are important to choosing the right language for a project. This section answers frequently asked, practical questions about OPS5.

Is it difficult to learn to program in OPS5?

OPS5 has a limited, simple syntax. It is easy for a person to learn all the actions, functions, and operators. The difficulty in learning OPS5 lies in becoming accustomed to how the rule interpreter works, and in learning how to write rules that produce meaningful results. Most nonprogrammers learn the language easily, as do programmers who are already familiar with more than one programming language. The people most likely to have difficulty learning the language are programmers who know only one other sequential language, perhaps because these programmers have never seen alternative approaches to control strategies.

Can an OPS5 program communicate with databases and programs that are written in other languages?

OPS5 has a call-out facility to communicate with routines written in other languages. The extent of this ability varies with the implementation; some OPS5 implementations can call to only routines written in LISP, others can call to numerous other languages and applications, including databases. Chapter 8, *External Routines*, discusses the use of external routines with OPS5.

*Expert systems are computer programs that perform a task in a specialized area of expertise. Their performance is usually expected to be comparable to that of a human expert.

Does OPS5 have mechanisms for reasoning with uncertainty? Does it provide an explanation facility?

Many of the early rule-based systems (such as MYCIN [Buchanan 1984b]) used certainty factors to express the relative degree of belief among hypotheses, and also had the ability to explain their reasoning to a user. There are no standard mechanisms for either of these capabilities in OPS5. These facilities must be developed by the programmer or development team, and often are written in a language other than OPS5.

Is OPS5 efficient during run-time?

The efficiency of OPS5 depends on the implementation. The efficiency of implementations that compile rules into executable code compares favorably to that of programs written in most sequential languages such as FORTRAN or PASCAL. Implementations that compile rules into data structures to be interpreted, as do many LISP-based OPS5 ones, could be noticeably slower, especially for large rule bases.

It is difficult, however, to compare the efficiency of a rule-based system to that of a sequential program because the kinds of problems the two are meant to solve differ. The worth of the ability of OPS5 to solve large, complex, nonalgorithmic problems with *acceptable* performance cannot be measured in central processing unit (CPU) seconds.

OPS5 programs can be written so as to maximize run-time efficiency. Chapter 10, *Efficiency*, explains what is and what is not efficient in an OPS5 program.

Is OPS5 good for prototyping?

OPS5 can be a good tool for prototyping. Most knowledge-intensive problems, even those with algorithmic solutions, can be structured as a set of IF–THEN rules. The advantage of prototyping in OPS5 is that the programmer can concentrate less on control statements and more on understanding and representing the knowledge of the domain. From the prototype, the algorithmic portions become apparent and can be reimplemented using a sequential programming language (see Chapters 11 and 12).

Can OPS5 be used in projects involving multiple programmers?

It is possible to develop an OPS5 program in modules of rules that represent functional units. These modules can be managed using standard code-management systems. More than one developer, therefore, can work on the same OPS5 program. Again, however, the ease of multiprogrammer development depends on the implementation of OPS5. Implementations that support modular compilation are more easily adapted to projects for which there is more than one programmer.

In Chapter 12, *Building and Testing OPS5 Systems*, we discuss developing large systems.

Is it difficult to maintain an OPS5 program?

Theoretically, an advantage of programming in a rule-based language is the ease with which rules can be added or removed from the rule base. In reality, many tasks cannot be performed adequately without substantial amounts of control; thus the OPS5 programmer must define control strategies that will restrict the knowledge that can be brought to bear at any given time. Within a defined control strategy, however, the rules are data-driven and are not interdependent. Maintenance within this framework is easier in an OPS5 program than in a sequential program, since control strategies do not have to be modified with every change in functionality.

Are there development tools for programming in OPS5?

The original OPS5 manual written by Charles Forgy at CMU [Forgy 1981] contained descriptions of a core set of debugging and run-time utilities. These have been extended in successive implementations, and many OPS5 implementations now include a multiwindow development environment.

In Chapter 6, *Debugging an OPS5 Program*, and Chapter 12, *Building and Testing OPS5 Systems*, we describe user-written tools that are useful in the development and maintenance of large-scale OPS5 programs.

1.5 Contrasting Sequential and Rule-based Languages

If you are already familiar with programming in one or more computer languages that are *not* rule-based, you may make assumptions that hold for most computer languages but that are not true of OPS5.

The most notable difference between OPS5 and other programming languages is that the control of program flow in OPS5 is not expressed in explicit control statements. The language is *data-driven*; the rule interpreter chooses the rule to execute depending on the data that match the rules. There are no conditional branches, calls to OPS5 subroutines or procedures, nor any iterative loops. When an OPS5 program executes, rather than there being a single thread of control that solves the problem, there can be many, parallel control paths. It is not useful to trace the paths through the program by looking at the code alone.

Since there is a need for some control over the order of steps in a rule-based program, OPS5 programmers have developed programming techniques that affect how groups of rules are chosen and executed. This level of control, however, is not part of the language's definition or syntax.

The entire state of an OPS5 program is described by the contents of working memory. Working memory is global in the sense that all rules are matched to all data; you can not make some data specific to a subset of rules or hide information. Also, rather than data being passed between program components, the data used by an OPS5 rule are obtained by matching patterns in working memory.

The differences in control structures and program state require programmers to develop OPS5 programming techniques that are different from the techniques for sequential languages. Although it is possible to simulate familiar control structures in OPS5, to do so is not making the best use of the language. This book describes the most effective ways to use OPS5.

1.6 Further Reading

Rule-based computer languages have been used primarily in the field of artificial intelligence, particularly for expert systems. One of the earliest expert systems, which has been written about extensively, is MYCIN [Buchanan 1984b]. An early work on expert systems by the original researchers in the field is *Building Expert Systems* [Hayes-Roth 1983]. A more practical, business-oriented introduction to expert systems is *Expert Systems* [Harmon 1985].

The field of artificial intelligence does not have one all-inclusive source of reference, but the three volumes of the *Handbook of Artificial Intelligence* [Barr 1981] provides a good technical introduction to the various sub-fields. Nilsson's *Principles of Artificial Intelligence* [Nilsson 1980] and Winston's *Artificial Intelligence* [Winston 1984] are both programming-oriented introductions to the field. Many of the seminal research papers of the field are collected in *Readings in Artificial Intelligence* [Webber 1981] and *Readings in Knowledge Representation* [Brachman 1985].

There have been studies of artificial intelligence languages that include OPS5, the earliest being in *Building Expert Systems* [Hayes-Roth 1983]. Brownston and associates in their *Programming Expert Systems in OPS5* [Brownston 1985], include a comparison of OPS5 with other tools. Definitive evaluations and comparisons of tools are difficult to find; Harmon compares tools using a common set of criteria [Harmon 1985, Harmon 1988].

One promising approach to the definition and use of higher-level control strategies in OPS5 programs is the RIME methodology [Marcus 1988]. Its effectiveness is discussed in [Soloway 1987].

Summary

- OPS5 is a rule-based language founded on the general computational strategy called a rule-based system, or production system.
- The components of a rule-based system are a rule base, a database called working memory, and a rule interpreter that is the machinery that runs the program. The rule interpreter matches the data to the rules and chooses which rule to apply.

- A rule base employs either forward or backward chaining. The terms "forward" and "backward" commonly refer to the direction of problem solving. A forward-chaining system uses the rules to move from a set of initial data to construct a goal. A backward-chaining system starts with a desired goal or hypothesis and derives the substantiating evidence for that conclusion.
- OPS5 is inherently a forward-chaining rule-based language that can be used for forward- and backward-chaining problem solving.
- OPS5 is suited for domains that are difficult to formulate as an algorithm, that require symbolic expression, for which there is a growing and or changing knowledge base, or in which the solution is "naturally" expressed in IF–THEN rules. A problem programmed in OPS5 should not require an optimal solution.
- The difference between OPS5 and most other computer languages is that OPS5 does not use explicit control statements, and it encodes program state as the entire set of elements in the database.

Exercises

1. Assume you plan to solve the following problems using rules. For each, decide whether you should use a forward- or backward-chaining approach. Explain your choices.
   a. Welding assistant: Advises junior welders on how they can improve their skills based on feedback from a quality-control mechanism that explains characteristics of faulty welds.
   b. Pharmacist's assistant: Keeps track of drugs prescribed to each customer to check for potentially harmful drug interactions, and for contraindications of drugs based on a customer's personal characteristics.
   c. Distribution manager: Advises how to use a fleet of trucks that distributes goods from several manufacturing plants.
2. Write a set of IF–THEN rules in English to supply a robot with the following capabilities. The robot knows how to do only four things:
   a. Lift a bin from storage.
   b. Place a bin on the belt.
   c. Lift a bin from the belt.
   d. Place a bin in storage.

   The robot can lift a bin from storage and place a bin on a belt only when it receives a GO signal from its controller and when there is a clear space on the belt. Conversely, the robot can lift the bin off the belt and place the bin in storage only when it receives a WAIT signal from its controller and there is a bin before it on the belt.

CHAPTER 2

OPS5 Syntax

THE PREVIOUS CHAPTER introduced the three components of a rule-based language:

1. *Rule base.* A collection of rules that make up the "program"*
2. *Working memory.* The database that holds the symbols that are matched to and manipulated by the rules
3. *Rule interpreter.* The machinery for matching elements in working memory to rules and for choosing the rule to execute

The basics of each of these components are covered in the following chapters. This chapter introduces the syntax for the language, by which we mean the notation for writing rules and for describing the elements of working memory. Chapter 3 explains how to write an OPS5 program. The rule interpreter is described in Chapter 4.

Although there is no official standard for the syntax of OPS5, Forgy's *OPS5 User's Manual* [Forgy 1981] is usually accepted as the de facto standard. The syntax in this chapter is based on Forgy's specification. In later chapters, we refer to extensions to the language provided by VAX OPS5™ and other OPS5 implementations in the context of advanced programming techniques. The differences between the syntax of the original LISP implementation and

---

*The rule base is also called *production memory* or *rule memory.*

VAX OPS5 are highlighted throughout this chapter and are summarized in Appendix A.

Most examples and concepts in this book use only the syntax that is introduced in this chapter. OPS5 syntax is very simple. The power of the language lies not in the constructs defined by the language, but in the programming techniques for using it. These techniques are the subject of subsequent chapters of this book.

This chapter can either be read as an introduction to the language syntax or used as a reference. It should be supplemented with the documentation for your specific implementation of OPS5. The chapter is organized so that topics are introduced in the same order that you encounter that topic when writing an OPS5 program: the structure of working memory, the elements of working memory, rules, and finally the functions.

2.1 The Room-Assignment Problem

The room-assignment problem is used to illustrate the points in this and subsequent chapters. The goal of this program is to assign students to temporary housing in an apartment complex while they attend training courses of various lengths.

The apartments vary by the number of occupants they can accommodate. There are four sizes: singles, doubles, triples, and quads. It is most economical to fill the largest apartments first. It is preferable to keep single apartments empty as long as possible to accomodate students who have special needs.

There are two factors taken into consideration when placing students in the same room: the students must be of the same gender, and they must either all be smokers or all be nonsmokers.

Note that this problem conforms to some of our criteria for a good OPS5 domain. There are two sets of symbolic data (rooms and students) that are fit together according to a set of constraints (gender and smoking preference). Using a brute-force method to enumerate all possible combinations of students and rooms is infeasible for large numbers of students. The heuristic approach, however, produces a satisfactory solution by describing the conditions under which students can be placed in the same room.

2.2 Working Memory

Working memory represents the state of computation of an OPS5 program. It is composed of the set of all *working memory elements*. In this book we refer to a working memory element as a *WME* (pronounced wimmie). In our example of an English grammar, each grammar symbol, such as S, could be represented in OPS5 by a WME. In practice, however, a WME typically contains many symbols. Thus, the *state* of working memory in OPS5 is defined by the WMEs and by their contents at a given point in time.

Working memory is the focus of an OPS5 program. Instead of approaching a problem with the question, "What is the *process* used to solve this problem?" in OPS5 the question is, "What are the main *entities* in this problem, and how are they manipulated?" Entity definitions help to define key WMEs, and entity manipulations help to define key rules.

Working memory is defined by both the structure of its WMEs and their contents. The first step is to define the structure of the elements that are in working memory.

2.2.1 The Structure of Working Memory: Element Classes

Each element in working memory is an instance of an *element class*. An element class defines a WME structure in the same way that a PASCAL data type defines the structure of entities in a PASCAL program. An element class is not an entity that can be manipulated; it is the mold from which instances can be made. An element class is identified by a *class name* and by a set of *attributes* that refer to relevant features that describe the entity. These roughly correspond to a PASCAL record type declaration, which defines the type and set of field names to access various values of the record.

For the room-assignment problem, the two main entities that are manipulated are students and the rooms to which they are assigned. From these entities, we define the element classes named `student` and `room`.

The attributes for the `student` element class hold information such as the student's name, the gender of that student, and whether or not she is a smoker. These are facts about the student that are given as program input. An attribute is also defined to specify whether or not a student has been assigned a room; this status information is used during program execution. The `student` element class is defined in Figure 2.1.

The `room` element class is given an attribute for a unique room number, and an attribute for the capacity that the room can accommodate. Both of these facts are given as program input. Information about the number of students that can be assigned to the room at any time is specified by the attribute named `vacancies`. This is another example of an attribute dedicated to program status information. Finally, when a room is partially filled, we need attributes for

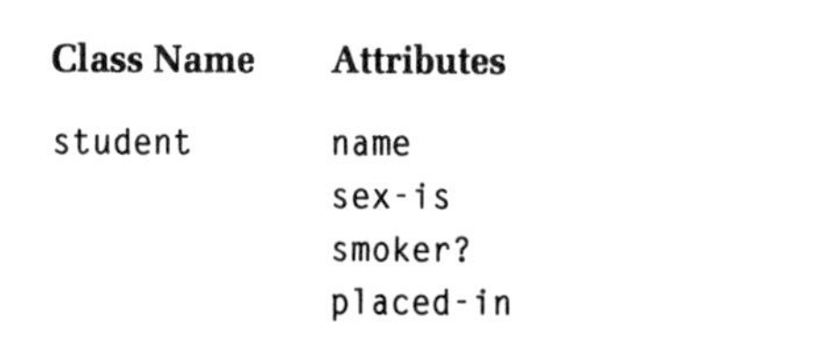

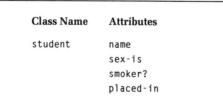

Class Name	Attributes
`student`	`name`
	`sex-is`
	`smoker?`
	`placed-in`

Figure 2.1 The student element class.

indicating the gender and smoking preferences of students already assigned that room. Figure 2.2 shows the structure of the `room` element class.

Note that the attributes in element classes represent different types of information. There are facts, such as a student's name or a room number, that are given as program input. There is also program status information, such as whether a student has been assigned a room or what the current number of students in a room is, that encodes the state of program execution.

Also note that the attributes in the previous examples are named mnemonically, stating as specifically as possible to what information the attribute refers. Program readability depends on well-named attributes. The addition of verbs, as in the attribute `sexes-are`, or punctuation marks, as in `smokers?`, is useful for improving readability.

Describing a set of element classes for a problem is an important and difficult step in writing a program. For instance, in Figure 2.2, the number of students a room can hold is represented by the attribute `capacity` and the number of students yet to be assigned that room by the attribute `vacancies`. In Exercise 2.1, you are asked to devise an alternate set of attributes for representing this information. See Chapters 4 and 11 for more detailed discussions about designing initial element classes and rules for an application.

2.2.2 The Contents of Working Memory: Working Memory Elements

As previously mentioned, working memory contains instances of element classes called working memory elements, or WMEs. Each WME consists of a class name and attributes, each of which has a *value* associated with it.

In this text, we often use the class name to refer to the WME. For example we call any WME that has the class name `room` a `room` WME, and any WME with the class name `student` a `student` WME.

Figure 2.3 is an example of a `room` WME. Attribute names are distinguished from their values by a preceding caret character (`^`). Each WME is enclosed in parentheses.

Class Name	Attributes

`room`	`number`
	`capacity`
	`vacancies`
	`sexes-are`
	`smokers?`

Figure 2.2 The room element class.

```
(ROOM ^NUMBER 213
      ^CAPACITY 3
      ^VACANCIES 1
      ^SEXES-ARE MALE
      ^SMOKERS? YES)
```

Figure 2.3 A room WME.

This room WME represents room number 213 which can hold three people. From the value of the ^vacancies attribute, we can see that there is only one space left in the room. The two current occupants of the room are male and are smokers.

Values in OPS5

All values in OPS5 are *atoms*. The significance of this representation is explained further in Chapter 8, *External Routines*, in the context of passing values to and from an OPS5 program. Atoms can be either symbolic or numeric. Some OPS5 implementations support only integer numeric atoms, others support floating-point atoms as an atomic type distinct from integer numeric atoms. Check your OPS5 documentation to determine the atom types supported in your implementation.

Although OPS5 atoms are typed, attributes are not. OPS5 does not allow type declarations to indicate what type of values can be used with an attribute name, even though some matches or computations can be performed between only atoms that are of like type. This allows for greater flexibility in the range of values used with an attribute name, but it also means that the compiler cannot be depended on to warn of inconsistent uses of values at run time.

Any attribute that is not given a value in a WME has the default value nil. Besides being the default value, the symbol nil does not have any other special status in OPS5.

OPS5 is case-insensitive.* Atoms are converted to uppercase characters when they are read by the compiler or by the run-time system. To prevent case folding, enclose the atom in vertical bars, as in |Carol|. Any atom enclosed in vertical bars is matched or printed exactly as it appears. So although the atom Carol matches to the symbol CAROL, the atom created as |Carol| matches to only those atoms that were created in the same manner.

---

*The issue of case sensitivity varies from one OPS5 implementation to another. OPS5 atoms in LISP-based OPS5 implementations are simply LISP atoms and follow the case conversion and sensitivity conventions defined for that LISP.

```
(ROOM ^NUMBER MH103
      ^SEXES-ARE MALE
      ^SMOKERS? NO
      ^CAPACITY 3
      ^VACANCIES 0
      ^OCCUPANTS RODRIGUES TEMPLETON WALSH)
```

Figure 2.4 A room WME with a vector attribute.

Vector Attributes

Unlike the attributes in Figure 2.3, not all attributes are followed by only a single value. A *vector attribute* is an attribute that is associated with more than one value. There can be at most one vector attribute in each element class.

For example, in the `room` element class, the attribute `^occupants` holds a vector of student names denoting people who share that room. A `room` WME with the `occupants` attribute is shown in Figure 2.4.

2.2.3 Declaring Attributes

All element classes and attributes used in a rule base must be declared prior to being used in OPS5 rules. These declarations must be placed in the rule base where they will be seen by the compiler before any rules are compiled. It is an error for any symbol in the rule base to be preceded by a caret character (`^`) before that symbol is declared.

Element classes are declared using the *`literalize`* declaration. Each `literalize` declaration specifies the element-class name and the attributes associated with that element class. The element classes introduced for the room assignment program, for example, would be declared at the beginning of the rule base by the following declarations:

```
(literalize student      ; An eventual room occupant
        name             ; Unique student identifier
        placed-in        ; Room number or NIL
        sex-is           ; MALE or FEMALE
        smoker?)         ; YES or NO

(literalize room         ; A place to put students
        number           ; Unique room identifier
        capacity         ; Integer: maximum students
        vacancies        ; Integer: openings left
        sexes-are        ; Once occupied: MALE or FEMALE
        smokers?)        ; Once occupied: YES or NO
```

Note that we have included a comment with each attribute name; a comment in OPS5 is delimited by a semicolon and line break.

When there is a vector attribute in the element class, it must also be declared a vector attribute with a *vector-attribute* declaration. By convention, the vector-attribute declaration follows the element class of which it is a part, and the vector-attribute name is also included in the literalize declaration of its element class. The vector-attribute declaration establishes the attribute as a vector attribute in all classes for which it is declared.

When we include the attribute occupants in the room element class, the declaration becomes

```
(literalize room          ; A place to put students
        number            ; Unique room identifier
        capacity          ; Integer: maximum students
        vacancies         ; Integer: openings left
        sexes-are         ; Once occupied: MALE or FEMALE
        smokers?          ; Once occupied: YES or NO
        occupants)        ; Once occupied: Vector of student
                          ;  names

(vector-attribute occupants)
```

You can list attribute names in any order in a literalize declaration without affecting how those names are used in rules.

2.2.4 The Representation of WMEs

This section presents a model of the internal representation of WMEs. This model is intended to help to explain the difference between correct and incorrect syntax. It can also help to explain how functions that are introduced later in the text such as litval and substr work, and how external routines pass values to and from an OPS5 program. If you are just learning OPS5, you can skip this section until you begin to manipulate vectors or use external routines.

A WME can be viewed as a vector of fields, each holding a single atom. The class name is in the first field of the vector. An attribute name is used as an *index* to a field in the WME that holds that attribute's value. The index is assigned to the attribute name by the literalize declaration.

When a WME is made (with the make action or command), a 1-based vector is created with nil as the default value of each field. The *current field index* for this WME is set to 1. When the class name is given, it is written into the first field and the index is incremented. When an attribute name is encountered, the current field index is set to the field associated with that attribute. The corresponding value is then written into the proper field and the current field index is again incremented. If several values occur together in the make action or command, they are written into adjacent fields starting at the current field index.

Suppose the room element class has the following field-position assignments for each attribute:

^number	assigned position 2
^capacity	assigned position 3
^vacancies	assigned position 6
^sexes-are	assigned position 8
^smokers?	assigned position 9

When the following WME is created

```
(ROOM ^NUMBER 111 ^CAPACITY 4 ^VACANCIES 4)
```

a vector representation of the WME is

1	2	3	4	5	6	7
room	111	4	nil	nil	4	nil

Since all fields initially contain the value nil, the values of the attributes ^sexes-are and ^smokers do not have to be specified explicitly.

A vector-attribute name is assigned a field position beyond all other non-vector attributes, so that the vector values do not overwrite values of other attributes. The vector-attribute declaration assigns this index. Like all other attribute names, the vector-attribute name is assigned only a single index, which is the position of the first value in the vector.

2.3 Rules

OPS5 rules are independent entities, each written to execute when a set of WMEs is found that match the rules' conditions. Rules cannot pass data to each other, cannot direct when another should execute, and cannot specify their own time to execute. They can execute only when they are matched by WMEs in working memory, and are chosen to execute by the rule interpreter.

Figure 2.5 is a template of the components of a rule. In an actual rule, the names rule-name, condition-element, and action are replaced with entities of that type. The three dots indicate that the preceding element can be repeated.

Each rule starts with a p for production. The p is followed by a unique rule name. No two rules in an OPS5 rule base can have the same name. The name of the rule should represent the purpose of the rule in the system. Rule names such as place-student-in-single are preferable to names like rule-17.

The two major parts of a rule are the *left-hand side* (*LHS*), which precedes the arrow (-->), and the *right-hand side* (*RHS*), which follows it. The expressions on the LHS are called *condition elements*. Each condition element states the

```
(p  rule-name
      (condition-element)  }
            :              } left-hand side (LHS)
   -->
      (action)             }
         :                 } right-hand side (RHS)
            )
```

Figure 2.5 A rule template.

conditions that WMEs must match. For a rule to be satisfied, all positive condition elements must be matched, and no negated condition elements must be matched. Negated condition elements are identified by a hyphen preceding a condition element. When the rule is matched and is chosen to execute, the expressions on the RHS, called *actions*, each perform some activity, usually that affects the state of working memory.

OPS5 owes its use of parentheses to the original LISP-based implementation. Parentheses surround the rule itself, each condition element, and each action.

The following section discusses the specific syntax for constructing the LHS and RHS of rules.

2.3.1 The LHS: Condition Elements

It is usually easier to specify what a rule should *do* (RHS actions), than it is to specify the conditions under which the rule should execute (LHS conditions). Correctly specifying the state of working memory that should exist for a particular rule to fire is the most difficult and important part of writing a rule. If an LHS is not specific enough about what working memory should look like, the rule may fire inappropriately. If an LHS is *too* specific, the rule may not fire as often as it should.

The key to learning how to write condition elements is understanding how a match is made between a condition element and a WME. When the OPS5 rule interpreter attempts to match WMEs to a condition element, the first step it takes is to eliminate all WMEs from consideration that do not have the class name specified in the condition element. This prunes all the WMEs except those that are from the same element class. Second, OPS5 applies the value test at the first attribute name in the condition element to the value* for that attribute in each of the remaining WMEs. If the WME value passes the test specified in the

*Remember, all attributes in a WME have a value, even if that value is the default `nil`.

condition element, matching proceeds to the next attribute and applies *its* value test to the WME's value. This continues for each WME until a value test fails, or until all value tests in the condition element succeed. In the latter case, a match has been made. The match process is covered in more detail in Chapter 3, *The Recognize-Act Cycle*, and in Chapter 10, *Efficiency*.

It is as important to be able to specify the conditions that must *not* exist in working memory for a rule to execute as it is to specify the conditions that must exist. Describing a condition may require specifying that certain data are *not yet* or are *no longer* in working memory. For example, the following condition element is satisfied only if there are no unoccupied single rooms available:

```
- (room ^capacity 1 ^vacancies 1)
```

In the match described previously by a *negated condition element*, the value tests `^capacity 1` and `^vacancies 1` test for only equality with the constant value 1.

In actuality, the condition element can specify value tests other than equality that a matching WME value must satisfy. Condition-element tests are constructed from the following components:*

- *Variables*—for matching to any value in the WME, or for defining a relationship between two values:

  ```
  ^name <student-name>

  ^capacity <slots-available> ^vacancies <slots-available>
  ```

- *Predicate operators*—for restricting the range of values that can match:

  ```
  ^vacancies > 0
  ```

- *Disjunctions*—for specifying a list of values, one of which must be equal to the value in the WME:

  ```
  ^capacity << 1 2 3 >>
  ```

- *Conjunctions*—for specifying a group of value tests that must be satisfied by one WME value:

  ```
  ^capacity { > 1 <> nil }
  ```

Each of these components of the LHS is discussed in the following sections.

*Some implementations of OPS5 also allow calls to user-written functions in condition elements. Check your OPS5 documentation.

Variables

The OPS5 variable bears little resemblance to the variable of most programming languages. OPS5 variables are not declared and are seldom explicitly assigned values. They cannot be passed from rule to rule, or defined globally to all rules.

A variable is any OPS5 atom that is enclosed in angle brackets. The following are all valid OPS5 variables:

```
<price>
<1>
<365th>
```

When an OPS5 variable is first used in a rule, it acts as a wildcard that matches and is assigned whatever value is in the same position in the WME. Variables provide you with a means of referring to and manipulating a WME value from the LHS of the rule without your knowing ahead of time what that value will be. You may know, for instance, that you have to assign a room number to a student, but the rule you write cannot specify the exact room number or the actual student name if it is to work for all rooms and all students. The variable for room number, then, holds the particular room number of a `room` WME matched to that rule.

For example, suppose we have the following condition element and WME:

Condition Element	**Working Memory Element**

`(student ^name <student-name>`
`        ^placed-in nil)`
	`(STUDENT ^NAME LEROY`
	`         ^PLACED-IN NIL`
	`         ^SEX-IS MALE`
	`         ^SMOKER? NO)`

For the WME to be matched to the condition element, the WME must first have the class name `student`. Second, the value of the WME's `^placed-in` attribute must be equal to the value `nil`. Assuming this is the first use of the variable `<student-name>` in the rule, that variable matches and is assigned the value `LEROY`.

The first time a variable is matched to a value in a WME, it is said to be *bound* to that value. Any subsequent use of the same variable in that rule represents the bound value. In the example, if the variable `<student-name>` is used again in the rule, on either the LHS or RHS, it represents the value `LEROY`. If the rule contained the action

```
(write <student-name> is a wanderer.)
```

and was selected to execute, it would produce the following output:

```
LEROY IS A WANDERER.
```

Variables provide a means of establishing relationships between different WMEs. For example, the relationship between a `student` WME and a `room` WME is that each student is assigned a room number. If we want to get more information about the room a student has been assigned, we can write a rule in which the variable for the student's `^placed-in` attribute is the same as the variable for the room's `^number` attribute. The first time the variable is matched, it is bound to a value; in its second use, it can match only the room whose number is the same as the room in which the student was placed. This forms a *consistent match.*

```
(p  print-an-assigned-student
      (student ^name <any-student>
               ^placed-in <room-number>)
      (room ^number <room-number>...
```

Variables can also establish relationships between values in the same WME. If you want to write a condition element that matches to a `room` WME that represents an empty room, for example, you can assign the same variable to the attributes `^capacity` and `^vacancies`, as in:

```
(room ^capacity <max-room-size>
      ^vacancies <max-room-size>)
```

It is especially important that variables are given names that reflect the values to which they are matched or the role they play in relation to other values. Since a bound variable can be used anywhere else in the rule, a representative name helps to establish to what value that variable refers once it is out of its original context.

Predicate Operators

Predicate operators are used with values in condition elements to state the relationship between the value in the condition element and the matching value in the WME. Until now, we have used the equal-to operator without explicitly writing it; we have assumed the value in the condition element must be *equal to* the value in the WME. Therefore, although we have used only the first, the following two representations are equivalent:

```
(room ^number <room-number>)

(room ^number = <room-number>)
```

A complete list of OPS5 predicate operators is presented in Table 2.1.

With predicate operators, a condition element can specify constraints on its matching values, rather than specify the value itself. Using the greater-than operator, for example, we can add a condition to the rule `assign-student-`

Table 2.1 Predicate operators.

Operator	Definition	Types Used With
=	equal-to	symbol, number
<>	not-equal-to	symbol, number
<=>	same-type-as	symbol, number
<	less-than	number
<=	less-than-or-equal-to	number
>	greater-than	number
>=	greater-than-or-equal-to	number

`to-room` that specifies that the room in which a student is being placed has vacancies. The value that matches the `^vacancies` attribute must be *greater than* 0:

```
(p  assign-student-to-room
      (student ^name <any-student>
               ^placed-in nil)
      (room ^number <room-number>
            ^vacancies > 0)
      ...
```

All the predicate operators described in Table 2.1 can be used to compare numeric values whereas only three can be used between symbolic atoms. These are the equal-to (=), the not-equal-to (<>) and same-type-as (<=>) operators.

Since OPS5 normally converts all characters to uppercase ones, you do not have to write rules in uppercase characters to have them match uppercased WMEs. However, if a WME value retains lowercase characters, by being either enclosed in vertical bars or created by external routines, it will be matched by only a condition element value with the same case preserved by enclosing vertical bars.

The first use of a variable in a rule, being the binding instance, must be used with the equal-to operator. Binding a variable in a condition element sets its value to be equal to the value in the matching WME. After the variable is bound, it can be compared with WME values using different operators. If the following two condition elements appeared in a rule, they could match only two different students (students that have different names):

```
(student ^name <1st-student>)
(student ^name <> <1st-student>)
```

The same-type-as operator (<=>) tests that the type (integer, floating point, or symbolic) of the WME value is the same type as the value in the condition element. The value used in the condition element as the model type can be any atom of that type or a variable bound to an atom of that type. It can be any integer if the value in the WME must be an integer, or any symbol if the value in the WME must be a symbol. In the following example, the first condition element can be matched by any `student` WME whose value for the attribute `^name` is a symbol; the second condition element can be matched by any `room` WME whose value for the attribute `^number` is an integer:

```
(student ^name <=> symbol)
(room ^number <=> 999)
```

A predicate operator used with a vector attribute applies to only the value that the operator precedes, not to every value in the vector. The following condition element matches a `room` WME in which the first value in the `^occupants` vector attribute is not `nil`. That is, there is at least one student assigned to this room. It does not matter what the other values in the vector are.

```
(room ^occupants <> nil)
```

To find the three students assigned to a triple, we could write

```
(room ^capacity 3 ^vacancies 0
      ^occupants <1st> <2nd> <3rd>)
(student ^name <1st>)
(student ^name <2nd>)
(student ^name <3rd>)
```

This example is presented only to illustrate how predicate operators work with the values of vector attributes. There are better techniques for manipulating vectors that are not dependent on the number of values in the vector. These are presented later in this chapter (Section 2.3.3).

Disjunctions

A *disjunction* is a value test that specifies a set of values, *one* of which must be equal to the value in the matching WME. The set of values is surrounded by double angle brackets.* A disjunction expresses a logical OR between possible matching values. So the OPS5 syntax

```
^capacity << 1 2 3 >>
```

specifies that the value for the `capacity` attribute in a matching WME must be 1, 2, or 3.

*In most OPS5 implementations, a space is required between the angle brackets and their contained values.

OPS5 treats all atoms* inside a disjunction as constants. Predicate operators and variables within the double angle brackets are treated as constants or as errors. The equal-to operator before each value is implied. For example, the symbol <room-size> in the following disjunction will only match the atom <ROOM-SIZE> in a WME, instead of having the usual variable semantics:

```
^capacity << 2 3 4 <room-size> >>
```

Conjunctions

A *conjunction* is a test that groups together value tests to be applied to the single WME value. The WME value must satisfy all the operators in the conjunction to match.

A conjunction is represented by enclosing all the value tests in braces ({}).

The following condition element is matched by only a room WME whose value of the ^vacancies attribute is greater than 0 but is less than the value of the ^capacity attribute. That is, the room is neither empty nor full.

```
(room ^capacity <capacity>
      ^vacancies { > 0 < <capacity> } )
```

When the first appearance of a variable on the LHS is in a conjunction, that variable is bound to the value in the WME that satisfies all the tests in the conjunction. For example, the following two condition elements are matched by two different student WMEs. The second student's name is different from the name bound to the variable <1st-student> and is not equal to LEROY. The WME value that satisfies these two conditions is bound to the variable <2nd>.

```
(student ^name <1st-student>)
(student ^name { <2nd> <> <1st-student> <> leroy })
```

Conjunctive syntax is simply shorthand for repeating the attribute name for each value test performed on the value indicated by that attribute. The second condition element can be written, for instructive purposes, in the equivalent form

```
(student ^name <2nd> ^name <> <1st-student> ^name <> leroy)
```

*This also applies to function calls for those OPS5 implementations extended to allow function calls in condition elements.

Since value tests may appear in any order after the class in a condition element, it follows that conjunctive tests also may appear in any order. For example, the following condition elements are equivalent:

```
(room ^vacancies { <spaces-left> > 0 })
(room ^vacancies { > 0 <spaces-left> })
(room ^vacancies > 0 ^vacancies <spaces-left>)
```

Disjunctions, being value tests, may also appear within a conjunction. The following test binds the variable <medium-sized-room> and restricts its value to the integer 2 or the integer 3.

```
^capacity { <medium-sized-room> << 2 3 >> }
```

2.3.2 The RHS: Actions

When all the condition elements on the LHS are matched by WMEs, and the rule interpreter chooses a rule to execute, the RHS actions are performed in the order they are written. Actions do things such as

- Create WMEs
- Change values in WMEs
- Remove WMEs from working memory
- Print output
- Stop the program

The actions covered in this chapter are make, remove, modify, write, halt, bind, and call.* These are the actions used most frequently in the examples in this book.

The make Action: Creating WMEs

The *make* action is used to create a WME. A template for the make action is

(make *rhs-pattern*)

An *rhs-pattern* is a combination of element class name (which is optional) followed by attribute names (also optional) and the attributes' values.

The following three make actions create three room WMEs:

```
(make room ^number 101 ^capacity 3 ^vacancies 3)
(make room ^number 102 ^capacity 1 ^vacancies 1)
(make room ^number 103 ^capacity 2 ^vacancies 2)
```

---

*See your OPS5 documentation for other available actions.

A `make` action need not assign a value to every attribute in the WME's element class. If an attribute is not assigned a value, its default value is `nil`. The attributes `^sexes-are` and `^smokers?` in the WMEs created in the previous example have the value `nil`, since students have not yet been assigned to the room.

If more than one value is accidentally assigned to the same attribute, the resulting value of the attribute is the last value assigned. After the following action is completed, the value for the attribute `^number` is `102`:

```
(make room ^number 101 ^capacity 3 ^vacancies 3
           ^number 102)
```

The modify and remove Actions: Modifying and Deleting WMEs

The *modify* action changes one or more values in a WME, leaving the rest of the WME intact. The *remove* action deletes one or more WMEs from working memory.

These two actions are presented together because they share an important argument. Both actions must refer to a specific WME on which to act. The `modify` action must refer to a WME to change, the `remove` action to a WME to delete. The argument that specifies the WME on which to act is called an *element designator* because it is used to *designate* the working memory *element* to modify or remove.

(modify *element-designator rhs-pattern*)

(remove *element-designator...*)

An action cannot refer directly to any WME in working memory. Only the WMEs that match the rule's condition elements can be acted on by the RHS.

There are two types of element designators: element variables and integer positions. The former is preferred and is used throughout the book. We introduce the latter only because it is included in the language definition; it is used by a relatively small number of programmers.

An *element variable* is an element designator that acts as a label to a condition element. It has the same syntax as does the value variables within condition elements; it is a symbol enclosed in angle brackets. As a convention, this text capitalizes element variables to make them visually distinct from value variables. Unlike value variables, however, an element variable is placed outside a condition element's parentheses. An element variable is associated with a condition element by surrounding braces. Within the braces, it may occur before or after the condition element it names.

The following example illustrates the two styles of placement of element variables. In both cases, the element variable `<Empty-room>` is outside of the condition element but is associated with it by a pair of braces around both the element variable and the condition element.

```
{ <Empty-room>
   (room ^number <room-number> ^capacity <max>
        ^vacancies <max>) }
```

```
 { (room ^number <room-number> ^capacity <max>
        ^vacancies <max>)                         <Empty-room> }
```

It is a matter of personal preference whether element variables are placed before or after the condition element. In this text, element variables are placed before the condition element on a separate line and column from their associated condition element. This style aligns all the element variables in one column, and all the left parentheses of condition elements in another.*

Be careful not to be confused by the two uses of braces: both for conjunctive value tests and for element-variable associations. The following example contains a condition element in which braces are used for both purposes:

```
{ <Student-wme>
   (student ^name { <student-name> <> nil }) }
```

Element variables and integer positions are used as element designators in modify and remove actions.

Figure 2.6 contains a rule that uses element variables with the modify action. The element variables <Unplaced-student> and <Empty-room> refer to the WMEs that match the first and second positive condition elements, respectively. In the modify actions on the RHS, the WMEs that match the student and room condition elements are indicated by these element variables. Values not specified in the modify actions remain unchanged in the modified WME.

Figure 2.7 shows the rule in Figure 2.6 modified to use numeric element designators. A numeric designator refers to the relative position of a condition element, counting only positive condition elements. The first action modifies the WME that matches the *first* condition element, the second modifies the WME that matches the *second* positive condition element. The negated condition element is not included in the count, since it would be meaningless to refer to it in an action—by definition, no WME matches a negated condition element.

The remove action can use one or more element designators in the same action, as in the following examples:

```
(remove <Student>)
(remove <Filled-room> <Graduated-student>)
(remove 3 4 5)
```

*Appendix B discusses stylistic decisions such as these.

```
(p  assign-student-to-empty-room
;
; If there are no vacancies in a compatible room, allocate
; another one and assign this student to the room.
;
   { <Unplaced-student>
      (student ^name <student-name> ^placed-in nil
               ^sex-is <gender> ^smoker? <smoke-pref>) }
      - (room ^vacancies > 0
              ^sexes-are <gender> ^smokers? <smoke-pref>)
   { <Empty-room>
      (room ^number <room-number>
            ^capacity <max-size> ^vacancies <max-size>) }
   -->
      (modify <Unplaced-student> ^placed-in <room-number>)
      (modify <Empty-room> ^occupants <student-name>
            ^sexes-are <gender> ^smokers? <smoke-pref>
            ^vacancies (compute <max-size> - 1)))
```

Figure 2.6 Using element variables as element designators.

```
(p  assign-student-to-empty-room
;
; If there are no vacancies in a compatible room, allocate
; another one and assign this student to the room.
;
      (student ^name <student-name> ^placed-in nil
               ^sex-is <gender> ^smoker? <smoke-pref>)
      - (room ^vacancies > 0
              ^sexes-are <gender> ^smokers? <smoke-pref>)
      (room ^number <room-number>
            ^capacity <max-size> ^vacancies <max-size>)
   -->
      (modify 1 ^placed-in <room-number>)
      (modify 2 ^occupants <student-name>
            ^sexes-are <gender> ^smokers? <smoke-pref>
            ^vacancies (compute <max-size> - 1)))
```

Figure 2.7 Using numeric positions as element designators.

It is preferable to use element variables rather than numbers as element designators. The positioning of condition elements on the LHS of a rule frequently changes during program development. Condition elements are added to or removed from the rule. If you use numeric element designators, each time one of these changes occurs, the relative position of the condition elements changes, so the arguments to the `modify` and `remove` actions must be changed as well. Checking for this consistency with every change to a rule is easy to forget. An incorrect element designator causes errors that may be difficult to diagnose. Element variables remain the same despite changes in the rule. In addition, when element variables are effectively named they also enhance readability, especially of large rules.

The write Action: OPS5 Output

The *write* action is used to produce all output from an OPS5 program.* By default, output is sent to the terminal.† The `write` action can be specified with any RHS expression containing constants, bound variables, or function calls. The template for the `write` action is

(`write` *rhs-pattern*)

Figure 2.8 contains a rule, two example WMEs that match the rule, and the output produced by the `write` action when the rule executes. Note that, because OPS5 converts all atom characters to uppercase ones, the output from the `write` action is in uppercase characters. Case can be preserved only by enclosing characters in vertical bars. Vertical bars treat all enclosed characters as a single, literal atom. That is, no variables or function calls are evaluated, and everything within the bars, including whitespace, forms a symbolic atom.‡ Since everything between vertical bars is considered a single atom, the number of characters that can be used between vertical bars is limited by the length limit of an atom.

Figure 2.9 shows the results of using vertical bars to preserve case while leaving variables outside the vertical bars to be evaluated.

The `write` action generates a space after any printed atom, including the period in Figure 2.9, but does not automatically generate new lines before or after output. The OPS5 functions for formatting output are covered in the next section.

---

*Note that OPS5's capability for input and output is limited. The actions and functions provided are useful for prototype systems, but are rarely used in actual applications. Most input and output is handled by user-written external routines.

†The default for output can be changed to an external file with actions such as the `openfile`, `closefile`, and `default` actions.

‡Various implementations may restrict the set of characters that may form an atom.

Rule

```
(p  print-assigned-student
      (student ^name <assigned-student>
               ^placed-in { <room-number> <> nil })
      (room ^number <room-number> ^capacity <room-size>)
   -->
      (write <assigned-student> has been placed
             in Room <room-number> .)
      (write The room holds <room-size> students.))
```

Working Memory

```
(STUDENT ^NAME MITCH ^PLACED-IN 411 ^SEX-IS MALE ^SMOKER? NO)
(ROOM ^NUMBER 411 ^CAPACITY 3 ^VACANCIES 2 ^SEXES-ARE MALE
      ^SMOKERS? NO)
```

Output

```
MITCH HAS BEEN PLACED IN ROOM 411 . THE ROOM HOLDS 3 STUDENTS.
```

Figure 2.8 Output from the write action.

Rule

```
(p  print-assigned-student
      (student ^name <assigned-student>
               ^placed-in { <room-number> <> nil })
      (room ^number <room-number> ^capacity <room-size>)
   -->
      (write <assigned-student> |has been placed in Room|
             <room-number> .)
      (write |The room holds| <room-size> |students.|))
```

Working Memory

```
(STUDENT ^NAME MITCH ^PLACED-IN 411 ^SEX-IS MALE ^SMOKER? NO)
(ROOM ^NUMBER 411 ^CAPACITY 3 ^VACANCIES 2 ^SEXES-ARE MALE
      ^SMOKERS? NO)
```

Output

```
MITCH has been placed in Room 411 . The room holds 3 students.
```

Figure 2.9 Output from the write action, preserving case.

The halt Action: Halting Program Execution

The *halt* action stops execution of an OPS5 program after the current rule firing. The halt action takes no arguments. The program stops execution only after the execution of all the actions on the RHS of the rule in which it is found.

The rule in Figure 2.10 halts the program when there are unplaced students but no vacancies remaining in any rooms.

It is appropriate to use the halt action when you can define the specific state of working memory for which the program is finished, or can describe unusual or emergency situations under which it is important for the program to terminate. A program also halts without the halt action when there are no more matches between WMEs and rules.

The bind Action: Binding a Variable on the RHS

The bind action is used to bind a new variable to a value on the RHS. The bind action takes one or two arguments: the variable name, and an optional value for the binding. The value specified for the variable can be a constant, another variable, or a function call such as compute. If the value is omitted, OPS5 will generate an atom for a default binding.

Variables are bound on the RHS for several reasons. The result of calculations that are performed more than once on the RHS can be stored in a variable to reduce the redundant computation:

```
(bind <openings> (compute <empty-slots> - 1))
(modify <Room> ^vacancies <openings>)
(write |There are now| <openings> |slots left.|)
```

In the following sections describing RHS functions, another situation arises where the bind action is necessary—when the result of one function must be used as an argument to another function.

```
(p  no-rooms-left
      (student ^placed-in nil)
      - (room ^vacancies > 0)
   -->
      (write |There are not enough room slots for everyone!|)
      (halt))
```

Figure 2.10 Using the halt action.

The call Action: Calling External Subroutines

The `call` action is used to invoke user-written subroutines. A subroutine is called for only its side effects, such as creating WMEs, or for input and output purposes, so it does not return a value. `Call` is specified with the name of the external routine and a list of the routine's arguments.

(call *subroutine-name argument...*)

For example, in the action

```
(call myprog <name> <date> <number>)
```

the external routine is named `myprog` and its arguments are bound to the variables `<name>`, `<date>`, and `<number>`.

This action is covered in more detail in Chapter 8, *External Routines.*

2.3.3 Functions

OPS5 provides a set of *functions* for use within actions and condition elements.* These functions should not be confused with user-written functions that are discussed in Chapter 8. This section describes some of the OPS5-provided functions, such as `accept`, `compute`, and the functions for formatting output. The functions `litval` and `substr` are given special attention because of their importance to the techniques for manipulating vector attributes that are presented in later chapters.

The accept and acceptline Functions: OPS5 Input

The functions *accept* and *acceptline* are used to read input to an OPS5 program. Input can come from the program user at the terminal or from an input file. In this discussion, we assume that input comes from the terminal, which is the default.

The `accept` function reads either a single atom or a list of atoms enclosed in parentheses. For example, consider the following rule:

```
(p  get-response
      (task ^name get-answer)
   -->
      (write |Please type the first value that comes to mind:|)
      (make response ^text (accept)))
```

When the rule executes, the `write` text is printed and the `make` action begins to make a WME with class name `response`, then waits for the user to supply

*A few implementations of OPS5 also permit function calls from the LHS.

a value for attribute `^text`. If the user types more than one value before the carriage return, as in

```
one two three
```

the resulting WME is the following:

```
(RESPONSE ^TEXT ONE)
```

and the rest of the input is buffered for the next call to `accept`. If the input from the user is a list of atoms enclosed in parentheses, as

```
(one two three)
```

the resulting WME is the following vector:

```
(RESPONSE ^TEXT ONE TWO THREE)
```

The `acceptline` function differs from `accept` in two ways:

1. It allows input of any number of values (without parentheses) until a carriage return, end-of-line, or end-of-file is encountered
2. It allows an argument that supplies default input values in case the input line is empty

The `acceptline` function is best suited to vector input, since multiple values do not have to be surrounded by parentheses. OPS5 places the values successively in the WME. Although `acceptline` can be used with any attribute, it should be used with only vector attributes, so that the list of values do not overwrite another scalar attribute.

The values in the parentheses with the `acceptline` function are used in place of input if the only input received is a carriage return. In the following example, the user is requested to supply a greeting message. If the user simply enters a carriage return, the default values `hello`, `and`, `good`, and `morning` are supplied as the values for the attribute `^message`. The four values are separate atoms, to be used as vector values if the user types only `RETURN`.

```
(write |Enter a greeting or type RETURN for the default|)
(make greeting ^message (acceptline hello and good morning))
```

The compute Function: Performing Mathematical Calculations

All mathematical calculations in OPS5 are accomplished with the *compute* function. The `compute` function provides the five arithmetic operators listed in the Table 2.2.

`Compute` expressions use infix notation (the operator is placed between two operands), and each expression is evaluated from *right* to *left*. There is no order

Table 2.2 **Compute operators.**

Operator	Description
+	addition
-	subtraction
*	multiplication
//	division
\\	modulus

of precedence between the operators; you must indicate with parentheses any order of evaluation other than right to left.

For example, the result of the following call to the `compute` function is the integer 1:

```
(compute 6 // 2 + 4)
```

But adding parentheses to the expression changes the order of evaluation, and the result is the integer 7:

```
(compute (6 // 2) + 4)
```

In some implementations of OPS5, the `compute` function may appear in condition elements as well as in actions. When the function is on the LHS, the value returned by `compute` is used to match a value in a WME. The following condition elements match a `room` WME with a value for the attribute `^vacancies` that is 1 less than the value for the `^capacity` attribute. Only one student has been assigned to this room.

```
(room ^capacity <max-size>
      ^vacancies (compute <max-size> - 1))
```

The `compute` function is clearly limited in its ability to perform mathematical calculations. It is intended to be used for performing only simple arithmetic. More complex calculations are typically performed by user-written external routines.

Crlf, rjust, and tabto: Formatting Output

Although OPS5 does not have extensive input or output capabilities, the three functions `crlf`, `rjust`, and `tabto` can be used with the `write` action to format output. Table 2.3 lists the arguments and descriptions of these functions.

Table 2.3 Formatting functions.

Function	Argument	Description
`crlf`	—	Moves to beginning of a new line
`rjust`	column-width	Right justifies output within a specified column width
`tabto`	column-number	Tabs to the specified column number

Crlf (carriage return line feed) is the most commonly used formatting function. The `crlf` function causes output to resume at the beginning of a new line. `Crlf` takes no arguments.

The *rjust* function right-justifies text or values within a specified column width. This function is most often used to align information in tables. It must immediately precede the atom to be right-justified. Whereas

```
(write (crlf) (tabto 25) (rjust 10) Column A)
```

is a valid expression,

```
(write (crlf) (rjust 10) (tabto 25) Column A)
```

will generate an error.

To advance to a specific column, use the *tabto* function. If that column is beyond the position currently being printed, the printing position will be advanced to that column on the next line.

The following action illustrates the use of the `crlf`, `rjust`, and `tabto` functions to set up the heading for a table:

```
(write (tabto 10) |Student|
       (tabto 40) (rjust 12) |Room Number|
       (tabto 10) |-------|
       (tabto 40) (rjust 12) |-----------|
       (crlf))
```

This action produces the following output:

```
         Student                        Room Number
         -------                        -----------
```

The following rule lists each student under these headings:

```
(p  print-results-in-table
     (task ^name print-results)
     (student ^name <student> ^placed-in { <room> <> nil } )
```

```
-->
   (write (crlf) (tabto 10) <student>
         (tabto 40) (rjust 12) <room> (crlf)))
```

After four firings of the rule `print-results-in-table`, the table contains four student entries:

```
Student                                   Room Number
-------                                   -----------
TANYA                                             212
RAMONA                                            434
SAM                                               611
MITCH                                             411
```

Manipulating Vectors: The litval and substr Functions

The difficulty with storing values in a vector in OPS5 is accessing vector values other than the first one. As with all attribute names, a vector attribute name is a pointer to a value in a WME. The vector attribute name points to only its first value. How can you access other values? How can you search through the values?

Vectors are typically used as a stack. For example, when a student is assigned to a room, his name is pushed onto the vector after the names of students previously assigned to that room are shifted one to the right to make the first position available. The vector retains the ordering of student assignments. If a room is overfilled by mistake, the student most recently assigned to the room can be popped off the vector to be assigned to another room.

There is no OPS5 function that searches for a value in a vector. The only way to access values in the vector, other than the first value, is to use empty conjunction braces to represent a value to skip, or to list a variable to match to each value preceding the one of interest. For example, to match the first and third values in the vector, you would bind variables for the first and third, and use an empty conjunction for the second.

```
^parts-list <first> {} <third>
```

This method of accessing vector values is impractical if the vector is large, the number of atoms in the vector varies, or if you do not know in which position the value of interest sits.

Accessing a specific vector value on the RHS requires referencing its position in the vector. The *`litval`* function is called with an attribute name as its argument and returns the numeric position assigned to the attribute. When the `litval` function is called with the attribute `^occupants`, for example, it returns the numeric position your OPS5 implementation assigned to that vector in the WME. In the following example, the position assigned to the attribute

^occupants is bound to the variable <student-names>. The value returned is the position of the first value of the vector.

```
(bind <student-names> (litval occupants))
```

The position values returned by litval are used as arguments to the substr function. The *substr* function (for *substring*) is used to copy a set of contiguous values from a WME. The copied values can be placed in either the same WME (presumably in different positions in the same WME) or in another WME.

The substr function takes three arguments. The first specifies the WME from which the values are being copied. This is an element designator—either an element variable or a number representing the position of the condition element on the LHS. The second and third are the positions from which to start and stop copying, respectively. These positions can be indicated by an attribute name (without the caret), by an integer representing the position, or by a variable bound to either an attribute name or an integer position.

Given the condition element

```
{ <Room>
   (room ^occupants <choice1> <choice2> <choice3>) }
```

the substr function can be used on the RHS of this rule to copy a single value from the WME, such as the value of the ^number attribute (copying begins and ends at the same position):

```
(modify <Student> ^placed-in (substr <Room> number number))
```

Or it can be used to copy all the values of the ^occupants vector attribute into either another vector, or in an action such as write:

```
(write (substr <Room> occupants inf) |are roommates.|)
```

The symbol inf is a special symbol in the context of substr that specifies that all values to the end of the vector should be copied. Copying stops after the last non-nil atom.

Suppose that a room is reclassified to a smaller size, and some students must be reassigned. The values of the vector attribute ^occupants must be "popped" for each student that exceeds the new room capacity. If the vector contains

```
^OCCUPANTS GREEN WESTON VALREZ
```

and the room has been reclassified as a double, we want to change the vector to

```
^OCCUPANTS WESTON VALREZ
```

The substr function can be used in the make action to copy the atoms WESTON and VALREZ and to place them as the first two values of the ^occupants attribute.

```
(p  relieve-overcrowding-problem
   { <Overcrowded-room>
      (room ^vacancies { <deficit> < 0 }
            ^occupants <last-one-assigned>) }
   { <Evicted-student>
      (student ^name <last-one-assigned>) }
   -->
      (modify <Evicted-student> ^placed-in nil)
      (bind <1st-position> (litval occupants))
      (bind <2nd-position> (compute <1st-position> + 1))
      (remove <Overcrowded-room>)
      (make (substr <Overcrowded-room> 1 occupants)
          ^vacancies (compute <deficit> + 1)
          ^occupants (substr <Overcrowded-room> <2nd-position> inf)))
```

Figure 2.11 Using litval and substr to remove the first value from a vector.

The `litval` and `substr` functions are used together in Figure 2.11 to change the assignment of students in overcrowded rooms. The `litval` function is used to calculate the `substr` argument that represents the position from which to start copying. To find the position of the second atom in the vector, an offset is added to the first position. So, if the `bind` action assigns the variable `<1st-position>` to the first position in the vector,

```
(bind <1st-position> (litval occupants))
```

then the variable `<1st-position>` is incremented by 1 to calculate the position of the second value in the vector.* The new index is bound to the variable `<2nd-position>`:

```
(bind <2nd-position> (compute <1st-position> + 1))
```

The variable `<2nd-position>` is then used in the `substr` function to indicate from which value to start copying. Copying stops at the last non-`nil` atom in the vector, as directed by the special symbol `inf`.

The values copied with `substr` from the vector attribute `^occupants` in Figure 2.11 are effectively shifted one position to the left.

*Since the OPS5 language does not allow `litval` to occur inside `substr`, the `bind` action is needed to hold the intermediate results of the `litval`.

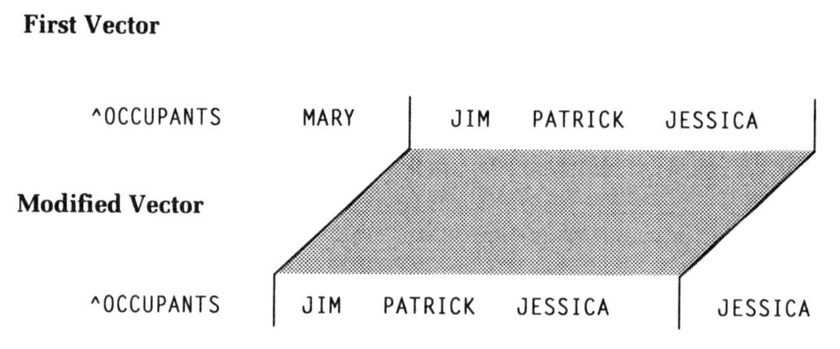

Figure 2.12 Using **substr** to shift the vector values, resulting in a trailing value.

If the vector is not to be written in its entirety, you may also use the `modify` action to shift vectors as follows:

```
(modify <Overcrowded-room>
    ^vacancies (compute <deficit> + 1)
    ^occupants (substr <Overcrowded-room> <2nd-position> inf)
               nil)
```

The trailing `nil` is required to overwrite the last atom in the original vector as the new vector will be shorter by one value. Figure 2.12 illustrates how the atoms in the first vector are overlayed by the new atoms when a `modify` action without the trailing `nil` is used, leaving the last atom unchanged.

Summary

- Working memory has a structure and actual instances. The structure is defined by element classes. The actual instances are called working memory elements or WMEs.

- The rule base is a collection of IF–THEN rules of the form: IF a set of conditions exists in working memory, THEN perform a set of actions. The IF portion of the rule, or left-hand side (LHS), consists of positive and negated condition elements that describe a set of WMEs that satisfy, or match, the rule. The THEN portion of the rule, or right-hand side (RHS), consists of actions that execute when the rule has been chosen.

- The LHS of rules can use variables, predicate operators, disjunctions, and conjunctions to specify the values in WMEs that can match the condition element.
- The RHS of rules include actions such as:
  - `make` for creating WMEs
  - `modify` for changing WMEs
  - `remove` for deleting WMEs
  - `write` for output
  - `halt` for stopping program execution
  - `bind` for attaching values to variables
  - `call` for invoking external subroutines
- The actions `remove` and `modify` make use of an element designator to specify the WME to be modified or deleted.
- OPS5 rules can also contain OPS5-provided functions that provide values to WMEs or that manipulate output or vectors, such as:
  - `accept` and `acceptline` for input
  - `compute` for mathematical operations
  - `crlf`, `tabto`, and `rjust` for formatting output
  - `substr` and `litval` for manipulating vectors

Exercises

1. When we created element classes for the room-assignment program, we represented the size and current number of occupants of a room by the attributes `^capacity` and `^vacancies`. Write the `literalize` declaration for a different representation of the `room` WME. Explain how this representation would be used to keep track of the students placed in a room.

2. Write the condition element that matches a student who has already been placed in a room.

3. Suppose the attributes of the `room` WME have been assigned the following indices by the `literalize` declaration:

`^number`	index 2
`^capacity`	index 3
`^vacancies`	index 6
`^sexes-are`	index 7
`^smokers?`	index 8

The following `make` action is syntactically correct but probably does not produce the WME the programmer expected:

```
(make room ^number 1135 ^capacity 2 ^vacancies 2 male no)
```

Draw the array that this WME represents. What problem will this WME cause during program execution?

4. It is important to understand the difference between using the not-equal-to operator (<>) in the condition element, and a negated condition element. Explain in English the condition being expressed by each of the following condition elements:

   a. `(student ^placed-in <> nil)`

   b. `- (student ^placed-in nil)`

   c. `- (student ^placed-in <> nil)`

5. What is the value of the `^number` attribute resulting from the following `make` action?

```
(make room ^number 301 ^number 302)
```

6. What is the output that results from the following `write` action? The variable `<room-no>` is bound to the value 322.

```
(write |There is a vacancy in room <room-no>|)
```

7. Now you can write some complete rules for the room-assignment program. Make sure to include the conditions that specify that a student can be placed only with those other students who have the same gender and smoking preference. Write rules that:

   a. Place a student in a partially filled room

   b. Place a student in an empty room

   c. Print the names of students that have been assigned rooms (use the formatting functions)

8. As this program is written, two students that have the same gender and smoking preference may not get assigned to a room if one other student with opposite gender or smoking preference was assigned to the last vacant room ahead of them. Can you think of a way for the program to schedule the two students together, rather than scheduling the single person first? In other words, think of a way that the rules can schedule the maximum number of students. Writing the rules is optional. Just think of a good solution.

CHAPTER 3

The Recognize-Act Cycle

UNTIL THIS POINT, we have referred to the rule interpreter as the black box that is responsible for driving the execution of a rule-based program. We know that the rule interpreter is what matches WMEs to rules, chooses the rule to execute, and executes the actions on the rule's RHS.

In this chapter, we look more closely at OPS5's rule interpreter and the *recognize-act cycle* algorithm. Each pass of the recognize-act cycle consists of three steps:

1. *Match.* Match all the WMEs to condition elements in all the rules
2. *Select.* Select one rule with matching WMEs from the set
3. *Act.* Perform the actions on the RHS of the chosen rule

3.1 New Terminology

Before we discuss each of the steps in the recognize-act cycle, we must introduce some new terminology.

An *instantiation* is a set of WMEs that satisfies a rule. That is, together they form a complete match of the positive condition elements of the rule. You can think of an instantiation as an *instance* of a matched rule. The set of instantiations collected as a result of the match step is called the *conflict set*. The process of selecting a single instantiation from the conflict set is called *conflict resolution*.

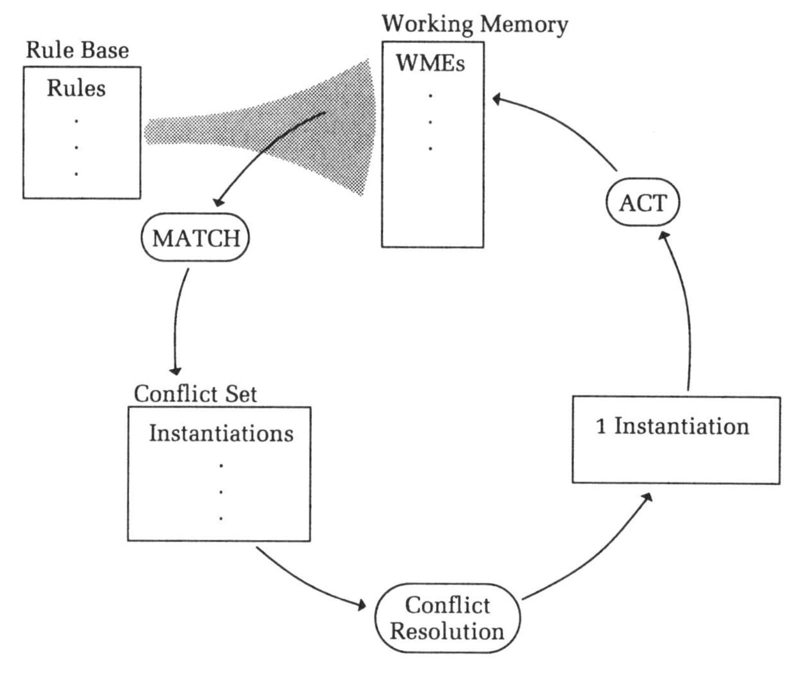

Figure 3.1 The recognize-act cycle.

Figure 3.1 illustrates the recognize-act cycle using these terms.

In the recognize-act cycle, WMEs are identified by their *time tag*. A time tag is a number OPS5 assigns to each WME when that WME is created, so that the WME has a unique identifier that indicates its creation time relative to other WMEs. Each time tag assigned is larger than the previous one was, although the time tags are not necessarily consecutive. Time tags have not been introduced previously because they can not be referred to or manipulated from within rules. Time tags are used only in the recognize-act cycle as a shorthand notation for referring to the WMEs themselves and as a basis for conflict resolution.

An instantiation is represented by a rule name and by the time tags of the WMEs that match each condition element. The time tags are listed in the order of the condition elements they match. In the following instantiation for the rule named `assign-private-room`, the WME with the time tag 47 matches the first positive condition element, and the WME with the time tag 12 matches the second one.

```
ASSIGN-PRIVATE-ROOM 47 12
```

Note that there is no way to tell from the instantiation alone whether the rule `assign-private-room` has any negated condition elements.

3.2 Match

A rule is considered successfully matched when all of its positive condition elements are matched by WMEs and there are no WMEs in working memory that match the rule's negated condition elements. The result of a successful match is an instantiation.

To understand what happens during match, we can decompose the process into two steps. In the first, called *intraelement match*, each condition element in the rule is matched to WMEs. Remember, however, that condition elements contain variables that can match any value in their first use on the LHS, but must match the bound value in any subsequent use in that rule. The second step of match, therefore, called *interelement match*, makes sure that the condition elements that contain the same variables are matched to WMEs with the same value for those variables.

When there are no variables shared among condition elements on the LHS, an instantiation is formed from each possible combination of the WMEs matching each condition element.* For example, Figure 3.2 contains the LHS of a rule, the WMEs matching each condition element, and the instantiations that are formed. Each WME that matches the first condition element can be combined with each element that matches the second condition element to form an instantiation.

Usually, there are variables that are used in more than one condition element on the LHS, so the number of instantiations is restricted by the requirement that variables with the same name must be bound to the same value. Figure 3.3 illustrates the instantiations formed with shared variables.

In Figure 3.3, although there are three matches to the first condition element (4, 12, and 15), and two matches to the second (7 and 9, but not 3), only two instantiations are formed. This is because the variables for the attributes `^sex-is` and `^smoker?` in the `student` WME must match the same values in the `room` WME. So, despite the number of matches that result from intraelement match, the number of instantiations is less than that in the previous example because of interelement match.

Even with the simple rule in Figure 3.3, the match process can be complicated for a human to simulate. OPS5 performs this match efficiently using a "many-pattern many-object match algorithm."† This algorithm is discussed in Chapter 10.

---

*If a rule has one condition element matched by M WMEs and another matched by N WMEs, and there are no variables shared between the two condition elements, there will be M × N instantiations of that rule.

†The phrase "many-pattern many-object" was the term Forgy used to refer to the matching algorithm implemented as the basis of OPS5 [Forgy 1982].

Rule

```
(p  assign-private-room
      (student ^name <some-name>
              ^placed-in nil ^special-consideration? yes)
      (room ^number <room-number> ^capacity 1
            ^vacancies 1)
   -->
      :
      :)
```

Working Memory

```
41 (STUDENT ^NAME DAWN ^SEX-IS FEMALE ^PLACED-IN NIL
       ^SPECIAL-CONSIDERATION? YES)
52 (STUDENT ^NAME PETER ^SEX-IS MALE ^PLACED-IN NIL
       ^SPECIAL-CONSIDERATION? YES)
9  (ROOM ^NUMBER 221 ^CAPACITY 1 ^VACANCIES 1)
12 (ROOM ^NUMBER 346  ^CAPACITY 2 ^VACANCIES 1)
17 (ROOM ^NUMBER 761 ^CAPACITY 1 ^VACANCIES 1)
```

Instantiations

```
ASSIGN-PRIVATE-ROOM 41 9
ASSIGN-PRIVATE-ROOM 41 17
ASSIGN-PRIVATE-ROOM 52 9
ASSIGN-PRIVATE-ROOM 52 17
```

Figure 3.2 Simple interelement match without variables.

For now it suffices to understand that one factor in OPS5's efficiency is that the conflict set is not recomputed each cycle. The results of both intraelement and interelement match are stored. Only the *changes* to working memory caused by a rule execution must be propogated to the conflict set each cycle. Those instantiations that are not affected by the WMEs that are created or deleted after a rule executes remain unchanged in the conflict set.

3.3 Conflict Resolution

The result of the match step is a conflict set that contains all the instantiations that are eligible for execution. During the conflict-resolution step a single instantiation is chosen to execute. The decision criteria and the method used to choose a rule are called a *conflict resolution strategy.*

There are many strategies a rule-based system can employ in choosing an instantiation from the conflict set, such as the first rule to enter the conflict

Rule

```
(p  place-in-partially-filled-room
      (student ^placed-in nil ^sex-is <m/f>
               ^smoker? <smoke>)
      (room ^number <room-num> ^capacity <max>
            ^vacancies { > 0 < <max> }
            ^sexes-are <m/f> ^smokers? <smoke>)
  -->
     .
     :)
```

Working Memory

```
4  (STUDENT ^NAME LEE ^PLACED-IN NIL ^SEX-IS MALE ^SMOKER? YES)
12 (STUDENT ^NAME KIP ^PLACED-IN NIL ^SEX-IS MALE ^SMOKER? NO)
15 (STUDENT ^NAME CINDY ^PLACED-IN NIL ^SEX-IS FEMALE ^SMOKER? NO)
7  (ROOM ^NUMBER 121 ^CAPACITY 2 ^VACANCIES 1 ^SEXES-ARE MALE
        ^SMOKERS? YES)
9  (ROOM ^NUMBER 355 ^CAPACITY 4 ^VACANCIES 2 ^SEXES-ARE MALE
        ^SMOKERS? NO)
3  (ROOM ^NUMBER 197 ^CAPACITY 3 ^VACANCIES 0 ^SEXES-ARE MALE
        ^SMOKERS? YES)
```

Instantiations

```
PLACE-IN-PARTIALLY-FILLED-ROOM 4 7
PLACE-IN-PARTIALLY-FILLED-ROOM 12 9
```

Figure 3.3 Interelement match with variables.

set, or the rule with the highest priority number associated with it.* In OPS5, conflict resolution is based on the following criteria:

- *Refraction.* The same instantiation is never executed more than once.†‡ Two instantiations are the same if they have the same rule name and the same time tags listed in the same order (that is, they have the same WMEs matching to the same condition elements).

*For a discussion and evaluation of conflict resolution strategies, see [McDermott 1978].

†The term *refraction* is from the use of the word in the neurosciences. The refractory period is the time period after a neuron fires during which that same neuron cannot fire again.

‡An exception to the refraction criterion is discussed in Chapter 7, *Programming Techniques.*

- *Recency.* The instantiation whose condition elements are matched by the most recent WMEs is chosen over all others. Recency is determined by a WME's time tag; WMEs that have the highest time tags are the most recent.
- *Specificity.* The instantiation of a rule with a more specific LHS is also given priority. A more specific LHS is one that contains more tests between condition elements and WMEs.
- *Arbitrary choice.* When the preceding criteria fail to select a single instantiation, an instantiation must be chosen at random.

These criteria are used in two strategies: the lexicographic-sort (*LEX*) strategy, and the means-ends-analysis (*MEA*) strategy. The LEX strategy is the simpler of the two, and is the default for conflict resolution. The MEA strategy is commonly used for control in large OPS5 programs. The two strategies are identical except for one step; the MEA strategy has an extra step that makes it more sensitive to the recency of the WMEs.

The following sections further elaborate on recency and specificity, and describe how these criteria are used in the LEX and MEA strategies. The different uses of the two strategies are discussed further in Chapter 5, in conjunction with control strategies.

3.3.1 Recency

Both the LEX and MEA strategies favor instantiations that contain recent data. The recency of a WME is judged by its time tag; a more recent, or newer, WME has a larger time tag. The instantiation with the largest time tag is chosen from the conflict set.

Usually, more than one rule is matched by the most recent WME. When this is the case, the rules matched by the most recent WME are compared by their second-most-recent WME. Likewise, the subset of instantiations that share the second-highest time tag are compared on the basis of the third-highest time tag. This process is repeated until one of the following conditions holds:

- One instantiation has a time tag higher than that of all other instantiations
- More than one instantiation is matched to WMEs with equal recency, but one instantiation has more time tags than the others do
- There are no time tags left to compare in any of the remaining instantiations

Figure 3.4 illustrates recency being used to select instantiations from the conflict set.

Recency treats instantiations as though they all have the same number of time tags to compare. If one instantiation has more time tags than another does, it is as though its extra time tags are compared to zeros. A larger number of

```
BEGIN-ROOM-SELECTION 6 18 4 19
QUERY-USER 6 19 7
POP-TASK 6
ASSIGN-DOUBLE-ROOM-FIRST 6 19 18 3
        |
        | select instantiations with the highest time tag (19)
        ↓
BEGIN-ROOM-SELECTION 6 18 4 19
QUERY-USER 6 19 7
ASSIGN-DOUBLE-ROOM-FIRST 6 19 18 3
        |
        | select instantiations with the next-highest time tag (18)
        ↓
BEGIN-ROOM-SELECTION 6 18 4 19
ASSIGN-DOUBLE-ROOM-FIRST 6 19 18 3
        |
        | next-highest (4)
        ↓
BEGIN-ROOM-SELECTION 6 18 4 19     instantiation to execute
```

Figure 3.4 Selecting an instantiation on the basis of recency.

time tags between two instantiations that are otherwise equally recent is always preferred.* Figure 3.5 illustrates choosing a rule with a larger number of time tags based on recency.

3.3.2 Specificity

The specificity of an instantiation is the number of value tests on the LHS of the rule. This number is calculated once and is stored with the rule. It is used only during conflict resolution, when the recency criteria fails to choose a single instantiation. Usually, a rule can be selected from the conflict set on the basis of recency alone—use of specificity during conflict resolution is a fairly rare occurrence.

Although rules with higher specificities fire before rules with lower specificities matching the same WMEs, it is not good programming style to use specificity to direct the order of rule firings. The specificity of rules is opaque to

*Note that, although it seems that an instantiation being preferred because it has greater number of time tags is an aspect of specificity (since more time tags implies more condition elements), it is in fact an element of the recency criteria. As discussed in the next section, a rule cannot be assumed more specific on the basis of a greater number of condition elements.

```
FILL-IN-DOUBLE-FIRST 76 3
FILL-IN-DOUBLE-FIRST 76 18
USE-SINGLE-IF-NECESSSARY 76 7 9 18
            |
            |  select instantiations with the next-highest time tag
            ↓
FILL-IN-DOUBLE-FIRST 76 18 0 0 0
USE-SINGLE-IF-NECESSARY 76 7 9 18
            |
            |  treat all instantiations as though they have the same
            |  number of time tags; compare an instantiation with
            |  more time tags to zeros
            ↓
USE-SINGLE-IF-NECESSARY 76 7 9 18
```

Figure 3.5 Comparing instantiations that have different numbers of time tags.

future readers or maintainers of the program (including to you). Whenever a rule is modified, its specificity can be affected; if a specific order of rule execution is expected and this order depends on rule specificity, modifying a rule can change the outcome of the program unexpectedly.

The detailed explanation of how specificity is calculated for a rule is given here mostly to help you with difficult cases of debugging. You can skip this level of detail if you are a new OPS5 programmer.

A rule's specificity is the number of value tests performed on the LHS. For example, the following value tests are counted:

- An *element class name* counts as one test.
- A *predicate operator with a constant* (including implied equal-to), such as <= 3, counts as one test.
- A *predicate operator with a bound variable,** such as > <variable>, counts as one test.
- A *disjunction*, such as << a b c d >>, counts as one test.
- Each *predicate or disjunction within a conjunction* counts as one test, so { <=> symbol << yes no maybe >> } adds two to the rule specificity.

*Note that the binding of a variable in its first use on the LHS is *not* a test; no comparison of values is required in this case.

We use the LHS of the rule place-in-partially-filled-room to illustrate how specificity is calculated:

```
(p  place-in-partially-filled-room
       (student ^placed-in nil ^sex-is <m/f>
                 ^smoker? <smoke>)
       (room ^number <room-num> ^capacity <max>
             ^vacancies { > 0 < <max> }
             ^sexes-are <m/f> ^smokers? <smoke>)
   -->
       :
       :)
```

In the first condition element there are two conditional tests. The bindings of the variables <m/f> and <smoke> are not considered countable tests.

element class name	student	1 test
predicate with a constant	^placed-in nil	1 test

The second condition element has five conditional tests:

element class name	room	1 test
each test in conjunction	{ > 0 < <max> }	2 tests
predicate with constant	^sexes-are <m/f>	1 test
predicate with constant	^smokers? <smoke>	1 test
		——
		7 tests

The rule has a total of seven conditional tests; the specificity number is 7.

3.3.3 The LEX and MEA Strategies

The four criteria introduced in Section 3.3 are used in the LEX strategy as follows:

1. Eliminate from the conflict set the instantiations that have already executed (refraction).

2. Order the instantiations based on the recency of the time tags in the instantiation. Select the most recent instantiation(s).

3. If more than one instantiation ties for the highest recency, order the most recent instantiations on the basis of the specificity of the LHS of the production. Select the most specific instantiation(s).

4. If more than one instantiation ties for the highest specificity, choose from the remaining instantiations arbitrarily.

The MEA strategy has an extra step, in which the recency criteria is used to compare all the time tags of the WMEs matching the first condition element in each instantiated rule. MEA first forms a subset of the instantiations whose first condition element is matched by the most recent WME. This step is used in programming techniques that are introduced in Chapter 5, *Control of OPS5 Programs*. The steps of the MEA strategy follow. The step that is different from the LEX strategy is highlighted by boldface characters.

1. Eliminate from the conflict set instantiations that have already executed (refraction).
2. **Order the instantiations based on the recency of the *first* time tag. Select the most recent instantiation(s).**
3. If more than one instantiation shares the highest first time tag, order these instantiations based on the recency of all the time tags in the instantiation. Select the most recent instantiation(s).
4. If more than one instantiation ties for the highest recency, order the most recent instantiations on the basis of the specificity of the LHS of the production. Select the most specific instantiation(s).
5. If more than one instantiation ties for the highest specificity, choose from among these instantiations arbitrarily.

Suppose we find the following conflict set:

```
FILL-DOUBLE-ROOM-FIRST 10 9 6 43
FILL-DOUBLE-ROOM-FIRST 10 43 9 3
SWAP-TO-SINGLE 12 23 17
SWAP-TO-DOUBLE 12  9 23
POP-TASK 9
POP-TASK 12
```

If we use the LEX strategy, first we find the subset of instantiations that have the highest time tag. Both instantiations with the rule name FILL-DOUBLE-ROOM-FIRST share the highest time tag (43). Both of these instantiations also share the time tags 10 and 9. Finally, the instantiation FILL-DOUBLE-ROOM-FIRST 10 9 6 43 is the instantiation chosen for execution, because its next highest time tag (6) is larger than the next highest of the other instantiation (3).

Using the MEA strategy, the first step compares the recency of all time tags matching the first condition element. This step eliminates all but the three instantiations whose first time tag is 12. From these three, all time tags are compared. Two of them have the highest time tag of 23. Only one instantiation, SWAP-TO-SINGLE 12 23 17, has the second highest time tag of 17, so it is chosen for execution.

The LEX and MEA conflict resolution strategies can produce substantially different results and are therefore used for different purposes. These strategies are discussed more fully in Chapter 5.

3.4 Act

Once an instantiation has been chosen by conflict resolution, that rule's RHS is executed during the act step. The `make` actions on the RHS are executed in the order they are written, so the last WME made on the RHS is the most recent.

Working memory is updated immediately as each action is performed. The affects on the matches between WMEs and rules are reflected in the conflict set as soon as the WME is created, deleted, or modified.

If the `halt` action is placed anywhere on the RHS, the rule completes executing all actions before pausing.

Summary

- The recognize-act cycle comprises three steps: match, select (conflict resolution), and act.
- Time tags are assigned to each WME by the rule interpreter to identify WMEs uniquely. Time tags are used in the recognize-act cycle, especially during conflict resolution.
- The match phase of the recognize-act cycle performs an intraelement match between each WME and each condition element, and an interelement match that checks that the same variable names used in different condition elements are matched to the same values.
- Conflict resolution chooses one instantiation from the conflict set using the criteria of refraction, recency, and specificity. If these criteria fail to select a unique instantiation, an instantiation is chosen arbitrarily from those that are equally recent and specific.
- The three criteria are combined into two conflict resolution strategies, the lexicographic-sort (LEX) and means-ends analysis (MEA) strategies.
- During the act phase, the actions on the RHS of the rule are executed in the order they are written. Any changes to working memory are immediately reflected in the conflict set.

Exercises

1. Use of a negated condition element in a rule constrains the number of instantiations that can form during match. A negated condition element is matched just as a positive condition element is; it is only during combination with WMEs matching other condition elements that matches to a negated condition element restrict the formation of instantiations.

   The rule in Figure 3.6 is the same as that in Figure 3.3, except that it contains a negated condition element. This condition element ensures that

Rule

```
(p  place-in-largest-partially-filled-room
      (student ^placed-in nil ^sex-is <m/f>
               ^smoker? <smoke>)
      (room ^number <room-num> ^capacity <max>
            ^vacancies { > 0 < <max> }
            ^sexes-are <m/f> ^smokers? <smoke>)
      - (room ^capacity > <max>
              ^vacancies { > 0 < <max> }
              ^sexes-are <m/f> ^smokers? <smoke>)
   -->
      .
      :)
```

Working Memory

```
4 (STUDENT ^NAME SAM ^PLACED-IN NIL ^SEX-IS MALE ^SMOKING? YES)
7 (ROOM ^NUMBER 121 ^CAPACITY 2 ^VACANCIES 1 ^SEXES-ARE MALE
      ^SMOKERS? YES)
9 (ROOM ^NUMBER 355 ^CAPACITY 4 ^VACANCIES 2 ^SEXES-ARE MALE
      ^SMOKERS? YES)
3 (ROOM ^NUMBER 197 ^CAPACITY 3 ^VACANCIES 0 ^SEXES-ARE MALE
      ^SMOKERS? YES)
```

Figure 3.6 Exercise 1: negated condition elements and matching.

the student is placed in the *largest* partially filled room. Given the rule and a set of WMEs matching each condition element, what will the contents of the conflict set be?

2. For each of the following group of instantiations, determine which instantiation is the most recent.

a.

```
PLACE-STUDENT-IN-SINGLE 84 9 1
PLACE-STUDENT-IN-SINGLE 3 6 21
PRINT-ASSIGNED-STUDENT 84 3 9
QUERY-USER 84 10
```

b.

```
PLACE-STUDENT-IN-SINGLE 9 12 6
PLACE-STUDENT-IN-SINGLE 7 12 1
PLACE-STUDENT-IN-PARTIALLY-FILLED 6 4 9 12
PLACE-STUDENT-IN-SINGLE 9 12 5
QUERY-USER 4 2
```

c.

```
PLACE-STUDENT-IN-SINGLE 9 12 6
PLACE-STUDENT-IN-SINGLE 7 12 1
```

```
PLACE-STUDENT-IN-DOUBLE 12 9 6
QUERY-USER 4 2
```

3. How many conditional tests occur on the LHS of the following rule?

```
(p  search-for-item
      (task ^name item-search)
      (item ^type <item-type-1>
            ^size { <size1> << 30 40 50 >> })
      (item ^name { <item-type-2> <> <item-type-1> }
            ^size { <> <size1> > 50 })
   -->
      .
      :)
```

4. For each of the following conflict sets, which instantiation will fire when the LEX strategy is used? Which will fire when the MEA strategy is used?

a.
```
RULE-ONE 34 67 4  (specificity 8)
RULE-TWO 36 2 3 (specificity 4)
```

b.
```
RULE-THREE 12 36 2 (specificity 5)
RULE-FOUR 12 2 36 7 (specificity 10)
```

c.
```
RULE-FIVE 13 8 5 (specificity 6)
RULE-SIX 5 13 8 (specificity 9)
```

d.
```
RULE-SEVEN 34 5 (specificity 5)
RULE-EIGHT 5 34 (specificity 5)
```

CHAPTER 4

Program Development

THE PRECEDING CHAPTERS have introduced the fundamentals of OPS5. This chapter concludes this introductory material by describing the mechanics of program development: How to start writing a rule base, how to comment, compile, and execute the rule base, how to initialize working memory, and how to interact with the executing program.

We refer to all the facilities of the OPS5 programming environment as the *run-time system*. The run-time system has two components:

1. The rule interpreter
2. The command interpreter

The *rule interpreter* implements the recognize-act cycle, as described in the previous chapter. During the execution of the recognize-act cycle, you can interact with the program through a set of commands. The *command interpreter* is the user-interface component of the run-time system that reads and executes these commands.

The room-assignment problem introduced in Chapter 2, Section 2.1 is used to illustrate program development and execution.

4.1 Creating a Rule Base

This section suggests ways to begin writing a rule base, and offers some basic rule writing and commenting conventions.

4.1.1 Writing the First Rules

When you start writing an OPS5 program, it is useful to write OPS5-like rules in English. Writing English IF–THEN rules helps you to formulate the steps of the problem without being restricted by OPS5 syntax or to your element-class representation. Then, from the English rules, you can begin to write experimental OPS5 rules. Alternating between English and experimental OPS5 rules can help you to determine how the element classes should be structured.

We begin by writing the rule or rules that address the crux of the problem. In the room-assignment problem, for example, we need a rule that assigns a student to a partially filled room, if possible. The English rule for that could be the following:

```
IF
  there is a student who needs housing
  and there is a room that has a vacancy but is not empty
  and the current occupants are of the same sex as the new
      student and have the same smoking preference
THEN
  assign the new student to that room
```

Once you have written a few OPS5 programs, the English you use to write rules will become more and more OPS5-like. You begin to anticipate which statements can and which cannot be represented with OPS5 syntax. You also develop an intuition for how to express a problem in element classes, so your English sentences start with class names and are followed by attributes. For example, the previous rule can be rephrased as

```
IF
  student: name, needs a room, sex, smoker?
  room: with number, has occupants and vacancies, occupants are
      same sex and smoking preference
THEN
  assign student to room: room number with student,
      and decrement room vacancies.
```

Next, we write more rules that solve the main problem. For these first rules, it is best to work as before, from English rules to OPS5, modifying the element classes when necessary. Once the element classes are adequate for most new rules you write, you may find it possible to skip the step of writing English rules. With stable element classes, it is easier to go straight from ideas to condition elements. However, you may still find English rules helpful for clarifying complex interactions among element classes.

After working out several main rules in a structured English form, you can infer the element classes needed to express these rules from the LHS of the rules, as shown Table 4.1.

Table 4.1 Element classes for room assignment.

Class name	Attributes
`student`	`name`
	`placed-in`
	`sex-is`
	`smoker?`
`room`	`number`
	`capacity`
	`vacancies`
	`sexes-are`
	`smokers?`

Note that the representations in Table 4.1 are not the only ones that we could have derived from the English rules, and we may find out later in program development that we need different or additional attributes. For example, the `room` element class may need a list of the current occupants of that room.

Chapter 11, *Designing an OPS5 Application*, carries this discussion further.

4.1.2 Rule-Writing and Commenting Conventions

A typical OPS5 rule base resides in a file or files, created with a text editor. The rules can be placed in any order in the file, but by convention they are grouped by similar functionality to enhance readability.

The rules themselves can be formatted according to any convention you find most readable; it is important only that you use the convention consistently. Appendix B presents OPS5 rule-writing conventions, and explains the motivation for the rule-writing conventions used in this book.

Like any program, an OPS5 rule base should be thoroughly commented. The OPS5 comment character is the semicolon (;). OPS5 ignores everything from the semicolon to the end of a line. Comments can be placed anywhere within and between rules, although there are five places in which comments are particularly important:

1. At the head of the rule base
2. Beside attribute declarations
3. Before a group of rules that share similar functionality
4. At the start of each rule
5. Within a rule if there is code that may be difficult for a reader to understand

Figure 4.1 is a template of a rule base that includes the appropriate placement of comments.

The attribute declarations, `literalize` and `vector-attribute`, are placed at the head of the rule-base file, since all attribute names must be declared before they are used in rules. If a rule base is divided into more than one file, as is allowed in most implementations of OPS5, then the attribute declarations can reside in a separate file that must be compiled first.

4.2 Compilation

All OPS5 rule bases are "compiled" in the sense that the rule base is converted to a discrimination network called the RETE network [Forgy 1982].* The network facilitates efficient matching between rules and working memory, and therefore increases the speed of program execution.

In LISP-based implementations of OPS5, the RETE network is built by converting the rules into memory-resident LISP data structures. Compilation occurs either when the rule starting with `(p...)` is entered at the LISP prompt, or when a file of rules is loaded:

```
lisp> (load 'room_assignment)
```

In non-LISP implementations of OPS5, the discrimination network is constructed by compiling and linking a source file into executable code. The `OPS5` command, for example, is used for compiling a VAX OPS5 rule base, which takes a source file (with default file type `.ops`) and produces an executable file (file type `.exe`).

```
$ ops5 /exe room_assignment
```

Check the documentation provided with your implementation of OPS5 for details on compilation.

4.3 The Command Interpreter

OPS5 provides a set of commands for interacting with a program during the recognize-act cycle, for setting up a programming environment, and for examining program components. In this chapter, we concentrate on only those commands that are essential to writing simple programs:

- Initializing working memory
- Running the recognize-act cycle
- Setting the conflict resolution strategy

---

*See Chapter 10 for a more complete description of this network.

```
;;;;;;;;;;;;;;;;;;;;;;;;;;;;;;;;;;;;;;;;;;;;;;;;;;;;;;;;;;;
;;; Rule file identification information and
;;; an initial comment at the head of the rule base
;;; can explain the purpose of the rules in this file.
;;;
;;;

;;;;;;;;;;;;;;;;;;;;;;;;;;;;;;;;;;;;;;;;;;;;;;;;;;;;;;;;;;;
;; Declarations and initialization

(literalize
                           ; Listing the possible values or
           :               ; the range of values an attribute
              )            ; can have is helpful

(vector-attribute ... )    ; Comments on the use of each
                           ; attribute should appear to its
           :               ; right
;;;;;;;;;;;;;;;;;;;;;;;;;;;;;;;;;;;;;;;;;;;;;;;;;;;;;;;;;;;
;; Rules

;; This comment describes the functionality of the following
;; group of rules. Some conventions use the number of
;; semicolons to indicate the type of comment (for example,
;; these comments are preceded by two semicolons).  The
;; comments at the head of the file of rules are preceded by
;; three semicolons.

; A comment can directly precede the rule.
(p  a-rule-name
;
; Or it can follow the rule name surrounded by two blank
; comment lines to set the comment apart from the rest
; of the rule.
;
     (..condition-element..)
     (..ce..)          ; and comments should follow non-intuitive
                       ; code within the rule: (ce) stands for
         :             ; condition element
  -->
     (..action..)
     (..action..)
         :
      )
     :
```

Figure 4.1 Commenting a rule base

Most of the other commands provided are used for debugging, and are discussed in detail in Chapter 6.

In a LISP-based OPS5, commands are simply function calls that can be invoked from the LISP top level or embedded in LISP applications. The OPS5 command interpreter refers to those top-level function calls in a LISP-based OPS5.

In VAX OPS5, the command interpreter is indicated by the `OPS5>` prompt that appears as the result of running the compiled OPS5 program.

```
$ run room_assignment
OPS5>
```

4.3.1 Initializing Working Memory

The execution of an OPS5 program requires some initial set of WMEs to be created each time the program runs. Creating the first set of WMEs is usually called *initializing* working memory. WMEs are created with the `make` command, an equivalent to the `make` action used in rules. There are various methods, however, of using the `make` command:*

- Typing `make` commands into the command interpreter
- Executing or loading a file of `make` commands
- Creating one "dummy" WME with a `make` command that matches to a rule that contains `make` actions

The stage of program development usually affects how working memory is initialized. In prototypes, or in any OPS5 program under development, working memory is usually initialized by loading a file of `make` commands, using different files for different test cases. In the final stages of OPS5 applications, working memory is usually initialized by calling an external routine from a rule or from a `startup` statement.

The make Command at the Command Interpreter

The `make` command is analogous to the `make` action found on the RHS of rules. It can create only WMEs whose element classes are declared with attribute declarations.

In LISP-based OPS5, `make` commands are entered as function calls at the LISP top level. However, WMEs can be created only after the attribute declarations are processed and after at least one rule has been compiled. If the `make` commands are entered at the LISP prompt, at least one rule must have already been typed in or loaded from a file.

*The first two methods of initializing can be included in the `startup` statement in VAX OPS5 rule bases. This is explained in Section 4.3.4.

The make command

```
OPS5>(make student ^name jsbach ^sex-is male ^smoker? no)
```

creates the WME

```
(STUDENT ^NAME JSBACH ^PLACED-IN NIL ^SEX-IS MALE ^SMOKER? NO)
```

Files of make Commands

All the make commands that initialize working memory should be grouped into a separate file. In LISP-based implementations, this file is loaded after the rule base has been loaded or after a single rule has been entered at the LISP prompt. In VAX OPS5, the at-sign command (@) is used at the command interpreter to load a file of interpreter commands.

For example, if a file, such as one called students.wm, contains the make commands:

```
(make student ^name charley ^sex-is female ^smoker? yes)
(make student ^name karen ^sex-is female ^smoker? no)
(make student ^name dot ^sex-is female ^smoker? yes)
```

then the commands can be executed at the command interpreter in VAX OPS5:

```
OPS5>(@ students.wm)
```

or loaded in LISP-based implementations:

```
lisp> (load 'students.wm)
```

and the following WMEs are created:

```
(STUDENT ^NAME CHARLEY ^PLACED-IN NIL ^SEX-IS FEMALE
         ^SMOKER? YES)
(STUDENT ^NAME KAREN ^PLACED-IN NIL ^SEX-IS FEMALE ^SMOKER? NO)
(STUDENT ^NAME DOT ^PLACED-IN NIL ^SEX-IS FEMALE ^SMOKER? YES)
```

A separate file of make commands can be created for each program test case.

LISP-based OPS5 programs may also have make commands appear at the end of the rule-base source files. This is not an efficient method of OPS5 program development, since it requires a full load of the rule base each time you want working memory initialized, which may be unnecessary. Once the program is debugged and in final form, however, you may decide to move the make commands into the rule base.

Initializing from within rules

The initialization of working memory can be built into the rule base itself by using make actions or a call to an external subroutine on the RHS of a rule. The WME that matches this initialization rule must still be created at the command interpreter. In the following example, the "dummy" WME (start) is created at the command interpreter (called "dummy" because its only purpose is to match to the first rule to execute), and the rule it matches calls to the external subroutine initialize. The RHS of this rule could have similarly included a set of make actions.

```
(p  initialize-working-memory
      (start)
   -->
      (call initialize))
```

In non-LISP implementations of OPS5, the method of initializing in which make commands are themselves in rules is used only in later stages of program development, when the initial state of working memory has stabilized. Otherwise, if the initial state of working memory changes frequently, the rule base must also be changed. If the rule base is large, it is inefficient to edit, compile and run it repeatedly.

4.3.2 Running the Recognize-Act Cycle

The run command starts the execution of the recognize-act cycle. The match-select-act steps repeat until there are no instantiations in the conflict set, a halt is encountered in a rule, or a break that was set from the command interpreter is encountered.

You can specify the number of recognize-act cycles to execute by including that number with the run command. For example, the following run command specifies that three recognize-act cycles (three rule firings) should execute. Trace information is generated by the program as it executes. In the following example, the trace information includes the number of the rule firing and the instantiation that fired.

```
OPS5>(run 3)
1:  INITIALIZE-WORKING MEMORY 1
2:  PLACE-STUDENT-IN-EMPTY-ROOM 87 44
3:  PLACE-STUDENT-IN-PARTIALLY-FILLED-ROOM 85 44
BREAK -- Pause

OPS5>
```

4.3.3 Setting the Conflict Resolution Strategy

Designating the conflict resolution strategy for a program run is called setting the strategy. The strategy is set with the *strategy* command with the keywords `lex` (the default in most implementations) and `mea`. The strategy should be set before any WMEs are created; once set, the strategy should not be changed until another execution of the entire program is performed.

Although it is not necessary to set the LEX strategy (when it is the default), it is always a good idea to declare explicitly which strategy is being used. This makes the strategy clear to the reader, and makes your code portable to implementations of OPS5 that do not use LEX as the default strategy. Specify the strategy as follows:

```
OPS5>(strategy mea)
```

or

```
OPS5>(strategy lex)
```

4.3.4 The startup Statement

`Startup` is a special statement that may appear only once in a VAX OPS5 rule base. `Startup` contains a set of interpreter commands and actions that are compiled with the rule base, and are executed immediately on running the executable rule base. The commands and actions in `startup` make preparations for that program run; the statement is particularly useful for working memory initialization. `Startup` can contain a number of `make` commands, can execute a file of `make` commands, can call to an external routine that creates WMEs, or can create the one WME that matches to the rule that initializes working memory.

```
(startup
      (strategy mea)    ; Set the conflict resolution strategy
      (make ... )       ; Initialize working memory with MAKE
      (make ... )       ;    commands
      (@ students.wm))  ; Execute a file of MAKE commands
```

If one of the commands in the `startup` statement is the `run` command, the program does not pause at the command interpreter but begins executing the recognize-act cycle. If `startup` includes the `(disable halt)` command, then OPS5 does not return control to the command interpreter when the recognize-act cycle is halted. Control is returned directly to the operating system. Including these two commands in the `startup` is the way to "suppress" the OPS5 prompt for users of an OPS5 application. These commands should not be used during program development since they disable important OPS5 debugging facilities accessible from only the command interpreter.

```
(startup
      (disable halt)      ; Suppresses the halt message and
                          ;  returns control to the operating
            :             ;  system after program terminates
      (run))              ; Begins the recognize-act cycle
                          ;  without displaying the command
                          ;  interpreter prompt
```

Summary

- To write a rule base, you can start by writing rules in English. From the English rules, you can write experimental OPS5 rules. Alternating between the two representations gives you a sense of the correct element-class representation for the problem.
- The OPS5 rule base contains the rules, the attribute declarations, and an optional `startup` statement, all appropriately commented.
- Compiling an OPS5 rule base transforms the rules into a discrimination network that makes the program efficient to execute. In VAX OPS5, the rule base is compiled with the `ops5` command. In LISP-based OPS5, the rule base is loaded from rule files, or rules are entered individually at the LISP prompt.
- OPS5 provides a set of commands with which you can interact with your program and with the recognize-act cycle. The command interpreter executes these commands. From the command interpreter, you can initialize working memory, run the recognize-act cycle, and set the conflict resolution strategy.
- The `startup` statement is a special construct in VAX OPS5 that contains commands and actions that are executed immediately on running the rule base, before the recognize-act cycle is started. There is only one `startup` statement; it is executed only once in a program run.

Exercises

1. The exercises in Chapter 2 asked you to write rules for the room-assignment program. In this exercise, you can finish and run the program.
   a. Collect your rules into a single file.
   b. Compile the rule base.
   c. Decide what WMEs have to be initialized at the start of the program, and choose a method of initialization.
   d. Set the conflict resolution strategy to LEX.
   e. Run the program.

CHAPTER 5

Control of OPS5 Programs

DATA-DRIVEN PROGRAMMING LANGUAGES such as OPS5 are notable for their lack of control structures. However, once you have written OPS5 programs, such as those introduced in the earlier chapters of this book, you may recognize that there is some sequentiality even in problems well suited to data-driven programs. This sequentiality corresponds not to the order of individual rule firings, but rather to the organization of larger sections of the rule base.

So how is the sequentiality of a problem expressed in a language that does not have traditional control structures? Although the conflict resolution strategy has some affect on the order of rule firings, the conflict resolution strategy is difficult for the programmer and obscure for the reader to depend on as a control mechanism. In some OPS5 programs, therefore, it is necessary to develop programming techniques for partitioning a large rule base into groups of rules, and for directing the order in which the groups of rules are used.

This chapter introduces the basic concepts and some common programming techniques for controlling groups of OPS5 rules. We stress the following qualities of a good control technique:

- Groups of rules should be used to enforce some degree of modularity on data-driven programming
- Control information should be made explicit as a particular type of problem knowledge, so that it can be maintained easily
- The manipulation of control information should be centralized in as few rules as possible

- Within functional units of the program, the rules should act strictly in a data-driven manner

5.1 The Sensor-Monitoring Problem

To illustrate the concepts introduced in this chapter, we use an OPS5 program that monitors a dynamic physical system through a collection of sensors. Most of the time, the program collects and analyzes data on the change of state of each sensor. When particular combinations of sensor inputs occur, however, the system takes corrective actions. In our example, those actions will be in the form of a summary of the problem, and suggestions to remedy the situation. A user of the system can then either accept or override each of the recommendations the system makes.

5.2 The Representation of Control

In this section we look at the fundamental components of any OPS5 control technique: rule clusters, control WMEs and condition elements, conflict resolution strategies, and the idea of "active" rule clusters.

5.2.1 Rule Clusters

The development of a control strategy in any computer program, whether in OPS5 or in a conventional language, begins during the design process. The initial phase of the design process of a conventional software program begins after the functional scope of the program has been determined. Modules are defined that represent the major functional areas of the program, and these are then further divided into the major routines, data structures, and module interfaces. Finally, the function of each module is fully mapped onto a set of routine specifications and data structures, and coding can begin.

The design process of an OPS5 program is rarely preceded by a functional specification. OPS5 is usually chosen for problems that are dynamically changing or difficult to specify algorithmically. These problems are often difficult to bound prior to some initial implementation.

Consistent with traditional design, an OPS5 problem is first divided into identifiable functional pieces, or *modules*. The modules represent functional units of a useful system, and are not biased by the ease or difficulty of OPS5 implementation. These modules are implemented in an OPS5 program as groups of related rules, which we call *rule clusters*.

In the sensor-monitoring program, we can identify primary modules such as

- Activate sensors
- Analyze data

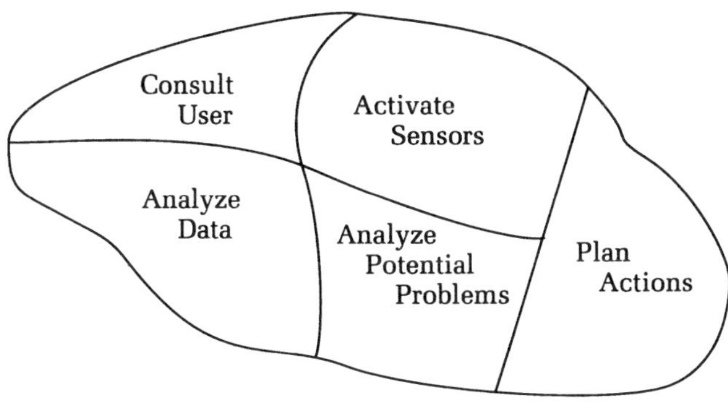

Figure 5.1 The sensor monitoring task and its subtasks.

- Analyze potential problems
- Plan actions
- Consult user

Whereas some of these modules will be implemented as one rule cluster, others may have to be further divided into more than one cluster.

The number of rules in a rule cluster varies greatly, so it should not be used to determine how a task is partitioned. Clusters should be identified by their functional integrity.

Some terminology related to control structures is used consistently in this book. The overall problem to be solved by the OPS5 program is called the *task*. The task of our example domain, for instance, is to monitor a dynamic physical process. The task of many expert systems, particularly during program design, often has amorphous boundaries that do not clearly differentiate what is and is not encompassed in the scope of the problem. In Figure 5.1, the outer perimeter of the entire form represents the task.

The modules that act together to accomplish the task, such as `activate sensors` and `analyze data`, we call *subtasks*.* The subtasks roughly carve the problem space into major functional units, and define the boundaries around groups of rules that work together to accomplish similar goals. Each of the divisions in Figure 5.1 represents a subtask.

*Rule clusters and subtasks are actually the same thing. A rule cluster, however, is seen from the point of view of the OPS5 implementation. A subtask is what we choose to call a rule cluster from the point of view of our domain. OPS5 programmers use many names other than subtask, such as context, goal, or task.

5.2.2 Control WMEs and Control Elements

Once we think we know the subtasks needed to solve a problem, we can develop a representation for them in OPS5. In the control techniques introduced in this chapter, we create an element class specifically for control. Using terminology already established, we call this element class `subtask` with an attribute `^name` that defines the specific subtask. We can call WMEs of this element class *control WMEs*, and condition elements matched by these WMEs *control elements*.

In any program in which we implement a control strategy we include the appropriate attribute declaration, such as

```
(literalize subtask
            name)
```

As you begin to use this technique, you see the advantages of using a separate element class for control. First, having a separate element class makes any manipulation of control explicit, because you always manipulate a WME of the control element class. Second, a uniform representation of all control information allows you to use special rules in the program that can work on *any* control WME.

Each subtask is named by a symbol that describes the functional purpose of that module. For example, our module that plans actions can be named by the symbol `plan-actions`. Each symbolic name for a subtask becomes a value of the attribute `^name` in the WME.

So how do we use the control element class? First, each rule in the program includes a control element that identifies to which subtask it belongs. For example, each rule that is part of the cluster of rules that plans actions for the sensor-monitoring program includes the condition element `(subtask ^name plan-actions)`, as in the following two rule fragments:

```
(p  plan-actions!close-condenser-valve
      (subtask ^name plan-actions)
                     ⋮
(p  plan-actions!right-forger
      (subtask ^name plan-actions)
                     ⋮
```

Notice the rule-naming convention introduced in these rules. The subtask name is listed first, followed by a name specific to the purpose of that rule. The subtask name and rule-specific name are separated by an exclamation mark. This convention helps to identify quickly to which rule cluster a rule belongs. It is particularly useful during rule traces (see Chapter 6, *Debugging an OPS5 Program*).

Once every rule includes a control element, we can "turn on" or "turn off" a group of rules just by creating or deleting their matching control WME. When a control WME is in working memory, all the rules that have that control element on their LHS are not prevented from being instantiated. They may or may not be instantiated based on the presence or absence of other WMEs needed for matching, but they are not actively prevented from matching as they are when the control WME is absent from working memory.

For example, when you make the following control WME, it is possible for the rules in the `plan-actions` subtask to be instantiated:

```
(SUBTASK ^NAME PLAN-ACTIONS)
```

As soon as the WME is deleted from working memory, the rules in that subtask cannot be instantiated. In addition, if there are no other control WMEs, no rules from other subtasks can interfere with the firing of the `plan-actions` subtask.

5.2.3 Control Using LEX and MEA Strategies

A fundamental part of a rule-cluster control technique is the underlying OPS5 conflict resolution strategy. Both the LEX and MEA strategies can be used to build successful control techniques.

The LEX strategy has been used effectively in some control techniques, but its applicability is somewhat limited. LEX was motivated by the pure production-system model, which encourages rule independence and discourages notions of control that extend over the entire rule base. As a result, it is difficult to develop cluster-level control techniques using LEX.

In our experience, systems of more than a few hundred rules developed using the LEX strategy have characteristic problems. If the rule base is not partitioned into clusters, there is excessive matching between WMEs and rules that are not instantiated or do not fire. Unnecessary matching can be extremely costly in an OPS5 program. It is also difficult to predict how adding or modifying rules will affect the execution of other rules in the program. Therefore, maintenance and debugging can become problematic.

It is possible to use the LEX strategy with rule bases that are partitioned into clusters, but we shall see in the techniques developed in the following sections that there are advantages to using MEA in these cases.

The development of the MEA conflict resolution strategy was motivated by a need for a much tighter and global control over choices made during conflict resolution. The focus on the first condition element of each rule presents a natural opportunity to use that element for cluster control. In our experiences developing OPS5 programs that have from a few hundred to several thousand rules, MEA has always been the strategy necessary for the required cluster control.

Although the MEA strategy provides a natural mechanism to implement control between subtasks, it retains purely data-driven behavior within each subtask. Instantiations from the same subtask share the first condition element, so they compete in the conflict set in a data-driven manner, as though using the LEX strategy.

5.2.4 Multiple active rule clusters using MEA

It should be clear that, if all rules contain a control element and working memory contains only one control WME at a time, only one rule cluster can be instantiated. But what if there is more than one control WME in working memory at the same time? Rules from more than one subtask can be instantiated. Do the subtasks interfere with one another? Which subtask's instantiations fire first?

To order the priority of instantiations of more than one subtask, it is easiest to use the MEA conflict resolution strategy. The MEA strategy orders instantiations in the conflict set based first on the relative recency of the WME matching each rule's first condition element. If every rule in a program is written such that its control element always appears as the *first* condition element, then the rules in the subtask that are matched by the most recent control WME are preferred over any of the rules that are matched by any other control WME. The priority of a subtask is determined by the recency of the time tag matching its control WME.

Suppose the following control WMEs are made:

```
1 (SUBTASK ^NAME PLAN-ACTIONS)
2 (SUBTASK ^NAME ANALYZE-POTENTIAL-PROBLEM)
3 (SUBTASK ^NAME ANALYZE-DATA)
```

and that the following hypothetical conflict set results:

```
ANALYZE-POTENTIAL-PROBLEM!CHECK-FOR-O-MISFIT 2 75 6 122
ANALYZE-POTENTIAL-PROBLEM!CHECK-GASKET 2 12 99
ANALYZE-POTENTIAL-PROBLEM!P-TERM-MISS 2 33 65 80
ANALYZE-POTENTIAL-PROBLEM!P-TERM-MISS 2 33 65 94
ANALYZE-DATA!CONDENSE-TERMS 3 7 16
ANALYZE-DATA!CONDENSE-TERMS 3 12 23
ANALYZE-DATA!ADD-ONS 3 47 32
PLAN-ACTIONS!SET-UP 1 19
PLAN-ACTIONS!SET-UP 1 21
PLAN-ACTIONS!STEP-A 1 82 104 98
PLAN-ACTIONS!STEP-A 1 82 104 115
```

Using the MEA strategy, all the instantiations in the conflict set from the subtask `analyze-data` will fire before any other instantiations that appear in the given conflict set.* This can be seen easily by inspection of the conflict set because only the first time tag in each instantiation has to be compared. Since the most recent control WME has the time tag 3, and this corresponds to

*We assume that none of the rules in that subtask modifies or deletes control WMEs.

the control WME with the value `analyze-data`, instantiations from that subtask have highest priority to fire. Given the conflict set shown, the next subtask's instantiations to fire would be `analyze-potential-problem`, and the last to fire would be from the `plan-actions` subtask.

5.3 Rule Cluster Control

So far, the components of our control strategy are

- Defining the subtasks that make up a program, each subtask accomplished by a rule cluster
- Representing subtasks in an element class (our choice was the element class `subtask` and the attribute `^name`)
- Including a control element in all rules as the first condition element
- Using the MEA strategy

The next step is to define methods of manipulating the control WMEs that are neither so strict as to make the ordering of subtasks inflexible, nor so loose that clusters of rules interfere with one another unproductively.

First, we introduce the methods of switching between subtasks. In the previous section, we saw that the recency of the control WME determined the priority of subtasks in the conflict set. Here we look at a single control WME and at how it might be manipulated in a program as part of a control strategy.

5.3.1 Modifying the Control WME

The most obvious method of controlling which subtask has highest priority in the conflict set is to allow only one control WME to exist at a time. In this case, only the rules that are matched by that control WME can be instantiated.

But then how do you switch from one subtask to another? One approach is to use a rule (or rules) in the subtask to *modify* the subtask name on the RHS. In Figure 5.2, a rule in the subtask named `plan-actions` modifies the control WME to the subtask named `consult-user` by modifying the `^name` attribute.

There are advantages in directing control by modifying the subtask name. Only instantiations from one subtask are in the conflict set at any one time. A homogeneous conflict set makes control very clear from the perspective of conflict resolution. The conflict set tends to be smaller with one subtask's instantiations than with more than one, and a small conflict set is desirable from the standpoint of efficiency.

The disadvantages of this technique, however, tend to outweigh its advantages. This technique violates our guideline that stresses modularity of control information. When a control WME is allowed to be modified on the RHS of any rule in the program, then the number of locations of subtask changes can be as large as the number of rules in the rule base! Modifying control WMEs

```
(p  plan-actions!done
   { <Subtask>
      (subtask ^name plan-actions) }
         :
   -->
         :
      (modify <Subtask> ^name consult-user))
```

Figure 5.2 Switching the active subtask by modifying the control element.

from within subtask rules causes problems similar to the problems in the use of the GOTO statement of sequential languages: When you modify the subtask name, the program cannot return control to the previous subtask when the next subtask is completed. Testing and maintenance of such a program is extremely difficult.

5.3.2 The Subtask Stack

A more flexible, maintainable technique for switching from one subtask to another uses what we call a *subtask stack.*

You can think of all the control WMEs in working memory as though they are organized as a stack. Each control WME represents a subtask. At the top of the stack are the control WMEs most recently added to working memory; at the bottom are those created earlier in the program. When more than one control WME is in working memory at the same time, the control WME at the top of the stack (that is, the most recent in working memory) identifies the subtask whose instantiations will dominate in the conflict set.

The stack analogy extends to the kinds of operations needed to use a subtask-stack control method. A *push,* for instance, is implemented by an RHS `make` action that adds a new, most recent, control element to working memory. Control WMEs must be pushed on the stack in the order opposite from that in which you intend them to execute. The last WME pushed on the stack has the highest time tag, so any rule matching that WME has higher priority in the conflict set.

One rule can push a group of control WMEs on the stack for a program, or for a section of a program. In the following example, the instantiation of rules in the `plan-actions` subtask have the highest priority in the conflict set. The instantiated rules in the `post-mortem-report` subtask do not execute until there are no rules instantiated in any of the other subtasks.

```
(p  analyze-potential-problem!go-with-it
        ...
   -->
      (make subtask ^name post-mortem-report)
      (make subtask ^name execute-actions)
      (make subtask ^name consult-user)
      (make subtask ^name plan-actions))
```

There are two problems that must be addressed regarding the subtask stack. First, we have not specified a method of removing, or *popping*, a control WME from the stack after all instantiations of that subtask have executed. Second, creating all control WMEs for a program implies that instantiations from all subtasks can be in the conflict set at the same time, which may be very inefficient.

5.3.3 Removing Control WMEs: The pop-subtask Rule

After the instantiations of rules matched by the most recent control WME have executed, it is best to remove that control WME from working memory. If it remains in working memory, it is possible that a rule in a later subtask will create WMEs that reinstantiate the rules from earlier subtasks. Since the rules of earlier subtasks are still matched by a control WME more recent than the currently active subtask, the new instantiations of the subtask will immediately take priority in the conflict set. It might be inappropriate to the execution of the program for these rules to fire again. For example, if the `plan-actions` subtask of the sensor-monitoring program is interrupted by the firing of a rule in the `activate-sensors` subtask, it may cause actions to be planned for sensory input unrelated to the current problem being solved.

One way to remove the most recent control WME after all of its instantiations have executed is to include one rule in the rule base that says, "Whenever there is a `subtask` WME, remove it." Using another analogy to stack operations, we call this a *`pop-subtask`* rule. Figure 5.3 shows the `pop-subtask` rule for a program in which the control element class has the class name `subtask`.

Because this rule does not specify the name of a subtask, it matches every subtask WME. Since it has only one conditional test (the class name `subtask`) on its LHS, and all other rules in a subtask, even if they have only one condition element, have at least two conditional tests (the subtask class name and the value of `^name` attribute), the `pop-subtask` rule is guaranteed to be the least specific rule of every rule cluster. All instantiations that match a particular control WME are at least as recent and are more specific, so they are always of higher priority than is the `pop-subtask` rule during conflict resolution. Therefore, the `pop-subtask` rule waits until all instantiations of a subtask

```
(p  pop-subtask
   { <Top>
      (subtask) }
   -->
      (remove <Top>))
```

Figure 5.3 The pop-subtask rule

have fired and then removes the control WME from working memory. Further execution of instantiations from this subtask are inhibited until a new control WME for it is created.

If you use the `pop-subtask` rule in your program, you should avoid other rules that remove or otherwise modify the control WME. Such rules artificially inhibit other rules in the same subtask, violate the assumption that subtasks run until completion, and, most important, make flow of control difficult to trace.

Notice the similarity between invoking rule clusters using the subtask stack with the `pop-subtask` rule, and function and procedure calling of sequential languages. One of the rules in a subtask can create a control WME on its RHS. The newly created control WME is the most recent in working memory, so all rules matching this control WME immediately have priority in the conflict set. The instantiations from the *calling* subtask (from which the new control WME was made) cannot fire until all the instantiations matching the new control WME have fired, and the `pop-subtask` rule has removed that control WME. The *called* subtask may create new control WMEs that *invoke* other subtasks, each of whose instantiations have higher priority in the conflict set. All the control WMEs must be removed with the `pop-subtask` rule before *control is returned* to the original subtask, by means of priority during conflict resolution. The important point here is that priority does return to the subtask from which new subtasks are created, thereby focusing control back on the place in the program from which control WMEs are created.

Remember that the flow of control to which we are referring here is among *clusters* of rules, not among the rules themselves. Our goal is to concentrate on one group of rules at a time, not to decide ahead of time the order of rule firings.

An advantage to using a subtask stack that is unlike procedural programming is that, when a subtask is enabled, there is no requirement that a rule in that subtask fire before the next subtask is enabled. If enabling a subtask does not yield any instantiations, the associated control WME is simply removed by `pop-subtask`. In fact, you do not have to have *any* rules in the rule base that are members of a subtask whose control WME is created. This encourages top-down design strategies, in which you can test a top-level skeleton before writing any of the lower-level subtasks.

5.3.4 Subtask Stack and Efficiency

It is possible that the subtask stack as presented thus far could cause an efficiency problem. When the subtask stack is initially created, all the rules that match those control WMEs can create one or more instantiations. Although the instantiations created do not fire inappropriately, a large conflict set is an indication that many rules were matched unnecessarily. Chapter 10, *Efficiency*, discusses the reasons that the match process is the efficiency bottleneck in OPS5 programs.

There are many ways to modify the subtask-stack control strategy such that the conflict set does not include instantiations from every subtask in the subtask stack. These modifications "block" the matching of all control WMEs except the most recent. The control WMEs other than the first contain an extra value that does not match to the control elements in rules.

One method for achieving a limited match is to add a `^status` attribute to the `subtask` element class:

```
(literalize subtask
            name
            status)
```

The values for the `^status` attribute can be either `active` or `pending`. The control element in the rules must now include the attribute and value `^status active`.

```
(p  plan-actions!close-condenser-valve
      (subtask ^name plan-actions ^status active)
                   ⋮
(p  plan-actions!right-forger
      (subtask ^name plan-actions ^status active)
                   ⋮
```

Only the control WMEs that have the value `active` for the `^status` attribute can match to rules and yield instantiations for the conflict set. Therefore, when we build the subtask stack, all but the most recent control WMEs have the value `pending` for the `^status` attribute.

```
(p  analyze-potential-problem!go-with-it
        ...
   -->
      (make subtask ^name post-mortem-report ^status pending)
      (make subtask ^name execute-actions ^status pending)
      (make subtask ^name consult-user ^status pending)
      (make subtask ^name plan-actions ^status active))
```

In the example, only the rules in the subtask `plan-actions` can create instantiations. All the other control WMEs are blocked from matching the control elements in their rules because the value for the `^status` attribute in each of those rules is `pending` rather than `active`.

Now we need a method of changing the value `pending` to `active` in a control WME when we want that WME to activate instantiations of the associated subtask. We can add one rule to the program that matches to all `subtask` WMEs whose value for `^status` is `pending`, and that modifies the value to `active`.

```
(p  pending-to-active
   { <Pending>
      (subtask ^status pending) }
   -->
      (modify <Pending> ^status active))
```

This control technique still requires use of the `pop-subtask` rule, since we still want to remove control WMEs whose instantiations have all fired. This rule is not changed by the additional `^status` attribute:

```
(p  pop-subtask
   { <Top>
      (subtask) }
   -->
      (remove <Top>))
```

Exercise 5.2 asks you to figure out the order that the `pop-subtask` rule, the `pending-to-active` rule, and the instantiations of a subtask fire in relation to one another. This is a necessary exercise for you to do to convince yourself that this technique works as intended.

This technique, in which control WMEs in a subtask stack are prevented from firing with the values of a `^status` attribute, meets our criteria for a good control technique. Namely,

- Groups of rules that work toward the same goal are considered a "cluster" and are represented by a unique name.
- The control information used in the program is made explicit in the `subtask` element class. We know that WMEs of this element class always contain information about a subtask and indicate whether that subtask is the "active" subtask or a "pending" subtask.
- The manipulation of the program's control information is now centralized in the creation of subtask stacks and by the removal of control WMEs by one `pop-subtask` rule.

The last criterion of a good control technique—that rules within a subtask should act in a strictly data-driven manner—is not a result of a particular control technique, but rather must be accomplished within the framework of the control strategy and enforced by the programmer.

5.3.5 Agendas

Although the subtask stack meets our criteria for a good control technique and can be made relatively efficient by "hiding" inactive subtask WMEs, the technique lacks elegance. Since each control WME is made separately, working memory does not highlight the ordering dependencies. It is also awkward to have to create subtask WMEs in the order opposite from that in which they will be enabled, just so the last created is the most recent.

This section presents the most common alternative to the subtask stack—the agenda. An *agenda* is a vector of subtask names listed in sequential order. Whenever all the instantiations of a subtask have executed, the current control WME is deleted and the next subtask name in the agenda is used to create a new subtask WME.

Representation of an Agenda

There are at least two ways to represent an agenda. First, the agenda can be a vector attribute added to the element class we have been using for control, as in the following:

```
(literalize subtask         ; The element class for control
     name
     agenda)

(vector-attribute agenda) ; The vector holding subtask names
```

Alternatively, the agenda can be represented in its own element class:

```
(literalize subtask  ; This element class used in
     name)           ; rules to designate the subtask

(literalize agenda   ; This element class used in the control
     subtasks)       ; rules to retrieve the next subtask name.

(vector-attribute subtasks)  ; The vector of subtask names
```

This chapter uses the latter representation. Determining the differences between this representation and that of including the agenda in the `subtask` WME is the subject of Exercise 5.5.

The rules within subtasks look the same whether you are using agendas or a subtask stack. Each rule's first condition element matches WMEs of the `subtask` element class:

```
(p  consult-user!request-current-data
      (subtask ^name consult-user)
```

To create a sequence of subtasks, we create an `agenda` WME from the RHS of a rule:

```
(make agenda ^subtasks plan-actions consult-user
       execute-actions post-mortem-report)
```

The agenda thus created contains the names of four subtasks that will be enabled in the order they are written. The subtask `plan-actions` is enabled first, followed by `consult-user`, `execute-actions`, and `post-mortem-report`.

Control Rules Used with Agendas

A control technique that uses agendas represented in a separate element class requires three control rules:

1. A rule to remove the currently active control WME (`pop-subtask`):

```
(p  pop-subtask
   { <Control>
      (subtask) }
   -->
      (remove <Control>))
```

2. A rule to create a new control WME using the subtask name at the head of the agenda (`next-subtask-from-agenda`):

```
(p  next-subtask-from-agenda
   { <Agenda>
      (agenda ^subtasks { <next-subtask> <> nil }) }
   -->
      (bind <first-position> (litval subtasks))
      (bind <second-position>
            (compute <first-position> + 1))
      (remove <Agenda>)
      (make agenda
         ^subtasks (substr <Agenda>
                           <second-position> inf))
      (make subtask ^name <next-subtask>))
```

3. A rule that removes the agenda WME when all of its subtasks have been used (remove-agenda):

```
(p  remove-agenda
   { <Used-agenda>
      (agenda ^subtasks nil) }
   -->
      (remove <Used-agenda>))
```

The first rule is the same as that introduced for the subtask stack in Figure 5.3. The pop-subtask rule will form an instantiation for each control WME. Its purpose is to remove the control WME when all other instantiations of that subtask have executed.*

Once a control WME is removed by pop-subtask, the new control WME is created using the next name in the vector of subtask names. The control rule, next-subtask-from-agenda, removes the next name from the agenda and creates a control WME from it. This rule executes *after* the pop-subtask rule, because the agenda WME is more recent than is any other control WME, once the most recent control WME is removed. (This is guaranteed, since the agenda is recreated every time the new control WME is made.)

The next-subtask-from-agenda rule may require some study. On the LHS, a condition element matches the agenda WME, and binds the variable <next-subtask> to the first element of the vector attribute ^subtasks. This variable is used on the RHS to build a new subtask WME:

```
(make subtask ^name <next-subtask>)
```

Notice that the new control WME is created *after* the modification of the agenda, so the control WME is more recent than is the agenda.

On the RHS of the rule, we have to modify the vector such that the first element is removed, and the rest of the values in the vector shift one position to the left.†

The third control rule of the agenda technique removes the agenda WME after all of the subtask names in the agenda have been used to make control WMEs. The rule detects this situation when the first value in the ^subtask vector attribute is nil.

It is important to understand what each of the control rules associated with the agenda are, and the order in which they execute to change the active subtask.

---

*For a review of the pop-subtask rule, see Section 5.3.3.

† See Chapter 2 Section 3.3 for a review of how values in vectors are manipulated.

5.3.6 Indirect Control Techniques

The control techniques introduced in this chapter thus far can be considered direct control techniques. A *direct control technique* is one that can map from program state onto rules that invoke subtasks appropriate to that program state. *Indirect control techniques* are those in which the mapping from program state to subtask is not directly encoded in rules before the program run.

For example, suppose the creation of an agenda in a program depends on user input. The user enters a keyword that, to the program, represents an agenda. This technique is indirect. There may be several keywords, each of which corresponds to a different list of subtasks.

One OPS5 implementation of a technique in which a keyword matches an agenda is the following. The program may have several WMEs of the element class `dispatch-list` that have an attribute `^keyword` and a vector attribute `^subtasks`. Every value of the `^keyword` attribute is associated with a unique vector of subtask names. The agenda WME is created by copying the values from the `^subtask` vector in the `dispatch-list` WME when the user input matches the value of that WME's `^keyword` attribute.

```
(p  activate-sensors!activate-requested-sensor-type
;
; The DISPATCH-LIST contains the vector-attribute ^subtasks
; holding subtask names.
;
      (subtask ^name activate-sensors)
      (user-input ^value <keyword>)
   { <D-list>
      (dispatch-list ^keyword <keyword>) }
   -->
      (make agenda
              ^subtasks (substr <D-list> subtasks inf)))
```

Another indirect control technique is one in which subtask names are obtained by calls to a user-supplied external routine. The external routine can be either a subroutine or a function;* for example,

```
(call make_agenda <keyword>)
```

or

```
(make agenda ^subtasks (get_next_subtask_list))
```

*See Chapter 8, *External Routines*, for a complete explanation of user-written functions and subroutines.

Menu-Driven Control

A menu-driven control technique in which the subtasks instantiated depend on a user's choice from a menu is another example of indirect control. The following example is domain independent, and can be used in any program and for more than one menu in the same program. All menus in this example are displayed in the form shown in Figure 5.4.

Two element classes are used. The first holds information about a particular menu:

```
(literalize menu
  menu-id            ; A unique identifier for this menu
  max-choices        ; The number of choices the menu contains
  display-counter    ; The number of the choice being displayed
  user-choice        ; The menu choice the user picks
  default-subtask    ; Subtask to execute if user chooses
                     ;  default
  menu-prompt)       ; The prompt for user input after menu is
                     ;  displayed
```

The second element class contains information about each line of the menu:

```
(literalize menu-line
  menu-id            ; The identifier to the menu of which this
                     ;  line is a part
  display-number     ; The number this line is, in order of
                     ;  display
  text-on-line       ; The text describing this choice
  subtask)           ; The subtask to execute if this choice is
                     ;  chosen
```

Given the two-element-class representation, at least five control rules are needed to manipulate a menu. One rule displays the menu; another prompts the user for a response. The user's response is acted on by a rule that invokes the

```
1) [text for first choice]
2) [text for second choice]
:       :
<max>) [text for last choice]

  [text of question ]:  ←— (cursor waits there)
```

Figure 5.4 The display menu.

appropriate subtasks. Special rules exist to check for the default response and for invalid responses. The rules that create the menu initially or delete WMEs from previously used menus have been left to the specific application.

```
(p  menu!display-each-line-on-menu
;
; Display all the choices on the menu.  The
; value of the ^display-counter attribute should
; be 1 when the menu WME is created.
;
      (subtask ^name menu)
   { <Display-control>
      (menu ^menu-id <id> ^max-choices <max>
            ^display-counter { <disp> <= <max> }) }
   { <Display-content>
      (menu-line ^menu-id <id> ^display-number <disp>
            ^text-on-line <text>) }
   -->
      (write (crlf) (tabto 10) (rjust 2) <disp> (rjust 1) |)|
         (substr <Display-content> text-on-line inf))
      (modify <Display-control>
         ^display-counter (compute 1 + <disp>)))

(p  menu!prompt-user
;
; User has not responded yet, and all choices have been
; displayed, so prompt user for a response
;
      (subtask ^name menu)
   { <Display-control>
      (menu ^max-choices <max> ^display-counter > <max>
            ^user-choice nil) }
   -->
      (write (crlf) (crlf) (tabto 5)
         (substr <Display-control> menu-prompt inf))
      (modify <Display-control>
         ^user-choice (acceptline default)))

(p  menu!valid-user-response
;
; When the user choice matches a menu number, match it
; to the corresponding menu list and create the
; appropriate subtask.
;
      (subtask ^name menu)
```

```
   { <Display-control>
      (menu ^menu-id <id>
            ^user-choice { <choice> <> default <> nil }) }
      (menu-line ^menu-id <id> ^display-number <choice>
            ^subtask <subtask>)
   -->
      (make subtask ^name <subtask>)
      (remove <Display-control>))

(p  menu!default-response
;
; The user chose the default, so convert
; into the correct subtask.
;
      (subtask ^name menu)
   { <Display-control>
      (menu ^user-choice default
            ^default-subtask <subtask>) }
   -->
      (make subtask ^name <subtask>)
      (remove <Display-control>))

(p  menu!invalid-response
;
; The user's choice does not correspond to
; one of the lines on the menu or to the
; default, so let her try again.
;
      (subtask ^name menu)
   { <Display-control>
      (menu ^menu-id <id>
            ^user-choice { <choice> <> default <> nil }) }
      - (menu-line ^menu-id <id> ^display-number <choice>)
   -->
      (write (crlf) (crlf) |Invalid menu selection...| (crlf)
        |Please reselect the number left of desired choice.|
        (crlf) |  (A blank response gives the choice in [ ])|)
      (modify <Display-control> ^selected nil))
```

5.4 Developing a Control Technique

The control strategies discussed in this chapter are rarely used as the single strategy in a large OPS5 program. From within a subtask that is part of an agenda, you can create a subtask stack. From within a subtask that is part of a subtask stack, you can create an agenda of subtasks. In addition, indirect control methods are always used in combination with other control techniques.

To maximize the maintainability of a control technique that you create, try to make the technique simple, and make the manipulation of control information explicit and centralized. These goals help you to make the program predictable and therefore easy to follow and maintain.

In programs in which all control WMEs are created immediately when the program begins, there will be a predefined path of subtasks instantiated during program execution. When the control path is predefined, maintenance is limited to ensuring that the proper knowledge is represented in each subtask.

Few OPS5 applications, however, have a predefined control flow. Usually control WMEs are created from many rules in the system, so the order in which subtasks are instantiated depends on the state of program execution. From each rule in which a control WME is created, there is a new possible path of instantiating subtasks. A large number of paths through a program is often the cause of maintenance difficulties. However, the large number of paths may be an inherent characteristic of the problem being solved, and may be the primary reason for using a data-driven rule-based language such as OPS5.

Regardless of what control technique or combination of control techniques is used in a program, it is important *not* to modify or remove the subtask WME name on the RHS of a rule *within* a subtask. A subtask should stay active until no more rules in that subtask can fire. If a rule in the subtask violates this practice and modifies the subtask name, then some rules in the subtask may never get the chance to fire because of lack of a control WME.

A control rule, such as `pop-subtask`, is designed to be selected by conflict resolution only when there are no more instantiations of the corresponding subtask. It is, therefore, accepted practice to modify the subtask name in a control rule. It is only modifying the subtask name from within the subtask that can cause rule interdependencies that stand in the way of easily extending the program.

Notice that, when a rule within a subtask creates a WME to invoke a subtask, this does not impede maintenance the same way that modifying the subtask does. Although creating a `subtask` WME instantiates a subtask that will have highest priority in the conflict set, when the newly created subtask's instantiations have finished firing, the control WME is popped and the previous subtask's instantiations again have high priority in the conflict set.

Summary

- The guidelines for creating a good control technique are that you seek modularity, explicit control, centralized control, and data-driven rules within the framework of the control technique.

- A rule cluster is a group of rules that work together to accomplish a particular task.

- A task is the overall goal of the program. A subtask is a functional unit needed to achieve the task. A subtask is the application view of a rule cluster.
- Control information can be uniformly represented in an element class, such as `subtask`. WMEs of this element class are called control WMEs. Each rule in an OPS5 program that is a part of a rule cluster contains a condition element that matches to a control WME. This condition element is called a control element.
- Although both the LEX and MEA strategies provide the basis for control techniques, MEA tends to be more useful for most applications. The MEA strategy is used to order the priority of a different subtask's instantiations by comparing the control WMEs matching to the rule's first condition element.
- Modifying the control WME on the RHS of a rule within a subtask may seem to be a direct way of manipulating a control WME, but it produces a complicated web of subtask paths through a program and makes changes to the subtask flow more difficult to trace.
- A subtask stack is a method of ordering control WMEs based on their order of creation. Control WMEs whose rules have already been instantiated and fired can be removed from working memory using a rule called the `pop-subtask` rule.
- An agenda is a control technique in which the subtask names are held in a vector. The vector can be either part of the control WME or in a separate element class. This is a compact and direct way of representing and storing subtask names.
- Indirect control techniques are those in which the order of subtask activation is determined by some outside input during program execution. For example, control techniques that require input from a user or an external routine to determine the order of subtask instantiation are examples of indirect control.
- No single control technique is used in isolation. Most programs use a combination of control techniques.

Exercises

1. Why is it important to have an element class for control? Why couldn't we use a single symbol to represent each subtask, such as `activate-sensors`, or `analyze-data`, and use these as values in condition elements in the LHS? For example, the rules could look like the following legitimate OPS5 syntax:

```
(p  plan-actions!close-condensor-valve
      (plan-actions)
         ⋮
```

What are the disadvantages to this control strategy?

2. When using a subtask stack and a `^status` attribute in the control WME to block matching, in what order do the following components of this technique fire?

   - The instantiations of a subtask
   - The `pending-to-active` rule
   - The `pop-subtask` rule

   Why do they fire in the order you specified?

3. Suppose you have a program, such as the room-assignment program, to which you would like to add the subtask-stack control strategy. What must you do to your program to add this control strategy?

4. Section 5.3.4 introduced one method of reducing the size of the conflict set using the `^status` attribute. Can you think of another way of blocking the matching of all control WMEs except the most recent?

5. Suppose you choose to represent a control technique that uses an agenda, but the agenda is included in the following `subtask` control WME:

```
(literalize subtask
            name
            agenda)

(vector-attribute agenda)
```

   What are the control rules that you would need to go with this representation?

6. Create a control technique that cycles through a set of subtasks repeatedly. For example, if an OPS5 program played a game between a computer player and human player, you might need a set of subtasks, such as `initialize-game`, `display-board`, `human-move`, `display-board`, `computer-move`, in which the last four subtasks would repeat until the game was over.

7. The strategies for masking subtasks discussed in this chapter do not take into consideration the masking of matches made to rules in subtasks that have been interrupted by a newer, active subtask. For example, in the following subtask-level control flow, **A** through **E** are subtasks, and an arrow —> represents a single RHS `make` action of the control elements following it:

   A rule in subtask **A** makes a control element for **B**:
   A —> B
   A rule in subtask **B** makes control elements for **C**, **D**, and **E**:
   B —> C, D, E

The subtasks **C** and **D** can be masked using the various strategies mentioned in this chapter, but although **E** is the *active* subtask, **A** and **B** are also considered active and are not masked. Subtasks **A** and **B** lose during conflict resolution because of recency. The problem is that subtasks **A** and **B** may cause substantial unnecessary matching.

Consider the following proposed solution. Create every subtask WME without specifying any value for the status attribute, then add the following two rules to the system in addition to a `revive-subtask` rule that changes a pending subtask back to active:

```
(p  hide-interrupted-subtask
;
; Hide the currently active subtask and
; make the interrupting subtask active.
;
  { <Interrupter>
      (subtask ^status nil) }
  { <Interrupted>
      (subtask ^status active) }
   -->
      (modify <Interrupted> ^status pending)
      (modify <Interrupter> ^status active))

(p  enable-new-subtask
;
; Do new ones before pending
;
      (subtask ^status pending)
   { <New>
      (subtask ^status nil) }
   -->
      (modify <New> ^status active))
```

Note that the very first subtask WME must be made with `status ^active`. Will this approach solve the problem? Why or why not? Are there any reasons why you might *not* want to solve this problem?

8. Describe what happens if the `agenda` WME is modified after the new control WME is made in the `next-subtask-from-agenda` rule:

```
(p  next-subtask-from-agenda
   { <Agenda>
      (agenda ^subtasks { <next-subtask> <> nil }) }
   -->
      (bind <first-position> (litval subtasks))
      (bind <second-position> (compute <first-position> + 1))
```

```
        (remove <Agenda>)
        (make agenda
           ^subtasks (substr <Agenda> <second-position> inf))
        (make subtask ^name <next-subtask>))
```

9. What would happen in the following next-subtask-from-agenda rule if the nil were not included in the modify action after the substr function? What would happen if an extra nil were added?

```
(p  next-subtask-from-agenda
   { <Agenda>
      (agenda ^subtasks { <next-subtask> <> nil }) }
   -->
      (bind <first-position> (litval subtasks))
      (bind <second-position> (compute <first-position> + 1))
      (modify <Agenda>
         ^subtasks (substr <Agenda> <second-position> inf)
                  nil)
      (make subtask ^name <next-subtask>))
```

CHAPTER 6

Debugging an OPS5 Program

THERE ARE TWO MAJOR TASKS involved in producing error-free programs. One is making early design decisions that facilitate writing, testing, and maintenance. The other is finding and correcting the unanticipated and inevitable errors that block the successful outcome of a program. The former is discussed in Chapter 11, *Designing an OPS5 Application*. This chapter is for use during those unfortunate moments when you are faced with finding and correcting errors in an existing OPS5 program.

Like most language compilers, OPS5 compilers consistently detect invalid syntax. Most OPS5 programming errors are not due to invalid syntax, however. The simplicity of the OPS5 language makes it easy for a programmer unintentionally to skip or transpose characters, atoms, or elements, and still to produce legal syntax that compiles but causes run-time errors. This chapter discusses common syntax errors and solutions that are largely independent of application domain logic.

The fundamental skill required for debugging is the ability to "think like" the mechanism that drives the executing program. In OPS5, the mechanism is the recognize-act cycle. You must be able to explain the behavior of the program in terms of rules, working memory, and the recognize-act cycle. This skill is valuable in diagnosing and correcting common programming errors.

OPS5 provides a set of commands that help you to detect the location and nature of an error: commands to examine working memory, the conflict set, and all matches between WMEs and condition elements in particular rules.

In this chapter, we organize the discussion of debugging into three parts:

1. Common syntax errors

2. The commands OPS5 provides to find errors during the execution of the recognize-act cycle

3. Guidelines for debugging

To illustrate the debugging process, we will work with the OPS5 room-assignment program introduced in Chapter 2 which assigns students to temporary housing.

6.1 Syntax Errors

Most syntax errors are detected by the OPS5 compiler. Errors such as unmatched parentheses or misspelled RHS action names are not difficult for the programmer to find and correct.

More difficult and persistent debugging problems are caused by simple programmer errors that are valid OPS5 syntax. Errors of this kind can occur frequently in OPS5 because of the language's simple, unrestrictive syntax. For example, if you omit a caret (^) before an attribute name, the compiler will compile the attribute name as a constant to be matched, which is not what you intended. The following are some common programming mistakes:

Unmatched parentheses, curly braces, or vertical bars. All OPS5 compilers are sensitive to balancing parentheses, curly braces, and vertical bars. Failing to balance these delimiters is an easy mistake to make, both on the LHS and RHS. On the LHS, delimiters such as curly braces are often used both within the condition element as conjunction delimiters, and outside condition elements, to define condition-element variables. The RHS can contain embedded functions that require extra parentheses that are easily miscounted. The best way to avoid this problem is to use an editor that helps you to match open parentheses, curly braces, and vertical bars.

A missing caret (^) before an attribute name. An attribute name missing its caret is not detected by the compiler; that name becomes just another symbolic value rather than an index to a value. Suspect this error when no match occurs for what at first appears to be a well-formed condition element. This problem can be detected by careful inspection of the rule.

Misspelled attribute names. All attribute names are kept in a symbol table that is created from the `literalize` declarations. This table holds the numeric index to which each attribute name has been assigned. The compiler issues an error message if a symbol following a caret has not been declared an attribute.

Variables that are supposed to be the same but are spelled differently. Variables with the same name are matched to the same values in WMEs. When variable names are spelled differently, each can be bound to a different value.

Rules that have this error typically create many more instantiations than they ought to (or fewer if the misspelled variable is in a negated condition element). This mistake is often difficult to find, particularly if the programmer uses abbreviated variable names. Since the OPS5 compiler cannot know whether you intended two variables to be the same or different, this error is not reported at compile time.

Missing conjunction delimiters around more than one test. Conjunctions are used to group more than one test or variable binding that are performed on a single value. Without the curly braces around the conjunction, the value in the WME pointed to by the attribute name must pass only the first test listed in the condition element. Successive tests in the condition element are performed on successive values in the WME. OPS5 implementations may issue a warning if this occurs after a nonvector attribute, but compilers do not warn the user if there are missing curly braces for multiple tests after a vector attribute.

Using an attribute in the wrong element class. OPS5 compilers traditionally do not detect the use of attribute names in element classes for which the names were not declared. An attribute name is assigned an index into a WME of any element-class type. The compiler assigns these indices such that two attributes that appear together in any `literalize` statement will have different indices. When attributes that were not defined together in a `literalize` statement are used together in a condition element, there is no guarantee that they will not be referencing the same value in a WME. Suspect this problem when you find unusual attribute values in WMEs, such as a numeric atom where you expected a symbolic atom.

Not-equal-to disjunction <> << a b c >>. According to the original language definition, only an implicit or explicit equal-to predicate may precede a disjunction of values. When a different predicate is used, the OPS5 compiler will interpret the open disjunction delimiter (<<) as a constant atom, and will produce a test for the five atoms starting at that location in a WME. Unintentionally using these predicates before a disjunction will result in a condition element that does not match the WMEs you expected. You can replace a not-equal-to disjunction with its logical equivalent: `{ <> a <> b <> c }`, if that is what you intended.

Omitting a space following an open disjunction delimiter (<<). The OPS5 language specifies that a double angle bracket (<<) must be followed by whitespace if it is to be interpreted as the opening delimiter for a disjunction. If the << is immediately followed by a disjunct value, the two are compiled as a single atom and the disjunction is lost. For example, whereas

```
^voltage << 120 240 >>
```

matches WMEs with either 120 or 240 for the attribute `^voltage`,

```
^voltage <<120 240 >>
```

matches only those WMEs with the three values `<<120`, `240`, and `>>`, starting at the attribute `^voltage`.

If the OPS5 compiler does not warn about the possibility of an omitted space, the programmer may not notice the problem until the rule containing this error does not match when expected.

Compute errors with symbolic atoms. This run-time error is fairly common. It typically occurs when a variable is bound on the LHS to a value that is not a number, and is then used in a `compute` function in an action.

The most frequent case of `compute` errors occurs when a value is not initialized to a number before it is used, and there is no type check where the variable is bound to ensure it is a number. In this case, the default `nil` value is used and creates an error in the `compute` function. For OPS5 implementations that allow the `compute` function on the LHS, many errors may be reported during the

Table 6.1 Debugging facilities.

Facility	Purpose
`watch`	Traces rule firings, working memory, and the conflict set
`pbreak`	Sets a breakpoint on a rule
`wbreak*`	Sets a breakpoint on a WME pattern
`run`	Runs the system a specified number of cycles
`back`	Backs up working memory a specified number of cycles
`matches`	Displays the WMEs matching each condition element in a rule and all combinations of condition elements
`cs`	Displays the conflict set
`next*`	Prints the name of the next rule to fire
`wm`	Lists WMEs, either all or by time tag
`ppwm`	Lists WMEs, either all or by pattern
`savestate*`	Saves the current state of working memory and the conflict set
`restorestate*`	Restores a previously saved state of working memory and the conflict set
`make`	Creates a new WME
`remove`	Removes a particular WME
`modify`	Modifies an existing WME
`excise`	Removes a rule from the system

* command specific to VAX OPS5

execution of the RHS of a seemingly unrelated rule. These errors are actually being caused by the matching of new WMEs to a rule with the LHS `compute`.

6.2 OPS5 Debugging Commands

This section presents important debugging facilities available in most OPS5 implementations. They are discussed in general terms to help you understand when to use them. Refer to your OPS5 language documentation for specific information about the commands available in your implementation. Table 6.1 lists the interpreter commands discussed in this section.

6.2.1 Tracing Program Execution

The OPS5 trace facility provides various levels of information about the execution of your program. You can choose to see information on the instantiations that fire, on the WMEs that are created and deleted, or on the instantiations that are added to and taken from the conflict set.

The amount of information that is generated is determined by the *trace level.* The trace level is set by the `watch` command used with one of four arguments, 0, 1, 2, and 3. When it is used without an argument, the `watch` command returns the current trace level. Table 6.2 describes each of these trace settings.

Trace level 0, `(watch 0)`, disables all execution tracing. Only program output is displayed during the run of this program. Figure 6.1 shows part of an execution of the room-assignment program from Chapter 2. With the watch level set to 0, the program output appears without any tracing information.

For many OPS5 implementations, the default trace level is 1, `(watch 1)`, which lists the instantiations that execute. Each rule firing is numbered. This trace level is usually considered the most useful amount of trace information. You see enough information to know what is happening during program execution, but you are not overwhelmed with detail. If rules are named mnemonically, program flow can be followed easily as the program executes, and un-

Table 6.2 Trace levels and their output.

Command	Description of Output
`(watch 0)`	Disables all trace information
`(watch 1)`	Lists the instantiations as they fire
`(watch 2)`	Same as `(watch 1)`, plus all WMEs that are created and deleted
`(watch 3)`	Same as `(watch 2)`, plus all instantiations that are added to or deleted from the conflict set

```
OPS5>(watch 0)

OPS5>(run 3)

Placing GEORGE in the QUAD numbered M104 with LESTER.
Placing TED in the QUAD numbered M104 with GEORGE LESTER.
Placing MICHAEL in the QUAD numbered M104 with TED GEORGE LESTER.
Pause.

OPS5>
```

Figure 6.1 Output from trace level 0 (watch 0).

expected rule firings are easy to detect. Figure 6.2 shows the same execution fragment as does Figure 6.1, but with trace level set to 1.

Trace level 2, `(watch 2)`, is generally used for closely tracking changes to the working memory when there is a known error. In addition to the information given in a `(watch 1)` trace, this level lists the WMEs that are being made or removed at each rule firing. When a WME is made, it is listed preceded by the symbol `=>WM:`. When a WME is removed, it is preceded by the symbol `<=WM:`. Following the symbol is the time tag of the WME, and between brackets is the name of the rule that created or last modified this WME.* A `nil` value in the

```
OPS5>(watch 1)

OPS5>(run 3)

6:  PLACEMENT!OLD-ROOM 17 45
Placing GEORGE in the QUAD numbered M104 with LESTER.
7:  PLACEMENT!OLD-ROOM 9 49
Placing TED in the QUAD numbered M104 with GEORGE LESTER.
8:  PLACEMENT!OLD-ROOM 8 53
Placing MICHAEL in the QUAD numbered M104 with TED GEORGE LESTER.
Pause.

OPS5>
```

Figure 6.2 Output from trace level one (watch 1).

*Not all implementations list the source rule name with a WME.

brackets indicates that the WME was made by the interpreter or in a `startup` statement.

Figure 6.3 shows a fragment of the execution of the room-assignment program with trace level 2.

The added information in the trace level 3, `(watch 3)`, is rarely necessary. It provides all the information of the first and second trace levels, and adds a record of every instantiation that is added or removed from the conflict set. Instantiations entering the conflict set are preceded by the symbol `->CS:`; those leaving the conflict set are preceded by `<-CS:`.

Trace information can also be redirected to an external file by changing the default for output using the `openfile` and `default` actions. This is an easier way to examine large amounts of trace output. See your reference manual for the correct syntax.

6.2.2 Controlling the Recognize-Act Cycle

Assuming you have found an error in the program output, the next step is to find where the error originated. This may be easy if, for example, the error message names the rule that made the error. On the other hand, the error may have occurred many cycles before the symptoms were detected. For example, the current problem may be caused by an error in the control flow, by some error in application logic, or by an unintentional error in rule syntax. If you have expectations about the rule-firing sequence, a rule-firing trace may be a valuable tool in identifying the error.

In either of the last two cases, you need to be able to stop the recognize-act cycle at an appropriate place and examine the current state of the solution. OPS5 provides several commands to control the recognize-act cycle. Most OPS5 implementations include the commands `run`, `pbreak`, and `back`. If enabled, control-C will also stop the recognize-act cycle at the completion of the current rule firing. Other commands are available with particular implementations. VAX OPS5, for example, also offers a `wbreak` command. This section covers the use of the commands `run`, `pbreak`, `back`, and `wbreak`.

If you know the number of recognize-act cycles you want to execute before stopping to examine the state of the program, you can use the `run` command with an integer that indicates the number of cycles to execute. The command `(run 1)` can be used to step through the program, firing one rule at a time.

Figure 6.4 illustrates the use of the `run` command to step through the first five recognize-act cycles of the room-assignment program.

If you know the name of a rule that executes at approximately the point in the program that you are interested in, you can set a breakpoint at that rule's firing with the `pbreak` command. The `pbreak` command causes the recognize-act cycle to pause immediately *before* executing the specified rule.

In Figure 6.5, a `pbreak` is set for the rule `placement!condense-compatible-roommates`. The program is run using a `(watch 1)` trace. When the recognize-act

```
OPS5>(watch 2)

OPS5>(run 3)

6:  PLACEMENT!OLD-ROOM 17 45
Placing GEORGE in the QUAD numbered M104 with LESTER.
->WM:  48 [PLACEMENT!OLD-ROOM] (STUDENT ^NAME GEORGE ^PLACED-IN M104
 ^SEX-IS MALE ^SMOKER? YES)
->WM:  49 [PLACEMENT!OLD-ROOM] (ROOM ^NUMBER M104 ^TYPE QUAD
 ^SEXES-ARE MALE ^SMOKERS? YES ^CAPACITY 4 ^VACANCIES 2 ^ASSIGNMENTS 2
 ^OCCUPANTS GEORGE LESTER)
<-WM:  45 [PLACEMENT!NEW-ROOM] (ROOM ^NUMBER M104 ^TYPE QUAD
 ^SEXES-ARE MALE ^SMOKERS? YES ^CAPACITY 4 ^VACANCIES 3 ^ASSIGNMENTS 1
 ^OCCUPANTS LESTER)
<-WM:  17 [NIL] (STUDENT ^NAME GEORGE ^PLACED-IN NIL ^SEX-IS MALE
 ^SMOKER? YES)
7:  PLACEMENT!OLD-ROOM 9 49
Placing TED in the QUAD numbered M104 with GEORGE LESTER.
->WM:  52 [PLACEMENT!OLD-ROOM] (STUDENT ^NAME TED ^PLACED-IN M104
 ^SEX-IS MALE ^SMOKER? YES)
->WM:  53 [PLACEMENT!OLD-ROOM] (ROOM ^NUMBER M104 ^TYPE QUAD
 ^SEXES-ARE MALE ^SMOKERS? YES ^CAPACITY 4 ^VACANCIES 1 ^ASSIGNMENTS 3
 ^OCCUPANTS TED GEORGE LESTER)
<-WM:  49 [PLACEMENT!OLD-ROOM] (ROOM ^NUMBER M104 ^TYPE QUAD
 ^SEXES-ARE MALE ^SMOKERS? YES ^CAPACITY 4 ^VACANCIES 2 ^ASSIGNMENTS 2
 ^OCCUPANTS GEORGE LESTER)
<-WM:  9 [NIL] (STUDENT ^NAME TED ^PLACED-IN NIL ^SEX-IS MALE
 ^SMOKER? YES)
8:  PLACEMENT!OLD-ROOM 8 53
Placing MICHAEL in the QUAD numbered M104 with TED GEORGE LESTER.
->WM:  56 [PLACEMENT!OLD-ROOM] (STUDENT ^NAME MICHAEL ^PLACED-IN M104
 ^SEX-IS MALE ^SMOKER? YES)
->WM:  57 [PLACEMENT!OLD-ROOM] (ROOM ^NUMBER M104 ^TYPE QUAD
 ^SEXES-ARE MALE ^SMOKERS? YES ^CAPACITY 4 ^VACANCIES 0 ^ASSIGNMENTS 4
 ^OCCUPANTS MICHAEL TED GEORGE LESTER)
<-WM:  53 [PLACEMENT!OLD-ROOM] (ROOM ^NUMBER M104 ^TYPE QUAD
 ^SEXES-ARE MALE ^SMOKERS? YES ^CAPACITY 4 ^VACANCIES 1 ^ASSIGNMENTS 3
 ^OCCUPANTS TED GEORGE LESTER)
<-WM:  8 [NIL] (STUDENT ^NAME MICHAEL ^PLACED-IN NIL ^SEX-IS MALE
 ^SMOKER? YES)
Pause

OPS5>
```

Figure 6.3 Output from trace level two (watch 2).

```
OPS5>(run 1)
1:  PLACEMENT!NEW-ROOM 20 28
LENNY will be the first one in the QUAD room number B104.
OPS5>(run 1)
2:  PLACEMENT!OLD-ROOM 19 30
Placing ANDY in the QUAD numbered B104 with LENNY.
OPS5>(run 1)
3:  PLACEMENT!OLD-ROOM 18 34
Placing ALAN in the QUAD numbered B104 with ANDY LENNY.
OPS5>(run 1)
4:  PLACEMENT!OLD-ROOM 17 38
Placing TOM in the QUAD numbered B104 with ALAN ANDY LENNY.
OPS5>(run 1)
5:  PLACEMENT!NEW-ROOM 16 26
JOE will be the first one in the QUAD room number M104.
Pause

OPS5>
```

Figure 6.4 Stepping through rule firings (run 1).

cycle is stopped, we use the next command * to show that the break occurred as expected, just before the specified rule fires.

Of course, if you do not know where the problem originated, you can use the back command to help find the error. This command is especially useful when the program halts unexpectedly, or if it is not feasible to rerun the program many times. When you spot a symptom of the error, you can stop the recognize-act cycle, then *back up* a number of recognize-act cycles using the back command.

The back command *undoes* what the previous recognize-act cycles have done by restoring working memory and the conflict set to the state that existed at that time. The back command requires extensive memory to keep track of previous states of the program, so in most OPS5 implementations you must enable the back feature before you can back up rule firings. Also, you can never back up beyond the rule firing at which it was enabled.

The back command restores *only* working memory and the conflict set. It cannot undo side affects that did not affect working memory or the conflict set, such as opening or closing files, writing to or reading from files or databases, or any side effects of external routines.

Figure 6.6 shows back being used with the room-assignment program.

Another way you can control the recognize-act cycle is to stop rule firings when a particular WME enters or leaves working memory. For example, this

*The next command is explained in Section 6.2.3.

```
OPS5>(pbreak placement!condense-compatible-roommates)

OPS5>run
7:  PLACEMENT!OLD-ROOM 9 50
Placing LINDA in the TRIPLE numbered M313 with WENDY.
8:  PLACEMENT!NEW-ROOM 14 22
SARAH will be the first one in the TRIPLE room number H213.
9:  PLACEMENT!OLD-ROOM 11 58
Placing SUZIE in the TRIPLE numbered H213 with SARAH.
10:  PLACEMENT!OLD-ROOM 10 62
Placing CINDY in the TRIPLE numbered H213 with SUZIE SARAH.
11:  PLACEMENT!NEW-ROOM 13 27
LESTER will be the first one in the DOUBLE room number M122.
12:  PLACEMENT!OLD-ROOM 12 70
Placing GEORGE in the DOUBLE numbered M122 with LESTER.
13:  PLACEMENT!NEW-ROOM 8 23
SUE will be the first one in the DOUBLE room number D12.
PBREAK encountered
BREAK -- break

OPS5>next
PLACEMENT!CONDENSE-COMPATIBLE-ROOMMATES 78 66 46

OPS5>
```

Figure 6.5 Setting a breakpoint (pbreak).

would be appropriate if the symptom of the error was a WME that was made or modified incorrectly. The `wbreak` command causes the recognize-act cycle to stop when a specified WME or pattern within a WME is created.

If you are using a control strategy that uses an element class for only control information, you can use `wbreak` to stop the recognize-act cycle when the control WME is made for the subtask in which the error occurs. This also allows you to stop processing at the subtask in which a rule in question is expected to be instantiated, but is failing to do so.

Figure 6.7 shows the use of the `wbreak` command to pause the recognize-act cycle when a particular WME is made.

6.2.3 Inspecting the State of the Match

In more difficult debugging situations, you often need to look closely at how rules are and are not being matched by WMEs. The final results of the match are the instantiations in the conflict set, which you may wish to examine using the `cs` command. You can also use the `matches` command to examine which

```
OPS5>(pbreak placement!condense-compatible-roommates)

OPS5>(run)
Placing LINDA in the TRIPLE numbered M313 with WENDY.
SARAH will be the first one in the TRIPLE room number H213.
Placing SUZIE in the TRIPLE numbered H213 with SARAH.
Placing CINDY in the TRIPLE numbered H213 with SUZIE SARAH.
LESTER will be the first one in the DOUBLE room number M122.
Placing GEORGE in the DOUBLE numbered M122 with LESTER.
SUE will be the first one in the DOUBLE room number D12.
PBREAK encountered
BREAK -- break

OPS5>(back 3)

OPS5>(watch 1)

OPS5>(run 3)

11:  PLACEMENT!NEW-ROOM 13 27
LESTER will be the first one in the DOUBLE room number M122.
12:  PLACEMENT!OLD-ROOM 12 70
Placing GEORGE in the DOUBLE numbered M122 with LESTER.
13:  PLACEMENT!NEW-ROOM 8 23
SUE will be the first one in the DOUBLE room number D12.
Pause

OPS5>
```

Figure 6.6 Backing up recognize-act cycles (back).

```
OPS5>(wbreak student ^name joe)

OPS5>run
WBREAK encountered
232 [PLACEMENT!MOVE-STUDENT] (STUDENT ^NAME JOE ^PLACED-IN NIL
 ^SEX-IS MALE ^SMOKER? NO)
BREAK -- break

OPS5>
```

Figure 6.7 Breaking at a WME (wbreak).

```
OPS5>cs
PLACEMENT!CONDENSE-COMPATIBLE-ROOMMATES 126 74 54
PLACEMENT!CONDENSE-COMPATIBLE-ROOMMATES 126 74 114
PLACEMENT!CONDENSE-COMPATIBLE-ROOMMATES 74 126 54
PLACEMENT!CONDENSE-COMPATIBLE-ROOMMATES 74 126 114
PLACEMENT!NEW-ROOM 3 21
PLACEMENT!NEW-ROOM 1 21
PLACEMENT!NEW-ROOM 5 21
PLACEMENT!NEW-ROOM 2 21

OPS5>next
PLACEMENT!CONDENSE-COMPATIBLE-ROOMMATES 126 74 114

OPS5>
```

Figure 6.8 Using the cs and next commands.

matches are made to each condition element in a rule and how these matches combine to form instantiations. OPS5 implementations that do not sort conflict set output by instantiation dominance may also have a command that displays the instantiation that will be chosen for the next cycle. In VAX OPS5, this command is `next`. These commands are discussed in this section.

If a rule does not fire when expected, the first step is to determine whether the rule ever completed an instantiation. If it was instantiated, then the next step is to discover why the rule was not chosen to fire during conflict resolution. If it was never in the conflict set, you must determine why the rule did not match and form an instantiation.

Figure 6.8 shows how the `cs` and `next` commands can be used to examine the conflict set and the dominating instantiation. A conflict set instantiation is displayed as a rule name followed by a list of one or more integers. These integers are the time tags of WMEs that match the rule to form the instantiation. In our VAX OPS5 example, there is no significance to the order in which instantiations are displayed. Instead of forcing the user to figure out which instantiation will fire next, VAX OPS5 supplies the `next` command to indicate which instantiation has been chosen by conflict resolution to fire next. Some OPS5 implementations provide sorted conflict-set output, so the `next` command is not necessary.

If a particular rule you were interested in does not appear in the conflict set, you may want to look more closely at how its condition elements are and are not being matched by WMEs. The `matches` command lists the WMEs that match each condition element, as well as the combinations that lead to an instantiation of a given rule.

For example, suppose that, at some point in our room-assignment program, we want to see how `placement!old-room` is matching working memory. The rule has three condition elements. The first matches a student who is not yet assigned to a room. The second condition element finds a room with one or more compatible students and space for another. The third condition element is a negated element that specifies that this room is the largest one available. When the rule fires, it assigns the student to that room. Figure 6.9 shows the result of a `matches` command when the rule `placement!old-room` has one instantiation.

The heading `matches for 1` refers to the unassigned student WMEs that match the first condition element in the rule. Time tags appearing after the heading `matches for 2` correspond to rooms with vacancies. The heading `matches for 1 2` refers to the consistent combinations of the WMEs that matched the first two condition elements. In this case, of all the unassigned students and rooms with vacancies, only one compatible pairing of `student` and `room` WMEs exist. The time tags appearing after the heading `matches for 3` correspond to WMEs that match the negated condition independent of the previous positive ones. Notice that the final output, `matches for 1 2 3`, lists instantiations of

```
OPS5>(matches placement!old-room)

>>> PLACEMENT!OLD-ROOM <<<
*** matches for 1 ***
1
2
192
*** matches for 2 ***
158
170
202
*** matches for 1 2 ***
192  202
*** matches for 3 ***
158
170
202
*** matches for 1 2 3 ***
192  202

OPS5>
```

Figure 6.9 Using the matches command.

the rule that may* appear in the conflict set. There apparently were no matches of the negated element that inhibited the partial instantiation `(192 202)` from proceeding.

Sometimes, it is obvious from the output of the `matches` command why a rule is not instantiated, such as when a condition element is not matched any WMEs.† Other times, all condition elements have matching WMEs, but the matching WMEs cannot combine to form partial instantiations. This is the case when the matching WMEs cannot create consistent variable bindings across condition elements.

6.2.4 Examining Working Memory

Since working memory can change during every step of the recognize-act cycle, it is important to be able to examine working memory at any cycle, looking for WMEs of a particular class or with particular values. OPS5 provides two commands for examining working memory—`wm` and `ppwm`. When either of these commands is used without arguments, it produces a listing of the entire contents of working memory.

Each WME is uniquely identified by its time tag. Time tags are used to refer to WMEs in the output produced by the `cs` command (conflict set) and the `matches` command (matches between WMEs and rules). After using the `cs` and `matches` command, you often need to examine the WMEs referred to by the time tags. To list a WME by its time tag, use the `wm` command.

Figure 6.10 illustrates the use of the `wm` command to display the WMEs listed in an instantiation reported by the `next` command.

Often, you want to examine a subset of working memory that contains a certain value or pattern of values. The `ppwm` command accepts zero or more WME value restrictions, including class name, to find the WMEs that contain that pattern. The pattern is specified as a condition element, except that, in most OPS5 implementations, predicates and functions cannot be included. In Figure 6.11, the `ppwm` command is used to display all WMEs with the class name `room` with the value `no` for the `^smokers?` attribute, and then to display the WMEs containing the pattern `student ^placed-in M104`.

As in the second level of trace, `(watch 2)`, the output from `ppwm` lists a WME with its time tag, the rule from which it was created or last modified, and the values for each attribute.

Two other commands available in VAX OPS5 are useful for debugging. The `savestate` command copies the contents of both working memory and the

---

*If a valid instantiation does not appear in the conflict set, then that particular instantiation has already fired and refraction has caused it to be removed from the conflict set so that it will not execute again.

† In the case of a negated condition element, consistently matched WMEs would, instead, stop the rule from matching any further.

```
OPS5>next
PLACEMENT!CONDENSE-COMPATIBLE-ROOMMATES 126 74 114

OPS5>(wm 126 74 114)
126 [PLACEMENT!NEW-ROOM] (ROOM ^NUMBER D101 ^TYPE SINGLE
 ^SEXES-ARE MALE ^SMOKERS? YES ^CAPACITY 1 ^VACANCIES 0 ^ASSIGNMENTS 1
 ^OCCUPANTS TED)
74 [PLACEMENT!OLD-ROOM] (ROOM ^NUMBER M122 ^TYPE DOUBLE
 ^SEXES-ARE MALE ^SMOKERS? YES ^CAPACITY 2 ^VACANCIES 0 ^ASSIGNMENTS 2
 ^OCCUPANTS GEORGE LESTER)
114 [PLACEMENT!NEW-ROOM] (ROOM ^NUMBER H213 ^TYPE TRIPLE
 ^SEXES-ARE MALE ^SMOKERS? NO ^CAPACITY 3 ^VACANCIES 2 ^ASSIGNMENTS 1
 ^OCCUPANTS JOE)

OPS5>
```

Figure 6.10 Using the wm command.

```
OPS5>(ppwm room ^smokers? no)
169 [PLACEMENT!CONDENSE-COMPATIBLE-ROOMMATES] (ROOM ^NUMBER M313
 ^TYPE TRIPLE ^SEXES-ARE FEMALE ^SMOKERS? NO ^CAPACITY 3 ^VACANCIES 0
 ^ASSIGNMENTS 3 ^OCCUPANTS MARY PENNY NANCY)
81 [PLACEMENT!CONDENSE-COMPATIBLE-ROOMMATES] (ROOM ^NUMBER M104
 ^TYPE QUAD ^SEXES-ARE FEMALE ^SMOKERS? NO ^CAPACITY 4 ^VACANCIES 0
 ^ASSIGNMENTS 4 ^OCCUPANTS SUE CINDY SUZIE SARAH)
158 [PLACEMENT!NEW-ROOM] (ROOM ^NUMBER M122 ^TYPE DOUBLE
 ^SEXES-ARE MALE ^SMOKERS? NO ^CAPACITY 2 ^VACANCIES 1 ^ASSIGNMENTS 1
 ^OCCUPANTS JOE)
42 [PLACEMENT!OLD-ROOM] (ROOM ^NUMBER B104 ^TYPE QUAD ^SEXES-ARE MALE
 ^SMOKERS? NO ^CAPACITY 4 ^VACANCIES 0 ^ASSIGNMENTS 4
 ^OCCUPANTS TOM ALAN ANDY LENNY)

OPS5>(ppwm student ^placed-in m104)
103 [PLACEMENT!MOVE-STUDENT] (STUDENT ^NAME SUE ^PLACED-IN M104
 ^SEX-IS FEMALE ^SMOKER? NO)
94 [PLACEMENT!MOVE-STUDENT] (STUDENT ^NAME SUZIE ^PLACED-IN M104
 ^SEX-IS FEMALE ^SMOKER? NO)
98 [PLACEMENT!MOVE-STUDENT] (STUDENT ^NAME SARAH ^PLACED-IN M104
 ^SEX-IS FEMALE ^SMOKER? NO)
90 [PLACEMENT!MOVE-STUDENT] (STUDENT ^NAME CINDY ^PLACED-IN M104
 ^SEX-IS FEMALE ^SMOKER? NO)

OPS5>
```

Figure 6.11 Using the ppwm command.

conflict set into a file. The state saved with `savestate` can also be restored to working memory and the conflict set with the `restorestate` command. These commands can be used in combination to save the state of the program at which an error occurs, and, after the necessary corrections are made, to restore this state to test whether the error has been fixed.

For example, in debugging a system that runs for many rule firings before arriving at the cycle of interest, you may want to use `savestate` once and then debug from that point using `restorestate`, instead of rerunning the application to that point each time you want to return to that cycle.

Since OPS5 cannot save the state of any external routines or open files, `restorestate` is of limited value in applications for which external state is important.

Other OPS5 implementations may have a similar save and restore capability. OPS5 developers using a LISP-based OPS5 implementation may either use a LISP environment save and restore facility, or, if adequate internal access is permitted, write a simple store and restore facility of their own. Remember that the save facility has to save copies of both working memory *and* the conflict set.

6.2.5 Changing Working Memory

While debugging, it is often convenient to change working memory of a running program. For example, control WMEs can be added or removed to alter the flow of the program, or erroneous WMEs can be fixed.

The command interpreter allows the user to modify working memory using several commands: adding WMEs with the `make` command, deleting WMEs with `remove`, and changing values with `modify`. The only difference between these commands and the corresponding RHS actions lies in how the specific WME to be removed or modified is indicated.

Remember from RHS syntax that `remove` and `modify` actions require either a variable or an integer as an element designator—the way of indicating which WME is to be removed and modified. An element designator is a variable or integer corresponding to a condition element. In the command interpreter, however, an element designator is a time tag of the WME to be modified or removed. You can determine the time tag of a WME by using the commands for listing working memory (`wm`, `ppwm`), the conflict set (`cs`), or the matches between WMEs and condition elements (`matches`).

Figure 6.12 illustrates the use of element designators in the OPS5 command interpreter. Notice that an asterisk (*) is used with the `remove` command to indicate that all WMEs should be removed.

Notice that, when a WME is modified from the interpreter, the name in brackets before the WME's name is changed to `nil`. The modified WME also has a new time tag.

```
OPS5>(ppwm student ^name lester)
142 [PLACEMENT!MOVE-STUDENT] (STUDENT ^NAME LESTER ^PLACED-IN H213
 ^SEX-IS MALE ^SMOKER? YES)

OPS5>(modify 142 ^smoker? no)

OPS5>(ppwm student ^name lester)
213 [NIL] (STUDENT ^NAME LESTER ^PLACED-IN H213 ^SEX-IS MALE ^SMOKER? NO)

OPS5>(remove *)

OPS5>(wm)

OPS5>
```

Figure 6.12 Using element designators with modify and remove commands.

6.2.6 Changing the Rule Base

Often, after you find the source of the problem, you want to make a temporary rule fix in the system and to continue program execution to test the changes. If the correction involves removing or modifying an existing rule, then it is convenient to be able to effect that change in the middle of the run.

The `excise` command is used to remove a rule from a running program. This command effectively deletes the rule from the executing program, but it does not affect the source code. Thus, it can be used temporarily* to test the system without that rule.

```
OPS5>(excise placement!move-student)
```

In a LISP-based OPS5 system, you can easily replace an existing rule with a new one simply by loading the new rule from a file or by typing it in directly. This adds the new rule to the match network,† replacing any rule by the same name.

VAX OPS5 provides the `build` action to enable rules to be created and compiled into a running OPS5 application. In applications that use this feature,

*When you add or remove rules from your running program, you permanently change your *current* environment. The `back` command will not undo rule-base changes.

†Early LISP-based versions of OPS5 did not match new rules against WMEs that existed before the rule was created. Only WMEs made *after* that point matched the new rule. In VAX OPS5, rules added at run time by the `build` action are matched against existing WMEs. See your documentation to find out how your implementation handles dynamic rule-base changes.

certain rules match WMEs that may partially or fully specify new rules to add to the application. The `build` action compiles a rule into the system and causes it to be matched against existing working memory.

The ability to add rules to a running application is useful for debugging. You can test alternate rule fixes in the application before permanently editing the source code. This may provide much faster testing of rule changes in a compiled OPS5 than does going through an edit/compile/link loop for each alternative.

6.3 Guidelines to the Debugging Process

As in any other language, there is no guaranteed method for finding and repairing programming bugs in OPS5. However, many common bugs are detected and resolved with a simple systematic approach. This approach is based on its counterpart in sequential languages, but it is specialized for OPS5.

This section outlines an approach to the process of finding and fixing minor* bugs in an OPS5 program. These guidelines assume that the rule set is large enough that the order of rule firings is not predetermined. This lack of predictability at the rule level is characteristic of large data-driven programs, and is a major source of difficulty in debugging.

The approach focuses on the following questions; this section discusses each of these questions with the relevant OPS5 commands.

- What are the symptoms?
- What WMEs are involved?
- Where did they come from?
- What is the real problem?
- How can it be corrected?
- How can the error be caught sooner next time?

6.3.1 What Are the Symptoms?

The first step in debugging is to determine how the bug is revealed in program output or behavior. The bugs in knowledge-based programs are often easier to detect than are those in traditional programs, because the knowledge is represented in a form that is closer to the user's view of it. Errors in the output often map clearly to errors in the program source. The symptom usually occurs close to the time that the rule that caused the error fired.

It may be useful to be able to reproduce and characterize the symptom with more than one case. This may be necessary to ensure that you understand how

---

*By *minor bugs* we mean those bugs that do not require massive editing or redesign of the source code.

extensive the problem is. If you solve problems without fully understanding them, you may only patch one that instead requires a complete reconstruction.

6.3.2 What WMEs Are Involved?

In most cases, working memory is corrupted immediately prior to when the error symptom occurs. You should be able to pinpoint the WMEs that contributed to the error by inspecting the rule that fired when the symptom occurred. To do this, back up the system to the cycle just before the error occurs. Figure 6.13 shows the use of the `back` command to view program state just before the error occurs.

If your implementation of OPS5 does not have a `back` command, you must start the program over and use the `run` command to rerun the program to an earlier cycle.

There are only a few cases in which minor bugs are not attributable to missing or incorrect WMEs. These cases are easily detected by inspecting the rule that fired when the symptom appeared and then proceeding with debugging from there. Another cause of an error unrelated to missing or incorrect WMEs is external routines. These errors typically arise from corrupted state information in external modules. You can use traditional debugging techniques for tracking down and fixing external-routine errors.

6.3.3 Where Did They Come From?

Assuming one or more WMEs are found to be incorrect, the next step in finding the real source of the problem is to backtrack to the source of the corruption.

```
         :
 ADDING 1 RA60-CA WHICH REPLACES    ←— this is the unexpected output
    YOUR RA81-AA.
Pause

OPS5> (back 1)

OPS5> (next)
REPORT-EDIT!ONLY-ONE-REPLACED 833 614 742

OPS5> (wm 833 614 742)
      :
```

Figure 6.13 Backing up to investigate an error.

Again, the `back` command is valuable for backing up cycles to determine where the problem started. If you do not have the `back` command, or you want to back up more cycles than your implementation allows, use the `run` command to run the program from the beginning to where the error may have occurred. Commands such as `wbreak` and `pbreak` are useful in pausing the program when particular WMEs are made or rules are about to fire. You can also use the `cs` or `next` commands to examine the conflict set and the dominating instantiation.

When VAX OPS5 displays WMEs, it includes the name of the rule that created or last modified the WME. This rule name, along with a first-level trace, is very useful in quickly tracking the source of a WME's error. With the `back` command available, start by looking at the rule name associated with the WME, and back up the program to the point at which that rule fired. This process may be repeated with WMEs matched by that rule until you determine the rule or rules that contain the error.

If the error seems to be due to the repeated firing of one or more rules, you must find which WMEs are involved. If there are very few rules that are repeating, the problem may be found most quickly by inspecting the instantiations as they fire. If the repetition involves many rules, you may want to create a file of the level 1, `(watch 1)`, trace that includes output from the execution of the program, from the start of the run to the problem. Then a visual inspection of the rule-firing trace can direct you to where the repetitions started.

6.3.4 What Is the Real Problem?

When the source of the corrupted WME is found, it is commonly due to one of three problems:

1. A rule has an error in an RHS action
2. A rule fires unexpectedly
3. A rule does not fire when expected

Errors in the RHS actions are most often caused by a typographical error, a missing caret (`^`), an attribute used in a WME for which it is not defined, or an incorrect element designator in a `modify`, or `remove` action, or the `substr` function. You can detect these errors by carefully reviewing the rule. Once the error is detected, it is easy to correct.

It is very common for a rule to fire unexpectedly, which introduces errors that are noticed only later in the program. For example, a rule may invoke a subtask before another rule could complete the necessary preparations for that subtask. Often the solution is simply to make the LHS of the rule more specific about when it should or should not fire.

For all but the simplest cases, however, avoid putting rules together in a subtask if there are implicit sequencing restrictions among them. Sequencing should be a concern at the subtask-control level only. Rule-firing sequence within a subtask should be completely data-driven and should not be predefined by the programmer. If two rules must fire in a particular order, separate them into two consecutive subtasks to ensure that they fire in the correct order. If this results in many subtasks with only a very few rules in each, you may want to consider rewriting your program in a more sequential language.

A rule may also fire unexpectedly because of errors in the LHS. For example, conditions may be underconstraining, or a variable may be misspelled. A misspelled variable may result in a free variable binding instead of a restricting variable test. When the misspelled variable is in a positive condition element, the rule may be underconstrained, and may match more than intended. When the misspelled variable appears in a negated element, the rule does not usually create the expected instantiations.

Another common problem, particularly for OPS5 beginners, is a repeatedly firing rule. This is usually caused by a rule whose `modify` action changes a WME that matches a condition element on the LHS, but does not restrict a subsequent match to the same condition element after modification. Refraction does not prevent the rule from firing again on these new WMEs. To avoid this problem, ensure either that, when a rule modifies a WME, it disables its match to the condition element to which it previously matched, or that there are one or more rules in the conflict set that always take priority over the rule's new instantiation.

If a rule with a negated condition element fires repeatedly when you expect refraction to prevent repeated firings, you may be encountering a peculiar aspect of the refraction rule. Refraction states that no instantiation will fire more than once, meaning that no rule can fire more than once matched by exactly the same data. However, when there is a negated condition element, the same data can form an instantiation *if a WME is made that matches the negated element and is then removed.* That is, a new "absence" of the data is created. It is as though OPS5 keeps track of what *is not* matching to the negated condition element as part of the instantiation.

For example, suppose there is an instantiation of a rule with a negated condition element, and the rule fires, restricting it from entering the conflict set again. If a WME that matches the negated element is created and subsequently deleted, instantiations of the rule can now enter the conflict set. There is no memory of instantiations that fired before the rule was barred from the conflict set. The solution to this problem often requires creating explicit values that keep the same data from matching the positive condition elements.

Finally, a rule that is expected to fire may not fire at all. If an existing rule does not fire or instantiate when expected, focus on the LHS for errors. The `matches` command can be used in this case to determine which conditions or combinations of conditions failed to yield a match. There will be a syntax error (see Section 6.1), an error in the logic of the condition elements, or a missing or incorrectly named WME.

6.3.5 How Can It Be Corrected?

Once you identify the problem and choose a solution, you can often test that solution by making temporary changes to the rules or WMEs from the command interpreter, by either adding or deleting rules or working memory.

If the solution involves deleting a rule from the program, or if you suspect a rule to be at fault and want to verify that it is, you may want to test the suspicion by removing the rule from your running program with the `excise` command.

If a rule needs minor changes in its actions, you can modify working memory after the rule fires, to make the changes that the rule should have if written properly. Use the `pbreak` command to stop the program each time that rule fires. Then use `(run 1)` to fire the rule. Next, edit working memory with the `make`, `modify`, and `remove` commands to do what you think the rule *should have* done. Finally, continue the program execution with the `run` command to verify that the corrections to working memory solved the problem.

If a new rule is to be added, you may want to do so at the point it is needed. If your OPS5 implementation does not support run-time addition of new rules, or if it does not match newly added rules against older WMEs, you must restart the program-development loop and add new rules to the rule base before compiling or loading the rules again.

6.3.6 How Can the Error Be Caught Sooner Next Time?

OPS5 represents program state globally. A rule can be written to look at and modify any WME. Rules can match and modify data whenever an instantiation is formed and then selected. This flexibility is gained, however, at the expense of data modularity. Some rules may match data that you did not anticipate, or may match data at an unexpected point in program execution.

One way of managing this flexibility is to define conventions for the semantics of and operations on particular element classes. For example, the application may require that no two `line-item` WMEs may have the same number; that all `part` WMEs must have a non-nil value for the `^name` and `^price` attributes; or that, for every `link` WME, there must be a `node` WME with the value for an `^id` attribute corresponding to the `link` WME's `^from` attribute. When conventions such as these are violated, problems result in rules that depend on these constraints.

The sheer number of implicit conventions in a large OPS5 program requires some organization and automated help. One useful approach is to define explicitly these conventions, and to write rules to ensure that the conventions are adhered to. In the comments for each subtask, you can explicitly state the assumptions that the rules in that subtask make about the state of working memory while they are active. The assumptions from the comments of all subtasks are then gathered into one module, and rules are written to ensure that the assumptions are not violated. These rules, often called *assumption-checking rules*, can be specific to a subtask or global to the entire program.

```
(p  unpriced-component
;
; If a component has no price, signal an error and mark it
; as unpriced.  Note where the error occurs.
;
   { <Component>
      (component ^price nil ^name <what>) }
      (subtask ^name <current>)
   -->
      (call internal_error <current>
         |Component| <what> |has no price..setting unpriced.|)
      (modify <Component> ^price 0 ^sale-status unpriced))
```

Figure 6.14 Assumption-checking rule: Correct the error.

Global assumptions are implemented as *demon* rules, which are discussed in Chapter 9.

For example, the rule in Figure 6.14 checks to see whether a `component` is in working memory without a price. If so, it calls a routine to signal the error and temporarily fixes the problem.

Note that, in addition to matching the WME that states the violation, the rule also matches a subtask WME that is unnamed and not placed as the first condition element. The instantiation of this rule that fires will match the most recent subtask WME which presumably is the one in which the error first occurred.* The rule then sends the name of the current subtask to a user-written external routine, along with a problem-specific message, to be printed or logged as an error. The component is temporarily repaired automatically, and the program can proceed.

As another example, the rule in Figure 6.15 checks to see whether a `link` is present in working memory without a corresponding `node`. In this example, the error is serious enough that there is no general recovery action. Instead the program simply halts the rule firings and leaves the developer to begin debugging the problem at the point of the error. Rather than making a simple fix or halting the firing cycle, a more sophisticated assumption-checking rule may invoke one or more subtasks to diagnose or repair the problem.

In addition to the somewhat autonomous checking being performed, another benefit of the assumption-checking rules is that they can be kept separate from the rest of the program. When the program is acceptably robust, the assumption-checking rules can be removed without affecting program behavior.

*Chapter 9 discusses how rules such as this may be prevented by mistake from firing as soon as the problem occurs.

```
(p  dangling-link
;
; Complain if you find a link without a ^from node.
;
      (link ^from <dangle>)
      - (node ^id <dangle>)
      (subtask ^name <current>)
   -->
      (write (crlf) |** Uh-oh.  I see a link without a parent node|
             (crlf) |** in the| <current> |subtask.|
             (crlf) |** I'm stopping here. YOU fix it.|)
      (halt))
```

Figure 6.15 Assumption-checking rule: Abort.

Summary

- Most common OPS5 programming errors are mistakes that result in valid OPS5 syntax but unintended semantics. These errors are often difficult to find but, once identified, they are easy to fix.
- The `watch` command produces several levels of trace information from an executing program.
- The recognize-act cycle can be controlled with the commands `run`, `pbreak`, `wbreak`, and `back`.
- The match phase of the recognize-act cycle is often the key point of debugging. The commands `matches`, `cs`, and `next` are useful in determining the results of rule matching.
- Working memory can be examined with the `wm`, `ppwm`, and `savestate` commands.
- Temporary fixes can be made to working memory with the `make`, `remove`, and `modify` commands.
- The rule base can be changed during execution by use of the `excise` command and by the run-time addition of new rules.
- An assumption-checking rule is used to ensure that no data conventions are violated. These rules can fix the bug, invoke a subtask to fix the problem, or simply stop the program. Assumption-checking rules can be removed from the program in a delivery environment.

Exercises

1. Consider the following OPS5 condition elements:

```
(number ^value > <x>)
```

and

```
(number value > <x>)
```

   a. What is the difference to OPS5 between these condition elements?

   b. Create a WME that would match each of the condition elements, if the variable <x> were bound to 12.

2. For each of the following condition elements, determine whether it is legal OPS5 syntax. For each legal condition element, write two sample WMEs that match. Assume that this is the first occurrence of <x> in the rule.

   a. (number ^value { <x> <> 100 <=> 9999 })

   b. (number ^value } <x> <> 100 <=> 9999 })

   c. (number ^value <x> <> 100 <=> 9999)

   d. (number ^value << nil > 0 >>)

   e. (number ^value <> << 0 100 >>)

3. Consider the following condition element from an OPS5 program:

```
(clipboard ^estimate <best-guess>
           ^receipt > (compute <best-guess> * 1.10))
```

   a. Modify the condition element to prevent it from generating a run-time compute error when the value of the attribute ^receipt is not a number.

   b. How else can you ensure that the compute error will not occur?

4. For each OPS5 interpreter command listed, briefly describe how it can be used effectively in the debug process.

   a. ppwm

   b. back

   c. run

   d. pbreak and wbreak

   e. watch

   f. cs and next

g. `matches`

h. `wm`

i. `make`, `modify` and `remove`

j. `excise`

CHAPTER 7

Programming Techniques

THIS CHAPTER DESCRIBES common programming techniques and the underlying philosophy to help you write better OPS5 programs. Other important programming techniques such as demons, and the use of external routines are covered in later chapters. The emphasis of this chapter is on simplicity, modularity, efficiency, and the tradeoffs among them. Note that the techniques presented here are programming conventions, and are not part of the OPS5 language definition.

This chapter occasionally asks you to consider the efficiency of a programming technique. In general, the relative efficiency of a technique is dependent on the content of working memory and its rate of change. Beginning OPS5 programmers do not need to grasp fully the issues involved in rule matching to gain an intuition about what is and what is not efficient. Chapter 10, *Efficiency*, presents an in-depth discussion of the RETE match algorithm and its implications for program efficiency; that presentation substantiates the intuitions you gain concerning efficiency in this chapter.

7.1 Association Values

There are four distinct roles for an OPS5 atom in a WME: classification, information, distinction, and association. Each OPS5 atom plays one or more of these roles.

To illustrate these roles, consider an OPS5 program that helps a user to select components for a personal computer. The following is one condition element from a rule in this program:

```
(component ^type disk-unit
           ^peak-transfer-rate <speed>
           ^identifier <unique>
           ^controller <link>)
```

The values referenced in this condition element play the following four roles:

1. *Classification.* The atom denotes a WME class, or subset of that class, for the purpose of determining meaningful attributes. Classification values are typically referenced as constants in a condition element. In the previous example, `component` and `disk-unit` are classification values. The value `component` serves as the WME class, defining the relevant attributes. The value `disk-unit` refines that classification, distinguishing it from another component, such as a `monitor`. The reference to `disk-unit` also makes it proper to reference the attribute `^peak-transfer-rate`, whereas a `component ^type monitor` may reference attributes about monitors, such as `^screen-color`.

2. *Information.* Some atoms are used to provide information. They have domain significance in relation to the WME class. We can imagine that the value of `^peak-transfer-rate` is used to provide information, such as in a computation or for comparison to other disk units, and does not play any other role in the program.

3. *Distinction.* The atom uniquely distinguishes this WME from others that are similar. The value of `^identifier` is unique to this particular component among all components. It may be used in a rule to distinguish this WME from others that may be similar. Examples of distinction values are discussed throughout this chapter.

4. *Association.* An atom may exist only to establish a relationship among WMEs. In this case, we can imagine that the value of the attribute `^controller` may match a unique identifier of another component, representing the disk controller.

Of these four roles, association is central to many useful programming techniques. An *association value** is a value that is shared among two or more

*The term "pointer value" might be appropriate for an association value that ties an association attribute to a distinguishing attribute.

WMEs to bring them together in an LHS match. Two such values can be matched with a single variable in an LHS to "find" the associated WME. This association is bidirectional—if either is uniquely matched, we can find the other using the shared association value. An attribute that is defined specifically for the purpose of containing an association value we call an *association attribute*. A variable that is used to match association values we call an *association variable*.

Figure 7.1 shows a rule that asks the user a question and then reads the answer. Questions and answers both require vector attributes. Since the OPS5 language limits a WME class to only one vector, association values must be used to tie together two WMEs, each with one vector attribute. In `interaction!ask-question`, the association variable `<q-id>` uniquely associates the question with its question text via the attribute `^question-id` in both the `question` and `question-text` WMEs. This association has the effect of finding the text for a question that is ready to be asked. The rule `interaction!ask-question` retrieves the question from the `question-text` WME, displays it to the user, and stores the response in the `question` WME.

The actual value that matches `<q-id>` is not important. Using the same variable in both places ensures that the matching values are equal. If the value of the attribute `^question-id` is distinct for each `question` and `question-text` pair, then this rule finds the unique `question-text` associated with this question.

To ensure uniqueness, association values can be generated by a call to the `genatom` function. `Genatom` is a built-in OPS5 function that returns a *new* symbol

```
(p  interaction!ask-question
;
;  Write out the question text for an OPEN question starting
;  at the TEXT vector attribute, and put the response into
;  the REPLY vector attribute.
;
      (subtask ^name interaction)
   { <The-question>
      (question ^status open ^question-id <q-id>) }
   { <The-text>
      (question-text ^question-id <q-id>) }
   -->
      (write (substr <The-text> text inf))
      (modify <The-question> ^status asked
         ^reply (acceptline)))
```

Figure 7.1 An example of using an association value.

each time it is called during program execution. For example, the question WME and the question-text WME may have been created as follows:

```
(bind <unique> (genatom))
(make question ^status open ^question-id <unique>)
(make question-text ^question-id <unique>
        ^text Enter one or more software package:)
```

Creating these pairs with a genatom function ensures that the association value of question and question-text WMEs is unique. Of course, association values do not have to be generated by the genatom function; they can also play other roles at the same time they are used to form unique associations among WMEs.

Association values enable you to represent associations, set membership, linked lists, graphs, and other complex WME structures by establishing relationships among two or more WMEs.

As an example of the use of association values in representing a graph, consider a program that attempts to color a map with a minimum number of colors such that no two regions that share a border are the same color. A region is represented by a region WME. Each border is represented by two directional neighbor WMEs. The following declarations define the region and neighbor WME classes:

```
(literalize region      ;; A bordered region on the map
    name                 ; Unique region name
    color)               ; Name of assigned color

(literalize neighbor    ;; Directional link between regions
    of                   ; Region name
    is)                  ; Neighboring region's name
```

A neighbor WME serves as a link between two neighboring region WMEs. The attributes ^of and ^is are association attributes that define borders between regions, forming a map. Note that a region may have many neighbors, signified by many neighbor WMEs with the attribute ^of matching the region's name.

The rule in Figure 7.2 uses the attributes of the neighbor WME to find and display neighboring regions. The variables <what> and <neighbor> are association variables that tie together a region with its neighbor, enabling the rule to report all the neighbors of a particular region.

7.2 Maximizing and Minimizing

In many OPS5 applications, there are rules that must match a WME that has a value that is an extreme. For example, there may be a need for a rule that matches on a node with the highest link count, a fact with the highest support

```
(p  report!display-neighbor
;
;  If a region is to be displayed, tell about a neighbor.
;
      (subtask ^name report)
      (region ^name <what> ^status display-neighbors)
      (neighbor ^of <what> ^is <neighbor>)
      (region ^name <neighbor> ^color <neighbor-color>)
   -->
      (write (crlf) |  borders the| <neighbor-color>
             |region named| <neighbor>))
```

Figure 7.2 Using association values in a graph problem.

value, or a plan that is the least expensive. As rules fire and working memory changes, the extremes may change as well, yet the rules matching the extremes must continue to match correctly.

7.2.1 Finding an Extreme

In the simplest case, one rule in the program must match a WME with a maximum or minimum value for a specified attribute. The general solution is to use two condition elements. One condition element is positive, specifying relevant constraints and binding a variable for the extreme value. The second condition element is negated, specifying the same relevant constraints but with a strict inequality on the extreme value. The negated condition element is used to represent an expression meaning *"There is no WME like that but with a higher (lower) value."* The role of the negated element is to prune away matches of the positive condition element that match to less than the extreme value.

For example, the rule in Figure 7.3 is from a hypothetical program that monitors manufacturing processes in a chemical plant. This rule selects the next external input to process based on the value of the attribute `^priority`. The rule matches to the `input` WME with a value for the `^priority` attribute such that there is no `input` WME with a higher value for that attribute.

Note that the negated condition element may not narrow down the match to only one input. There may be several inputs with the highest priority. Since the programmer did not specify the sequence in which inputs with equal priorities should be processed, OPS5 arbitrates according to its conflict-resolution rules—the most recently created or modified of the highest priority inputs are processed first.

```
(p  select-input!choose-next-input
;
;  Find the input with the highest priority and
;  select it for processing next.
;
      (subtask ^name select-input)
   { <Top-input>
      (input ^status received ^priority <highest>) }
      - (input ^status received ^priority > <highest>)
   -->
      (modify <Top-input> ^status processing)
      (make subtask ^name process-input))
```

Figure 7.3 Finding a WME with a maximum value.

7.2.2 Keeping Track of an Extreme

If there are several places in a program where a particular extreme is used, it is often more efficient to have a few rules identify and mark the extreme with a constant than it is to include the positive-negative condition element pair in each rule. Any rule that subsequently accesses that extreme can do so by including that constant in a positive condition element, eliminating the need for the negated condition element and its relatively expensive pruning action. The need to limit the pruning activity increases if the WME containing the extreme value is changing frequently.

For example, suppose that, in our chemical-manufacturing application, inputs are arriving asychronously, creating `input` WMEs at arbitrary times during the program.* Several rules in the system may be interested in the `input` WME with the highest priority at any time. The first condition element in the following pair matches an `input` WME with some priority; the negated condition element ensures that it is among the ones with the largest value for the `^priority` attribute:

```
(input ^status received ^priority <max>)
- (input ^status received ^priority > <max>)
```

Rather than these two condition elements being included in each rule interested in the highest priority, two rules can track the maximum by keeping it marked with the attribute and value `^highest-priority yes`. Figure 7.4 shows two rules that track the inputs with the highest priority as input WMEs are cre-

*Techniques for handling asynchronous events in OPS5 are detailed in Chapter 8.

```
(p  note-highest-priority
;
; If you find an input with the highest priority
; that is not marked, then mark it.
;
   { <Unmarked-maximum>
      (input ^status received ^priority <max>
             ^highest-priority <> yes) }
      - (input ^status received ^priority > <max>)
   -->
      (modify <Unmarked-maximum> ^highest-priority yes))


(p  no-longer-highest-priority
;
; If you find a highest-priority input beat by
; another one, unmark the smaller one.
;
      (input ^status received ^priority <max>
             ^highest-priority yes)
   { <No-longer-maximum>
      (input ^status received ^priority < <max>
             ^highest-priority yes) }
   -->
      (modify <No-longer-maximum> ^highest-priority no))


(p  retiring-highest-priority
;
; If a previously highest priority input is being
; removed, then mark another input as highest before
; this one is unmarked.  This is necessary because
; note-highest-priority may only match old INPUT wmes
; after the highest one is removed, and thus never fire.
;
   { <Retiring-champ>
      (input ^status <> received ^highest-priority yes) }
   { <Unmarked-maximum>
      (input ^status received ^priority <max>
             ^highest-priority <> yes) }
      - (input ^status received ^priority > <max>)
   -->
      (modify <Retiring-champ> ^highest-priority no)
      (modify <Unmarked-maximum> ^highest-priority yes))
```

Figure 7.4 An example of maintaining an extreme.

ated and removed during the run, and a third rule to jump in and mark a next-highest input.

The rule named `note-highest-priority` finds an input with the highest priority, that is not marked `^highest-priority yes`, and marks it with the constant `yes`. This rule fires either when a new input of equal or higher priority is received, or when all previously marked inputs are processed and removed, so that the next-higher-priority inputs become the highest.

When an input is received with a priority higher than that of those currently marked, `note-highest-priority` marks it with `^highest-priority yes`. At this point, the rule named `no-longer-highest-priority` resets these previously highest-priority inputs to `^highest-priority no`.

The third rule, `retiring-highest-priority`, stands by just in case a next-highest-priority input is not already marked when a highest-priority input changes status. In such a case, the `note-highest-priority` could instantiate but may never fire.

With rules such as these to keep the highest-priority input marked, each rule that needs to match the highest priority can do so with the single condition element

```
(input ^status received ^highest-priority yes)
```

instead of with the less efficient two condition element pair. For example, the rule in Figure 7.3 can be written as follows:

```
(p  select-input!choose-next-input
;
;  Find the input with the highest priority and
;  select it for processing next.
;
      (subtask ^name select-input)
   { <Top-input>
      (input ^status received ^highest-priority yes) }
   -->
      (modify <Top-input> ^status processing)
      (make subtask ^name process-input))
```

By referencing `^highest-priority yes` instead of using a negated condition element to find the input with the highest priority, this rule and others like it are simpler and save execution time by letting the two rules in Figure 7.4 do the work of finding the extreme. If only one or two rules need to match the highest-priority input, however, you should use the solution with the negated condition element. In that case, there is no real savings in writing rules to maintain a marker on the highest-priority input.

7.3 Nonmodifying Iteration

Nonmodifying iteration is an iteration technique in which a rule fires exactly once on each member of a set of WMEs without modifying it. Since this technique does not modify matched WMEs, the refraction step in conflict resolution prevents it from firing more than once on any instantiation.

There are several benefits to writing rules that do not reinstantiate themselves when they fire. First, by not changing the matched WMEs, the rule uses refraction to avoid problems with uncontrolled looping. Second, rules that do not modify the WMEs they match usually are simpler than are rules that modify WMEs and that therefore have the potential of matching to the same data again and thus of looping uncontrollably. Because they make few or no changes to working memory, nonmodifying rules may also execute faster than do rules that modify their matched WMEs.

Although using refraction in a programming technique can eliminate uncontrolled loops and can result in simpler rules, there are also drawbacks to using nonmodifying iteration. Refraction is limited to the lifetime of an instantiation of a subtask. When a subtask is invoked another time by making a new control WME for that subtask, then the new subtask WME creates new instantiations with the old data—the old refraction no longer holds and the rules iterate again. Therefore, the usefulness of a nonmodifying iteration technique is limited to one execution of a subtask. Of course, this limitation is an advantage in situations in which it is desirable for the program to iterate over a set of WMEs each time a subtask is invoked.

Furthermore, to depend on refraction is often dangerous. If the WMEs matching rules that depend on refraction are modified at any time before that subtask is exited—either by rules in that subtask, by rules in a subtask invoked from there, or from rules firing independent of the subtask control*—then the effect of refraction is lost and the iterating rules begin again, posing the risk of an infinite loop.

These "infinite loops" are a common mistake made by new OPS5 programmers, who mistakenly believe that the refraction step in conflict resolution will prevent a rule from firing repeatedly. Remember that, when a WME is modified, it receives a new time tag, and it is the *time tag* that distinguishes one WME from another in conflict resolution.

The following subsections present two typical cases of the use of nonmodifying iteration: reading from and counting a set of WMEs.

7.3.1 Reading From a Set of WMEs

One good use of nonmodifying iteration is in writing a rule that must match particular WMEs only once to read specific information from them.

*The use of rules that do not follow a program's control conventions is the subject of Chapter 9.

```
(p  report!display-region
;
;  Match a region and report its color assignment.
;
      (subtask ^name report)
      (region ^name <region-name> ^color <assigned-color>)
   -->
      (write (crlf) <region-name> |is colored|
             <assigned-color>))
```

Figure 7.5 Using nonmodifying iteration to read WMEs.

For example, the rule in Figure 7.5 writes out a list of all map regions and the colors assigned to them by our map-coloring program. The rule `report!display-region` fires for each region WME and reports the color assignment. Refraction prevents it from firing more than once on any `region` WME while in this subtask. Note the absence of a `modify` or `remove` action.

The tradeoff in using nonmodifying iteration in this situation is between ordering and speed. Since the rule `report!display-region` makes no change to working memory, the OPS5 program can fire it for each region WME without spending any time matching rules to WMEs between firings. However, you have no control over the order in which it fires on the region WMEs. If firing order is not important, and if the risk of unanticipated WME modification from other rules is minimal, then nonmodifying iteration may be acceptable for reading WMEs.

7.3.2 Counting a Set of WMEs

Another common application of nonmodifying iteration is in counting a set of WMEs. Typically, counting need not proceed in any particular order and does not require any changes to working memory, so it can be accomplished using nonmodifying iteration.

Suppose that, in our map-coloring program, in addition to the color, we also want to report the number of borders each region shares with another region. Your first inclination may be to write a rule such as the `count-neighbors!incr-neighbor-count` rule shown in Figure 7.6. Unfortunately, this rule loops infinitely.

The problem with this rule is that the modification of the value of `^border-count` creates a new `region` WME, which reinstantiates the rule. Since the rule does nothing to inhibit the LHS from matching on the modified WME, the rule will fire again on the newly modified `region` WME, creating an infinite loop.

```
(p  count-neighbors!incr-neighbor-count
;
; Increment our count of borders for each neighbor we see.
;
      (subtask ^name count-neighbors)
      (neighbor ^of <region>)
    { <Region>
      (region ^name <region> ^border-count <so-far>) }
    -->
      (modify <Region> ^border-count (compute <so-far> + 1)))
```

Figure 7.6 A first attempt at counting borders.

One way to prevent the counting rule from looping on the same region is to match the `neighbor` WMEs separately from the `region` WME. The rules in Figure 7.7 use nonmodifying iteration to count neighbors of each region, and to put the result into the `region` WME.

Refraction is used in Figure 7.7 by the first rule, `count-neighbors!note-neighbor`. This rule neither makes changes to the WMEs it matches, nor makes any WMEs that would reinstantiate the rule. So the first rule fires once for each `neighbor` WME, creating a corresponding `neighbor-noted` WME that is counted as it is removed by the second rule, `count-neighbors!count-neighbor`. The second rule does not use refraction. The rule `count-neighbors!count-neighbor` removes the `neighbor-noted` WMEs as it increments the corresponding region-border count, thus inhibiting itself from counting any neighbor more than once.

The use of special WMEs for counting is a bit cumbersome, and is most often done only in prototype software. In production applications, an external routine is often employed to do the counting. Figure 7.8 contains rules to perform the same counting task as do those in Figure 7.7, but these rules use the following three user-written external routines.

- `increment_counter`: This is a subroutine that is passed the name of a counter and an integer increment. If no value is associated with this counter name yet, `increment_counter` initializes the counter with the increment value.* Otherwise, the subroutine adds the increment value to the value associated with the counter name.

- `counter_value`: This is an RHS function that returns the current value for a given counter name. If there is no counter by that name, it returns 0.

*This approach eliminates the need for a counter initialization routine, which avoids unnecessary complications for the rule writer.

```
(p  count-neighbors!note-neighbor
;
;  Create a WME to take note of a particular neighbor.
;
      (subtask ^name count-neighbors)
      (neighbor ^of <region>)
   -->
      (make neighbor-noted ^of <region>))

(p  count-neighbors!count-neighbor
;
;  Count the noted neighbor and remove it.
;
      (subtask ^name count-neighbors)
   { <The-Region>
      (region ^name <region-name> ^border-count <borders>) }
   { <The-Addition>
      (neighbor-noted ^of <region-name>) }
   -->
      (modify <The-Region> ^border-count (compute <borders> + 1))
      (remove <The-Addition>))

(p  report!display-region
;
;  Match a region and report its color and border count.
;
      (subtask ^name report)
      (region ^name <region-name> ^color <assigned-color>
              ^border-count <borders>)
   -->
      (write (crlf) <region-name> |is colored|
             <assigned-color> |and has|
             <borders> |neighboring regions.|))
```

Figure 7.7 Counting with refraction.

- clear_counter: The subroutine clear_counter resets the value associated with the given counter name to 0.

Since these rules do not affect working memory, they can execute quickly. Using simple external routines such as these, the rules can count neighbors and display regions without incurring any match time while the rules fire. Refraction combined with external routines is recommended for nonmodifying iteration when execution speed is important.

```
(p  count-neighbors!incr-neighbor-count
;
; Increment our waiting counter for each neighbor
;
      (subtask ^name count-neighbors)
      (neighbor ^of <region>)
   -->
      (call increment_counter <region> 1))

(p  report!display-region
;
;  Match a region and report its color and border count.
;
      (subtask ^name report)
      (region ^name <region-name> ^color <assigned-color>)
   -->
      (write (crlf) <region-name> |is colored|
             <assigned-color> |and has|
             (counter_value <region-name>)
             |neighboring regions.|)
      (call clear_counter <region-name>))
```

Figure 7.8 Counting with refraction and external routines.

7.4 Modifying Iteration

Nonmodifying iteration can be an effective technique in many situations. But in some cases, particularly when the rule interacts with the user or external routines, there is a restriction on the sequence in which WMEs are processed. Defensive programming suggests that you not depend on refraction, since subtle bugs may be introduced when someone writes another rule that modifies the WMEs you are processing.

For example, consider the rule in Figure 7.5. Users may desire to see region reports sorted alphabetically, by color, or by size rather than in an arbitrary order. Likewise, external routines may require interactions in a specific sequence, such as that required to navigate through a database.

Section 7.3.2 discusses a counting technique partially based on refraction. The rules in Figures 7.7 and 7.8 assume that no `neighbor` WME is modified in the `count-neighbors` subtask, and no `region` WME is modified in the `report` subtask. If these assumptions hold, refraction causes the rules to fire exactly once on each matching WME. If the assumptions do not hold, and WMEs are modified in these subtasks, then the rules fire more than once for each WME, possibly causing an uncontrolled loop. You may not want to make those assumptions if you anticipate further work in these subtasks.

This section presents the following four techniques that allow you to regain control over the sequence of WME processing, to limit dependence on refraction, and to avoid the infinite-looping problems associated with the rule in Figure 7.6.

- Mark a WME when it is processed by setting one of its attribute's values ("changed" attributes)
- Leave a trail of separate WMEs that indirectly mark which WMEs have been processed (change marker WMEs)
- Process WMEs using an available ordering (selective processing)
- Create a temporary set with members that are already processed (temporary sets)

These are called *modifying iteration* techniques because they iterate over a set of WMEs, allowing WME modification during the iteration but without the potential of uncontrolled loops.

7.4.1 "Changed" Attributes

Perhaps the most straightforward and efficient technique to avoid looping is to include an attribute in the WME whose value is changed to some constant to indicate that the WME has been processed. This approach gives the fastest match time and takes only one rule firing for each WME processed.

In Figure 7.9, for example, the rule `count-neighbors!new-neighbor` marks a `neighbor` WME with the attribute value pair `^counted yes` when it is accounted for in the region-border count. By marking a `neighbor` WME when it is counted, the rule inhibits that neighbor from being considered again, since the rule looks for only those `neighbor` WMEs with a value other than `yes` for the attribute `^counted`.

```
(p  count-neighbors!incr-neighbor-count
;
; Increment our count of borders for each neighbor we see.
;
      (subtask ^name count-neighbors)
   { <Region>
      (region ^name <region> ^border-count <so-far>) }
   { <Neighbor>
      (neighbor ^of <region> ^counted <> yes) }
   -->
      (modify <Region> ^border-count (compute <so-far> + 1))
      (modify <Neighbor> ^counted yes))
```

Figure 7.9 Modifying iteration using a "changed" attribute.

This technique is simple and efficient, but has several drawbacks that may limit its usefulness in some situations. First, if several modifications had to be made to the WME, each one would need its own "changed" attribute to mark that the corresponding change has been made. Also, if the WMEs were to be processed more than once, the "changed" attribute in each WME would have to be reset before each pass. For example, our map-coloring program may have to count borders each time they are redefined by the addition of a new country. The extra reset pass would be pure overhead due to the technique used and would cloud the main task of the program.

7.4.2 Change Marker WMEs

A partial solution to the disadvantages of using an attribute to mark changes is to use a separate WME to record changes made to another WME. Instead of looking for an unmarked WME and marking it when it is processed, we look for the absence of a corresponding marker WME for this change, and make the marker WME when the change is made. One representation for this marker is to use a separate element class called `marker`.

For example, in Figure 7.10 we match against only those `neighbor` WMEs for which a `marker` WME has *not* been created, then create the `marker` WME at the same time as we modify the `region` WME. If we need to count neighbors again, we can remove the `marker` WMEs using a rule such as `post-counting!remove-marker` (also in Figure 7.10) in another subtask after all the `neighbor` WMEs have been counted.

The WME marker technique has several advantages over the "changed" attribute marker technique for certain cases. Although you still need a reset pass if you want to iterate over the WMEs again, this technique does not require a separate attribute for each type of change. The change is described by the value of the attribute `^reason`, so new reasons for a change do not require a specific "changed" attribute in the `neighbor` WME. Also, the WME marker technique may be more efficient, since it does not modify the `neighbor` WME. If `neighbor` WMEs match many other rules, it may be less efficient to mark the `neighbor` WME than to use a separate WME class.

Although this technique is more easily and efficiently extendable than is the technique that uses special attributes to mark changes, it still suffers the disadvantage that markers must be removed if the attribute changes more than once, and that we lack control over the order in which WMEs are marked as changed.

7.4.3 Selective Processing

If the WMEs to be processed have an inherent ordering, you can use that ordering to control the iteration process, and avoid the need for a reset pass. We call this technique *selective processing.*

```
(p  count-neighbors!incr-neighbor-count
;
; Increment our count of borders for each neighbor we see.
;
      (subtask ^name count-neighbors)
   { <Region>
      (region ^name <region> ^border-count <so-far>) }
      (neighbor ^of <region> ^is <neighbor>)
      - (marker ^reason border-counted
                ^region <region> ^neighbor <neighbor>)
   -->
      (modify <Region> ^border-count (compute <so-far> + 1))
      (make marker ^reason border-counted
                ^region <region> ^neighbor <neighbor>))

(p  post-counting!remove-marker
;
; Remove all border-counted markers around.
;
      (subtask ^name marker-cleanup)
   { <Obsolete-marker>
      (marker ^reason border-counted) }
   -->
      (remove <Obsolete-marker>))
```

Figure 7.10 Modifying iteration using marker WMEs.

For example, in our map-coloring program, suppose each `neighbor` WME has a unique integer value for the distinguishing attribute `identifier`. We may count `neighbor` WMEs according to the order of their identifier values.

Figure 7.11 contains three rules that use the selective-processing technique to count `neighbor` WMEs, assuming they have been assigned unique integer identifiers. When the subtask is created for `count-neighbor`, the only rule that can fire is `count-neighbors!initialize-neighbor-count`. This rule creates a WME that is used to guide the selection of `neighbor` WMEs counted. Once the `neighbor-count` WME is made, both of the other rules will match. However, because the rule `count-neighbors!remove-neighbor-count` always matches a subset of the elements matching `count-neighbors!count-next-neighbor-wme`, it is not chosen to fire until `count-neighbors!count-next-neighbor-wme` can no longer fire.

The selective counting is performed by the rule `count-neighbors!count-next-neighbor-wme`. This rule matches the next `neighbor` WME to be processed by specifying that its identifier is greater than the last one processed, and that *there is no neighbor with an identifier between this one and the last*

```
(p  count-neighbors!initialize-neighbor-count
;
; Initialize the count by making a neighbor-count
; WME with a value for ^last-identifer lower than
; any real neighbor identifer.
;
      (subtask ^name count-neighbors)
   -->
      (make neighbor-count ^last-identifier 0))

(p  count-neighbors!count-next-neighbor-wme
;
; Increment our count of borders for the region
; corresponding to the next uncounted neighbor WME,
; and update the neighbor-count identifier.
;
      (subtask ^name count-neighbors)
   { <Neighbor-count>
      (neighbor-count ^last-identifier <done>) }
      (neighbor ^identifier { <next> > <done> } ^of <region>)
      - (neighbor ^identifier { < <next> > <done> })
   { <Region>
      (region ^name <region> ^border-count <so-far>) }
   -->
      (modify <Region> ^border-count (compute <so-far> + 1))
      (modify <Neighbor-count> ^last-identifier <next>))

(p  count-neighbors!remove-neighbor-count
;
; In general, remove the neighbor count WME.
; This is a general case of the above rule, so it
; will not fire until all neighbors are counted.
;
      (subtask ^name count-neighbors)
   { <Neighbor-count>
      (neighbor-count) }
   -->
      (remove <Neighbor-count>))
```

Figure 7.11 Counting WMEs using selective processing.

one processed. When the border count of the corresponding region WME is incremented, the rule resets the value of ^last-identifier in the neighbor-count WME to be the identifier of the neighbor WME just matched. This reset prevents the rule from counting this neighbor again.

Instead of using the expensive technique of positive-negated element pairs, we could have begun with the minimum identifier and then have counted neighbors sequentially. The counting rule would match the neighbor WME with the same value for ^identifier as in the ^next-identifier attribute of the neighbor-counted WME. The action would increment the count and increment the value of ^next-identifier. This rule would fire until there was no neighbor WME with the value of the ^identifier attribute matching the value of the ^next-identifier attribute of the neighbor-counted WME. This technique assumes, however, that the identifiers for neighbor WMEs are assigned consecutively and there are no deletions or reassignments that would create gaps in the sequence of identifiers. The rules in Figure 7.11 skip over gaps, and do not require consecutively assigned identifiers. So we may decide that not requiring consecutive identifier values is worth the extra processing required for the rule to find the next neighbor to count.

If there is no convenient ordering inherent in the WMEs to process, it is easy to establish an arbitrary ordering of your own. If you want only to distinguish one item from another, you can tag each WME with a value returned from the genatom function. However, if you want to establish an *ordering* among a set of WMEs, then a unique integer assignment is necessary.

The rule in Figure 7.12 is responsible for assigning an integer value for the identifier attribute for any unmarked neighbor. A map-state WME made in startup holds a counter in the ^neighbor-count attribute that is initialized to 0. The rule augment-map!assign-neighbor-identifier assigns a new identifier number to any neighbor WME that does not yet have a value for its ^identifier attribute. It then computes a new neighbor count, and uses that count as the value for ^identifier and ^neighbor-count. By setting the identifier, it no longer matches that neighbor WME again, since it matches only those neighbor WMEs that have a nil identifier value.

Like the other techniques discussed, selective processing has advantages and disadvantages. The advantages include control over the sequence of processing WMEs, independence from the dangers of refraction, and elimination of a marker reset pass. However, selective processing does require an integer ordering among the set of WMEs to be processed, which may have to be assigned specifically for this technique. In addition, there may be considerable run-time cost in processing the WMEs in order, if you allow the possibility of gaps in the ordering sequence.

7.4.4 Temporary Sets

The final modifying iteration technique presented in this chapter uses *temporary sets.* When WMEs are to be processed, an empty set is created to represent

```
(p  augment-map!assign-neighbor-identifier
;
; Assign a unique identifier for any neighbor WME and
; update the neighbor count in the map-state WME.
;
      (subtask ^name augment-map)
   { <New-neighbor>
      (neighbor ^identifier nil) }
   { <Map-state>
      (map-state ^neighbor-count <sofar>) }
   -->
      (bind <neighbor-id> (compute <sofar> + 1))
      (modify <New-neighbor> ^identifier <neighbor-id>)
      (modify <Map-state> ^neighbor-count <neighbor-id>))
```

Figure 7.12 Assigning distinguishing integer identifiers.

the WMEs that have been processed so far. The processing rule finds a WME that is not yet in the set, processes it, and puts it in the set. Once all the WMEs have been processed, the set is discarded.

The temporary-set technique has three advantages over the previous modifying iteration techniques:

1. It requires only one attribute in the processed WME class, regardless of the number or types of modifications to be made when processing WMEs
2. It does not require a reset pass between processing loops
3. It does not require an ordering of the processing WMEs, so it does not suffer from the inefficiencies of selective processing

Let us again use our example of counting borders of regions in our map-coloring program. Figure 7.13 shows rules that use the temporary-set technique to count `neighbor` WMEs. On entering the subtask, a new set identifier is created with the `genatom` function. By using `genatom`, we guarantee that the set is empty; that is, none of the `neighbor` WMEs are associated with this set. Once the `set` WME is made, the next rule fires for each `neighbor` WME that has not yet been associated with this set, signified by a different value for the attribute `^member-of-set`. When the rule fires, it increments the associated region-border count and associates the `neighbor` WME with the set by putting the set identifier into the neighbor's `^member-of-set` attribute.

The beauty of this technique is that the attribute `^member-of-set` can be used to record modification of different sets of WMEs for different reasons, simply by creating a new unique set identifier for each modifying iteration process. If, for example, another subtask counted only the borders of a particular region, it would be similar to the one in Figure 7.13, with one rule generating a unique

```
(p  count-neighbors!initialize-counted-set
;
; Initialize the count by making a temporary set for
; neighbors that you have counted.
;
      (subtask ^name count-neighbors)
   -->
      (make set ^identifier (genatom)
               ^membership counted-neighbors))

(p  count-neighbors!count-neighbor-wme
;
; Find a neighbor that has not yet been counted and
; increment our count of borders for the region
; corresponding to the next uncounted neighbor WME,
; and associate the neighbor with the count set.
;
      (subtask ^name count-neighbors)
      (set ^identifier <counted-set>
           ^membership counted-neighbors)
   { <Neighbor>
      (neighbor ^of <region>
               ^member-of-set <> <counted-set>) }
   { <Region>
      (region ^name <region> ^border-count <so-far>) }
   -->
      (modify <Region> ^border-count (compute <so-far> + 1))
      (modify <Neighbor> ^member-of-set <counted-set>))

(p  count-neighbors!remove-temporary-set
;
; In general, remove the counting temporary set.
; This is a general case of the above rule, so it
; will not fire until all neighbors are counted.
;
      (subtask ^name count-neighbors)
   { <Completed-set>
      (set ^membership counted-neighbors) }
   -->
      (remove <Completed-set>))
```

Figure 7.13 Counting using a temporary set.

set identifier, another processing the neighbor WMEs, and a third removing the set WME. Each time a temporary set was used, the old value for the ^member-of-set attribute of the neighbor WME would become obsolete and would be overwritten by the new set identifier.

The major disadvantage of the temporary-set technique is the requirement that the value of the ^member-of-set attribute of the neighbor WME stay constant until the modifications on the entire set are complete and the set WME is removed. If another subtask is instantiated during the processing of a set, the ^member-of-set attribute cannot be changed by the nested subtask. If the value of ^member-of-set is changed again in a WME, then, when the subtask is popped, the previous subtask will process that WME a second time.

Another disadvantage to some programs is that this technique modifies the WME it is processing, thereby causing matching time in rules that also match that WME. Since there is no reset pass, however, the temporary-set technique incurs much less of this overhead than does the attribute-marker technique.

7.5 Attribute-Value Shadowing

Many OPS5 programs require rules to monitor certain changes to a WME that indicate the need for immediate attention. For example, changing a node in a graph may signal the need to propogate changes to the adjacent nodes. This section discusses a technique called *attribute-value shadowing*, which uses redundancy of data in WMEs to detect changes. By making a duplicate copy of a value, we can detect a value modification by comparing it with its unchanged duplicate.

Attribute-value shadowing can take place in the same WME or in different WMEs. As a simple example, consider an OPS5 program that plays a game where players can gain or lose money in a variety of situations. The rules in Figure 7.14 notice when a computer-controlled player gains or loses cash, and react if the change is significant. The rule player-cash-changed uses the attribute ^old-cash to detect a change in the value of the attribute ^cash. When the values of these attributes differ, this rule updates ^old-cash and records the percentage change in ^delta-cash. If the player's cash has been reduced to less than 70 percent of its previous value, the rule complain-about-loss writes a complaint message. If the player's cash has more than doubled, the rule gloat-over-gain causes the player to cheer. To prevent the rules from firing again, should the player WME be changed in other ways, both these rules reset the value of ^delta-cash to 1.0.

Attribute-value shadowing is a good technique for improving the modularity of a program. Once rules like player-cash-changed are written, the programmer no longer needs to be aware of shadow attributes such as ^old-cash. Any change to the ^cash attribute of a computer-controlled player, regardless of where in the program it occurs, is implicitly checked by these rules. The programmer does not have to remember to add an action to invoke a subtask of these rules each time a shadowed attribute is changed. The data-driven nature

```
(p  player-cash-changed
;
; Notice when a computer player's cash changes, for whatever reason.
;
   { <The-player>
      (player ^type computer
              ^old-cash { <old> <> 0.0 }
              ^cash { <new> <> <old> }) }
   -->
      (modify <The-player> ^old-cash <new>
              ^delta-cash (compute <new> // <old>)))


(p  complain-about-loss
;
; Complain when my cash decreases more than I would like.
; I would like to keep more than 70 percent.
;
   { <The-player>
      (player ^type computer ^name <loser>
              ^delta-cash < 0.70) }
   -->
      (write <loser> : |"Nuts!  That's too much!"| (crlf))
      (modify <The-player> ^delta-cash 1.0))


(p  gloat-over-gain
;
; Gloat when my cash increases by more than 100%.
; That is, when delta-cash is > 2.0.
;
   { <The-player>
      (player ^type computer ^name <loser>
              ^delta-cash > 2.0) }
   -->
      (write <loser> : |"Hurray!  That's a tidy sum!"| (crlf))
      (modify <The-player> ^delta-cash 1.0))
```

Figure 7.14 Attribute-value shadowing in a single WME.

of OPS5 causes rules such as the ones in Figure 7.14 to fire whenever shadowed values change.

7.6 Techniques for Handling Common Problems

This section discusses methods of handling several minor problems you may encounter in programming with OPS5. These problems stem from subtle restrictions in the OPS5 language, so many of them may disappear as the language evolves.

7.6.1 Combining Condition Elements

The LHS of an OPS5 rule consists of a conjunction of positive and negated condition elements. A rule is satisfied if all the positive conditions and none of the negated ones are matched consistently. Sometimes, however, you may want the expressive power to specify a disjunction of two or more conditions, or for negating a group of condition elements.

Recall our process-monitoring application for a chemical plant. Sensors placed in critical positions in the manufacturing floor are polled at regular intervals. Suppose we want to write an OPS5 rule representing the following domain concept:

> If an input is received, and if either the associated sensor is known to be unreliable or the manufacturing line has temporarily been shut down, then ignore the input.

We may initially attempt to express this concept in a single OPS5 rule such as the one in Figure 7.15. Unfortunately, OPS5 syntax does not permit disjunction delimiters around condition elements, so this rule would not compile correctly.

Two solutions generally are used for this problem. One is to split the rule into two rules as in Figure 7.16, with one member of the disjunction in one rule and the other in the second rule. The remainder of the rules remain unchanged, and the action of both rules implements the domain concept. Unfortunately, this solution introduces redundant code, which increases the maintenance costs of the program.

The second solution is to change the representation so that the disjunction can be captured in a single attribute. This approach often requires redundancy in the values in working memory rather than in rules; the solution can be written concisely with one rule, using an attribute value disjunction, rather than being split over two very similar rules.

The need to negate a group of condition elements can be solved by either a "propose and prune" technique in which multiple rules are used to propose WMEs to operate on and then discard the inappropriate combinations, or by data redundancy. The following examples elaborate these two techniques.

Consider a rule in our map-coloring example that reports each region that has more borders than do any of its neighboring regions. A first attempt at writing

```
(p  accept-input!reject-useless-input
;
; If an input is received, and either the associated sensor
; is known to be unreliable, or the manufacturing line has
; been temporarily been shut down, then ignore the  input

      (subtask ^name accept-input)
   { <Useless-input>
      (input ^status received ^sensor-id <sensor>) }
   <<    ←— invalid syntax!
      (sensor ^sensor-id <sensor> ^reliability low)
      (process-line ^status shutdown)
   >>    ←— invalid syntax!
   -->
      (remove <Useless-input>))
```

Figure 7.15 An attempt to use disjunct condition elements.

```
(p  accept-input!reject-unreliable-input
;
; If an input is received, and the associated sensor
; is known to be unreliable, then ignore the input.
;
      (subtask ^name accept-input)
   { <Useless-input>
      (input ^status received ^sensor-id <sensor>) }
      (sensor ^sensor-id <sensor> ^reliability low)
   -->
      (remove <Useless-input>))

(p  accept-input!reject-shutdown-inputs
;
; If an input is received, and the manufacturing line has
; been temporarily been shut down, then ignore the input.
;
      (subtask ^name accept-input)
   { <Useless-input>
      (input ^status received) }
      (process-line ^status shutdown)
   -->
      (remove <Useless-input>))
```

Figure 7.16 Splitting rules to implement condition element disjunctions.

```
(p  report!display-crowded-region
;
;  Display each region that has more borders than any
;  of its neighbors.
;
      (subtask ^name report)
      (region ^name <region-name> ^border-count <max>)
      - (neighbor ^of <region-name> ^is <neighbor>)
      - (region ^name <neighbor> ^border-count >= <max>)
   -->
      (write (crlf) <region-name>
        |has more borders than any of its neighbors.|))
```

Figure 7.17 An attempt to negate associated condition elements.

this rule may produce a rule such as the one in Figure 7.17. This rule, unlike the rule in Figure 7.15, is legal OPS5 syntax, but it has a meaning different from that which we intended.

This rule also demonstrates a mistake many OPS5 programmers make. The negated conditions do not inhibit the match only when the region has a neighbor with at least as many borders. In fact, the two negated conditions act independent of one another. The first negated condition effectively eliminates from the match any region that has any neighbors at all. The second negated element inhibits the match if there is any region on the map with at least as many borders as the one being considered. Since the region matching the second condition element also matches the second negated element, the rule is contradictory and cannot fire. Both instances of the variable `<neighbor>` are useless, since the scope of a variable bound in a negated element is limited to that element. The second occurrence of `<neighbor>` is another negated element binding, unrelated to the first. Clearly, this behavior is not what we intended.

The "propose and prune" technique splits the rule in Figure 7.17 into three rules. The first rule suggests that any region is a candidate for having more borders than any of its neighbors has. The second rule disqualifies each region that has a neighbor with a higher border count. The third rule writes out the candidates that remain. This technique may be desirable because of the simplicity of the individual rules, but that benefit must be weighed against the cost of potentially many rule firings and of high-level control, which complicates the overall solution.

The alternate technique uses the concept of data redundancy. Figure 7.18 shows two rules that display regions that do not have any neighbors with a higher border count. We identify these regions by storing the value of `^border-count` in `neighbor` WMEs as well as in `region` WMEs. The rule `count-neighbors!update-neighbor` maintains a redundant copy of a neighboring re-

```
(p  count-neighbors!update-neighbor
;
;  Propogate a region's border-count to all its neighbor links.
;
      (subtask ^name count-neighbors)
      (region ^name <neighbor> ^border-count <sum>)
   { <Neighbor-link>
      (neighbor ^is <neighbor> ^border-count <> <sum>) }
   -->
      (modify <Neighbor-link> ^border-count <new>))

(p  report!display-crowded-region
;
;  Display each region that has more borders than any
;  of its neighbors.
;
      (subtask ^name report)
      (region ^name <region-name> ^border-count <max>)
      - (neighbor ^of <region-name> ^is <neighbor>
                  ^border-count >= <max>)
   -->
      (write (crlf) <region-name>
        |has more borders than any of its neighbors.|))
```

Figure 7.18 Redundant-data solution for the problem of negated condition elements.

gions' border count in `neighbor` WMEs. With the border count in the neighbor WME, the negated element in `report!display-crowded-region` exactly expresses the intent of the rule: to find a region for which there is no neighbor of that region with a higher border count. A disadvantage of the data-redundancy approach is that it requires the overhead of rules whose purpose is solely to maintain the integrity of the redundant data during a run.

With both the association value and the maximizing value in a single WME, the solution to the problem of negating a group of condition elements involves that of matching extremes, discussed in Section 7.2.

7.6.2 Disjunctions Involving Predicates or Variables

For mostly historical reasons, OPS5 treats all disjunctive values as constants. That is, atoms with variable syntax are treated as quoted atoms, and are not evaluated as variables. The test `<< waiting pending <x> >>` translates to a disjunctive test over the values `waiting`, `pending`, and the three-character atom `<x>`. This translation is often a source of surprise to new OPS5 programmers, who expect the variable inside the disjunction to be evaluated.

Testing for values outside a numerical range may tempt you to use a construct such as << < <min> > <max> >>, perhaps to signal an out-of-range error. Because OPS5 treats all values inside disjunctions as constants, this syntax is accepted by OPS5 and is translated into a disjunction over the atoms <, <min>, >, and <max>.

Suppose that, in our manufacturing-process-monitoring program, we are told that inputs received from sensors should be checked against the sensor-signal range. If the input does not fall within the tolerance limits of the sensor, then the input data are not reliable and should be ignored. The rule in Figure 7.19 would work as intended if predicates and variables were evaluated inside disjunctions—unfortunately, however, they are not.

Two common ways of expressing a disjunction with nonconstants are breaking the rule into one for each disjunct case, and using a negated condition element to turn the disjunction into a conjunction.

For example, splitting the rule in Figure 7.19 yields the two very similar rules in Figure 7.20 that detect when the input signal is unreliable. One matches an input signal that is below the minimum tolerance of the associated sensor. The other matches an input signal that is higher than the maximum tolerance. The remainder of the original rule is duplicated in the two new rules.

The other technique for expressing a disjunction requiring a predicate or variable uses a distinguishing value to perform the out-of-range match in one rule. The WME of interest is matched, and a negated condition element, associated by the distinguishing value, confirms that the WME cannot match the in-range test.

Figure 7.21 shows how this technique applies to our problem of detecting an unreliable input WME. A particular input WME matches the third condition

```
(p  accept-input!reject-input-beyond-limits
;
; If an input is received with a value outside the normal
; range of this sensor, suspect that the sensor is on
; the blink.
;
        (subtask ^name critique-input)
        (sensor ^sensor-id <sensor>
                ^min-tolerance <min> ^max-tolerance <max>)
     { <Unreliable-input>
        (input ^status received ^sensor-id <sensor>
                ^signal << < <min> > <max> >>) }
     -->
        (remove <Unreliable-input>))
```

Figure 7.19 Incorrectly specified variables in a disjunction.

```
(p  accept-input!reject-too-low-input
;
; If an input is received with a value lower than the
; minimum range of this sensor, suspect that the sensor is on
; the blink.
;
      (subtask ^name critique-input)
      (sensor ^sensor-id <sensor> ^min-tolerance <min>)
   { <Unreliable-input>
      (input ^status received ^sensor-id <sensor>
             ^signal < <min>) }
   -->
      (remove <Unreliable-input>))


(p  accept-input!reject-too-high-input
;
; If an input is received with a value higher than the
; maximum range of this sensor, suspect that the sensor is on
; the blink.
;
      (subtask ^name critique-input)
      (sensor ^sensor-id <sensor> ^max-tolerance <max>)
   { <Unreliable-input>
      (input ^status received ^sensor-id <sensor>
             ^signal > <max>) }
   -->
      (remove <Unreliable-input>))
```

Figure 7.20 Expressing a disjunction using two rules.

element, binding the (distinguishing) variable `<unique>` to the distinguishing value of `^identifier`. The negated condition also matches an input with the same identifier value, restricting it to looking at exactly the same WME. A test is made on the value of `^signal` in this negated element to see whether the value is in range. If the negated condition element successfully matches, then the input is fine and the rule is inhibited from firing on that `input` WME. If the negated element does not match, we know that the value of `^signal` is *not* within the acceptable range defined in the `sensor` WME. So the rule will match and should eventually remove the unreliable `input` WME.

Rule splitting, data redundancy, and the use of distinguishing values are all useful tools in developing techniques to solve representation problems that arise in OPS5 programming.

```
(p  accept-input!reject-input-beyond-limits
;
; If an input is received with a value outside the normal
; range of this sensor, suspect that the sensor is on
; the blink.
;
      (subtask ^name critique-input)
      (sensor ^sensor-id <sensor>
              ^min-tolerance <min> ^max-tolerance <max>)
   { <Unreliable-input>
      (input ^status received ^sensor-id <sensor>
             ^identifier <unique>) }
      - (input ^status received ^identifier <unique>
             ^signal { >= <min> <= <max> })
   -->
      (remove <Unreliable-input>))
```

Figure 7.21 Using a negated condition to express an out-of-range test.

7.7 Programming Style and Philosophy

As mentioned earlier, the OPS5 language provides little guidance on how to make the best use of it. There are no built-in constructs for control or for the definition of aggregate data structures. However, many developers have chosen OPS5 over other languages because of OPS5's simplicity and efficiency in pattern matching and in execution of large rule-based systems. As our experience with using the language grows, rules of thumb are emerging that create a philosophy and style of OPS5 programming.

Think in terms of rules and state.

New OPS5 programmers often concentrate on program control and rule-base structure too early in the development process. The key is in proper representation of the domain, and in the central rules of the system. Thinking of rules that handle the crux of the problem is the first step in designing a good representation. You should ensure that these central rules execute properly before you concern yourself with aspects of control. The OPS5 application design process is discussed in considerable detail in Chapter 11, *Designing an OPS5 Program.*

Strive for rule independence.

Ideally, rules in an OPS5 program should be independent. That is, if one is plucked out, only a small piece of knowledge is gone, and the system performs at a slightly less competent level. Likewise, competence increases as knowledge is incrementally added in the form of rules.

In reality, it can be quite difficult to implement an OPS5 program with rules that are truly independent. Atomic pieces of domain knowledge do not always map onto single OPS5 rules. This lack of correspondence results in small pockets of rules that are dependent on one another. This problem is minimized if these rule dependencies are localized and are made explicit.

You should not write rules that force artificial dependencies among rules in distinct subtasks. Specifically, you should not create a WME or a value in one rule expressly for a particular rule in another subtask. These "private" messages between particular rules complicate readability of the program and therefore make that program more difficult to maintain. Furthermore, WMEs that contain private messages are not intrinsic to the problem being solved; they merely add control information. In general, strive for coherence within a subtask, and for independence among subtasks.

Subtasks should be defined so that the ordering of rule firings within each one is unimportant. The sequence of rule firings in a subtask should be completely data-driven—the programmer should not try to force or even presuppose the firing sequence when writing the subtask. Rules should fire until there is no more work left in the subtask. In general, if there is no need for sequencing actions in a subtask, the ordering should be left unspecified.

Avoid conflict-resolution tricks, such as matching irrelevant WMEs just to make one rule dominate over another because of recency or specificity. For example, instead of matching a subtask element multiple times to secure a rule's dominance, design a priority-control method, or separate rules into subtasks and control the rules at the subtask level. If you are specific in the description of the problem state at hand, the correct ordering of rules usually follows.

Use refraction when it is safe to do so.

We have presented refraction as the basis of efficient WME iteration techniques. Rules that use refraction can be efficient and simple. However, relying on refraction, especially in potentially large or sophisticated applications, can make your application more prone to certain bugs. When you write rules that depend on refraction to avoid looping, document the dependence clearly in the rule and subtask comments so that other rule writers will be aware of it.

Use general and special case rules.

Programs written in OPS5 often have general case rules and special case rules. The general case rules match broad classes of situations and take the most commonly applicable action. For a similar but more specific situation, a special case rule may be written that matches a superset of those WMEs that match the general case rule. A special case rule must have more condition elements or condition element tests than its general case rule does. These rules apply in specific situations in which you want the program to behave differently from the way it would in the general case.

If you find yourself counting condition element tests to find out whether the general or special case rule dominates in the conflict set, then you should reexamine your solution. You may need to refine your representation to allow clearer distinctions among cases.

Special case rules have advantages, but incur a cost. They are efficient, since the OPS5 match algorithm does not duplicate effort in matching the similar parts of general case rules. Special case rules are often closely related to the way experts express their knowledge, and are therefore a convenient representation of that knowledge. However, the redundancy of the condition elements shared by the general and special case rules hampers maintenance. Any changes made to the LHS of a general case rule also must be applied to the associated special case rules.

Try an exception-driven design.

Often the best OPS5 program design is one that is reactive rather than proactive. That is, the bulk of the knowledge is applied in correcting an approximated solution rather than in advancing toward the final solution itself. This advantage may not be initially intuitive, but practice has shown that designs that make the assumption that the general cases are true and look to act on only the exceptions are often the cleanest and most efficient.

For example, one approach to choosing a distinct color for each region on a map may be to choose a single color for all regions as a first approximation. The coloring process may be then handled by a rule that finds two neighboring regions of the same color and selects another color for one of them.*

In general, a reactive, or exception-driven, design involves a set of rules that pursues a naive solution, and another set of rules that monitor the process, making corrections to the naive solution along the way. Exception-driven designs are commonly developed for planning and scheduling applications.

Try to make control knowledge explicit and separate from the domain knowledge.

An OPS5 application consists of control knowledge and domain knowledge. Control knowledge is the high-level procedural knowledge of how to move through the subtasks to reach a solution. It should be designed to help guide developers in representing and placing new knowledge in the system. Domain

*This approach may not result in a minimal coloring, but it will be adequate if it is not important to use the fewest possible colors.

knowledge encompasses the expertise necessary to perform the task with proficiency. Keeping control and domain knowledge separate in your application helps to minimize maintenance costs by making the program easier to read and update.

Realistically, control knowledge cannot always be easily separated or even distinguished from domain knowledge, since domain knowledge may involve decisions about subtask control flow. It is the responsibility of the programmer to decide whether specific knowledge is control, domain, or both.

Even if the separation of control and domain knowledge is unclear, the control should be as clear and predictable as possible. For example, avoid writing subtask rules that abort a subtask by modifying or removing the control element. Subtask rules that modify the control element force you to depend on the firing sequence of other rules in that subtask, and are often a source of errors. Each subtask should be designed so that, when it is invoked, all instantiations of its rules will be allowed to fire before the subtask is terminated.

Summary

- Association values are central to many programming techniques. They allow you to represent relationships among WMEs to form abstractions such as sets, lists, graphs, and arbitrary connections.

- Two techniques are presented for finding a WME that has a maximum or minimum value. The first uses two condition elements—one positive, the other negated. The second maintains a constant marker on the extreme WME. The first is simple and concise; the second is more efficient when many rules are required to find the same extreme.

- Nonmodifying iteration is a technique in which a rule fires exactly once on each member of a set of WMEs without modifying it. Examples are reading from and counting a set of WMEs. Use of refraction combined with external routines is a recommended practice when execution time is important and firing order is not an issue.

- In modifying iteration techniques, each member of a set of WMEs is visited and possibly is modified along the way. We discussed four of these techniques:
  constant-value markers, WME change markers, selective processing, and temporary set creation for changed WMEs. These techniques allow you to regain control over the sequence of WME processing, to limit dependency on refraction, and to avoid uncontrolled looping.

- Attribute-value shadowing is a method for monitoring changes in WMEs by keeping duplicate copies of data, one of which is involved in some dynamic process and one of which is static and is used for comparison to detect change.

- Rule splitting, data redundancy, and the use of distinguishing values are all useful tools in developing techniques to solve representation problems that arise in OPS5 programming.
- Good OPS5 programming style and philosophy suggest that you think in terms of rules and state, strive for rule independence, use refraction when appropriate for efficiency and simplicity, use special case rules, try exception-driven designs, and try to maintain a separation between control and domain knowledge.

Exercises

1. Explain each of the values in condition elements of the rule `report!display-neighbor` in Figure 7.2 (on page 123) in terms of the four roles described in Section 7.1. Focus on the primary role played by each value.
2. Answer the following questions pertaining to extremes matching.
   a. Describe what the behavior of the rule in Figure 7.3 would be if the greater-than predicate (>) were changed to a greater-than-or-equal-to predicate (>=).
   b. Modify the rules in Figure 7.4 such that only one input is ever marked as highest priority at any time, even if others share that priority value.
3. What are the benefits of using nonmodifying iteration? What are the drawbacks?
4. To avoid depending on refraction, use modifying iteration techniques to write rules similar to `report!display-region` in Figure 7.5 that reports each region and its color assignment.
   a. Use the attribute and value `^printed yes` to mark the region as it is printed.
   b. Use a `marker` WME to mark regions displayed.
   c. Use the temporary-set technique with a `set` WME.
   d. Write rules that display regions grouped by color, using whatever modifying iteration technique you wish.
5. Suppose that each region has an attribute `^population` that holds an integer estimate of the population of that region. Given the following WME classes, add attributes and write rules that use attribute-value shadowing to maintain a sum of the populations of each color.

```
(literalize region      ;; A bordered region on the map
    name                ; Unique region name (distinguishing)
    color               ; Name of assigned color
    population)         ; Current population, integer
```

```
(literalize color        ;; Information about a color
    name                  ; Distinguishing attribute
    population-total)     ; Sum of regions of this color
```

6. Data redundancy is a valuable aid in solving representation problems. How can you keep redundant values consistent?

7. Write rules that assign colors to regions in our map-coloring program, and run them on an OPS5 representation of the following map. Absolute minimal coloring is not a requirement, but try to limit the number of colors used. The only requirement is that neighbors that share a border must have different colors.

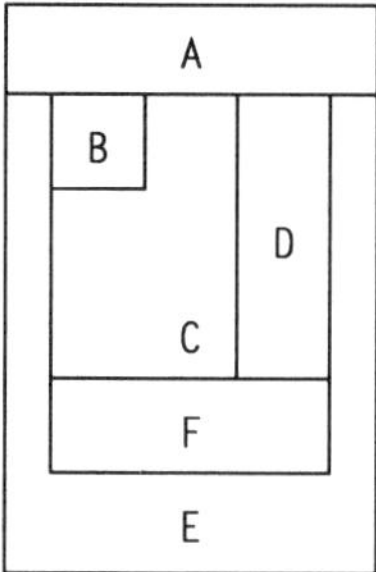

[*Hint:* Consider using techniques such as counting, extremes matching, data redundancy, and attribute-value shadowing.]

CHAPTER 8

External Routines

ALTHOUGH IT IS POSSIBLE to use the OPS5 language for almost any purpose, OPS5 is specialized for simple and efficient pattern matching. Certain tasks require computation that is awkward or impractical to implement in rules, such as

- Purely algorithmic procedures
- Database access
- Operating system interfaces
- Complex numerical calculations and
- Sophisticated input–output processing

To be successfully integrated into a larger computer-system environment, a rule-based language must support non-rule computations. There are two ways this integration can take place: the rule-based language can contain its own procedural language component, or it can provide an interface for calling routines written in other languages. OPS5 takes the latter approach.

Rather than make procedural language extensions to the language, OPS5 provides support for calling routines written in other languages. The advantage to this approach is that the capabilities and strengths of other programming languages are made available to the OPS5 programmer, rather than the programmer being restricted to one procedural language with its inherent limitations. This approach also encourages reuse of software; standard interfaces, packages, or modules already written and available in other languages can be called directly from OPS5 rules.

The integration of an OPS5 program with external routines is often part of an evolutionary step during program development. In many projects, OPS5 programming is used for the entire task to help clarify ill-defined portions. The development of an OPS5 prototype helps to elucidate problem-solving methods that, once defined, may be better suited to a different language or tool.

This chapter introduces OPS5's external-routine interface. We attempt to introduce the subject independently from the OPS5 implementation or the external language used. For illustrative purposes, however, we use a VAX OPS5 implementation that calls external routines written in C, BASIC and PASCAL, and a LISP-based OPS5 implementation that calls external routines written in COMMON LISP. Your OPS5 documentation should contain the specific descriptions of OPS5 interface routines and the calling mechanisms provided by your implementation.

8.1 The Result Element

Recall the vector representation of a WME introduced in Chapter 2. An OPS5 WME is just a vector of fields. Each field holds one value. An attribute name is an index to the field in the WME that holds its value.

The *result element* is a template for a WME. It contains a vector of fields that is identical to a WME, but that sits outside of working memory. OPS5 uses the result element extensively during rule firing, in particular to implement actions.

Most actions are implemented in two steps. First, OPS5 builds a "prototype" of the WME or of the pattern of values used in the action in the result element. Second, OPS5 takes the specified action on that prototype. For example, the `make` action first builds the WME in the result element based on the RHS pattern specified in that action, and then copies that WME into working memory. The

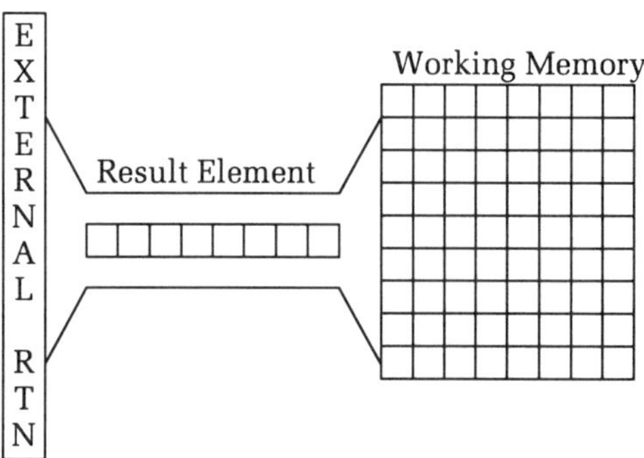

Figure 8.1 Passing data between OPS5 and an external routine through the result element.

modify action first copies the WME to be modified into the result element, then overwrites the values that have been specified to be changed, and finally copies the WME back to working memory. The write action fills the result element with the values listed in the action, and then prints each value separated with a space.

The result element is important to the discussion of external routines because it is the *only* interface between the external routine and OPS5 (Figure 8.1). An external routine can neither search working memory nor remove or modify WMEs directly from working memory. Instead, the OPS5 rule fills the result element with values as arguments to send to the external routine, and the external routine fills the result element with values if it is sending a WME back to the OPS5 program.

8.2 Overview of External Routines

The following steps are used when writing external routines for an OPS5 program:

- An external routine is determined to be a function or a subroutine
- User-written routines must be declared before they are called from a rule
- Calls to the external routine must be placed appropriately in rules
- The application-building process must incorporate all the routines into the executable system

Each of these steps is described briefly in the following sections.

8.2.1 Calling External Routines: Subroutines and Functions

All external routines are either *subroutines* or *functions*. The two can be distinguished by their placement in an OPS5 rule, and by the use of their results.

Subroutines are used purely for their side effects, such as calling databases to create WMEs, or implementing input and display routines. They are called using the RHS call action. The call action takes the name of the subroutine and an RHS pattern as arguments:

(call *rhs-subroutine rhs-pattern*)

For example, a subroutine called retrieve_component reads information from an external database and creates WMEs that represent database items. The following is a call to this subroutine:

```
(call retrieve_component <part-name> <supplier-code>)
```

The call to a subroutine uses the result element as an argument-passing mechanism. In this example, the variables `<part-name>` and `<supplier-code>` are bound to values that are placed in the result element and are used as arguments to the external routine.

External functions are used to return a result to the executing or matching rule; they are used in the same way that OPS5-provided functions such as `compute`, `substr`, or `crlf` are used. External functions are used for numerical calculations such as computing square roots or logarithms, for counters, or for queries to a database that return a single value.

A call to an external function is embedded in an RHS action or, in some implementations of OPS5, in a condition element. The name of the function with its parameters is enclosed in parentheses. In the following example, the function `retrieve_count` is called from inside the `make` action. This function call does not pass any arguments. The value returned by `retrieve_count` becomes the value at the field indexed by the attribute `^id-counter`.

```
(make item ^name <newpart> ^id-counter (retrieve_count))
```

8.2.2 Declaring External Routines in the Rule Base

The names of all external routines used in an OPS5 program must be declared for the compiler with the `external` declaration. Figure 8.2 contains a representative declaration of two RHS subroutines (`increment_count` and `get_inventory_records`), and one RHS function (`retrieve_count`). There are no syntactic differences in the declarations of functions and subroutines. Like attribute names, names of external routines must be declared before they are used in a rule, so they are usually placed at the head of the rule base or file of rules.

OPS5 does not allow for the number and type of arguments to an external routine to be declared in an `external` declaration. However, extended implementations may allow parameter-type declarations for type checking and automatic-type conversion.

```
(external
    increment_count          ; Sub: incr external counter
    retrieve_count           ; Fun: retrieve external counter
    get_inventory_records)   ; Sub: fetch from database
```

Figure 8.2 Using the external declaration.

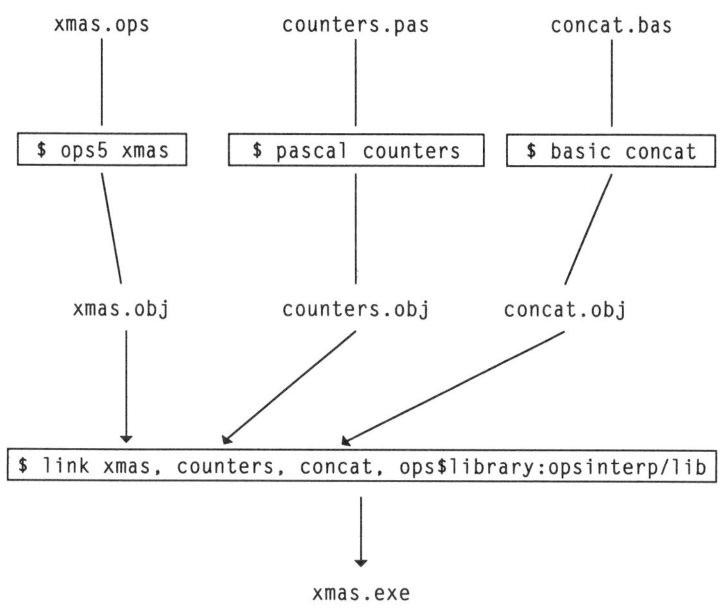

Figure 8.3 Compiling and linking external routines with a VAX OPS5 program.

8.2.3 Building an Application with External Routines

External routines that are called from a rule base must be present in OPS5's program image at execution time. In a LISP-based OPS5 implementation, the routines must merely be present in the LISP environment. In VAX OPS5, the routines must first be compiled by a corresponding language compiler into object code, and the object code must be linked together with the compiled rule base to produce an executable image.

Figure 8.3 illustrates compiling and linking a VAX OPS5 rule base that contains external routines. First, the sources for the OPS5 rule base and each external-routine module are compiled using their respective language compilers to produce object files. The module `counters.pas` is compiled by the VAX PASCAL™ compiler, and the module `concat.bas` is compiled by the VAX BASIC™ compiler to produce object code `counters.obj` and `concat.obj`. The OPS5 rule base, `xmas.ops`, is compiled by the VAX OPS5 compiler, producing `xmas.obj`.* The object files are then linked together with the rule interpreter, in the library `ops$library:opsinterp`.

*VAX OPS5 allows for modular compilation of a rule base spread over several files.

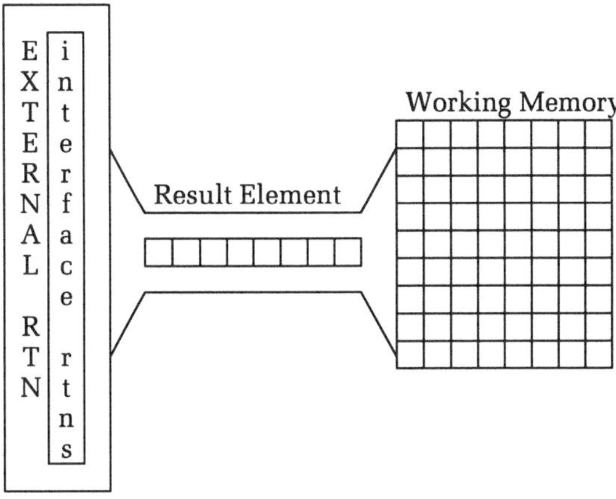

Figure 8.4 Interface-support routines used in the external routine.

8.3 Fundamental Routine-Interface Issues

The difficulty in the communication between any two programming languages lies in passing values between the two, and in having the values from one language understood by the other. In this section, we introduce OPS5's approach to that communication, and describe how OPS5 handles data-type conversion when it is necessary.

8.3.1 Interface-Support Routines

The interface that OPS5 provides for communication with other languages consists of a set of interface routines that we refer to as *interface-support routines*. Interface-support routines are used by external routines (shown in Figure 8.4) that communicate with OPS5 for

- Converting to and from atomic data when necessary
- Placing atoms in the result element
- Retrieving atoms from the result element
- Copying the contents of the result element into working memory
- Testing the type of atoms

In VAX OPS5, the names of these routines are always prefixed with `OPS$`; in LISP-based OPS5 implementations, the functions are prefixed with a dollar sign (`$`) and may be defined in a COMMON LISP package prefix (`OPS:`). In this book, when we talk about these routines independent of a specific example, we use only the name of the routine, with no implementation-dependent prefix. When we refer to a specific example, we use the full name as used by that OPS5 implementation.

When interface-support routines are used in an external routine, they must be declared. Each language has its own mechanism for declaring routines. The following is an example of declaring the VAX OPS5 interface-support routines named OPS$CVAN, OPS$CVNA, and OPS$INTERN in an external routine written in VAX BASIC:

```
EXTERNAL LONG FUNCTION OPS$CVAN (LONG BY VALUE)
EXTERNAL LONG FUNCTION OPS$CVNA (LONG BY VALUE)
EXTERNAL LONG FUNCTION OPS$INTERN (STRING BY REF,
                                   LONG BY VALUE)
```

You can create a file of all declarations specific to each language you use for all the interface-support routines, and include that file each time you write a routine in that language. VAX OPS5 supplies files containing OPS5 interface-support routine declarations for several languages.

8.3.2 Data-Type Conversion

Recall the discussion of OPS5 values in Chapter 2. All OPS5 values are represented as atoms. An atom is an integer encoding of an OPS5 value. This representation of data simplifies pattern matching, because any two values can be compared during match in one machine instruction. When an atom is passed to an external routine, however, the external routine may need to convert the atom into a data type meaningful in the routine's language.

No atom conversion is necessary in LISP-based implementations of OPS5. The routines external to a LISP-based OPS5 program are also written in LISP. Since OPS5 atoms are the same as LISP atoms, they can be used without checking for their type and converting. Users of LISP-based OPS5 implementations may therefore choose to skip this section.

In non-LISP implementations of OPS5, however, routines written in other languages cannot rely on a shared understanding of the atom. Most procedural languages represent data as integers, floating-point numbers, characters, booleans, and other structures. To use data from an OPS5 program in routines written in another language, OPS5 provides a set of interface-support routines that convert atoms into the appropriate representation for that language. OPS5 also provides routines that convert the representation in the external routine into OPS5 atoms when sending values to the OPS5 program.

Table 8.1 lists the OPS5 interface-support routines used for atom conversion that are supplied by VAX OPS5. We show only the OPS$ names for these routines, since the routines are not used with LISP-based OPS5 implementations. Analogous routines should exist in any non-LISP OPS5 implementation that allows calls to external routines.

Table 8.1 VAX OPS5 atom conversion routines.

Routine	Argument	Purpose and Return Value
OPS$CVAN	(atom)	(OPS5 ConVert Atom to Number) Converts an integer atom to an integer. Returns the integer.
OPS$CVNA	(integer)	(OPS5 ConVert Number to Atom) Converts integer to integer atom. Returns the atom.
OPS$CVAF	(atom)	(OPS5 ConVert Atom to Floating) Converts a floating-point atom to a floating-point number. Returns the floating-point number.
OPS$CVFA	(floating)	(OPS5 ConVert Floating to Atom) Converts a floating-point number to a floating-point atom. Returns the atom.
OPS$PNAME	(atom, character_buffer, buffer_size)	(OPS5 Print NAME) Fills the character buffer with the print-name of the atom. Returns the number of characters in the buffer.
OPS$INTERN	(character_buffer, buffer_size)	(OPS5 INTERNal symbol) Converts contents of the character buffer to a symbolic atom. Returns the symbolic atom.

To know which routine should be used to convert an atom that is passed from OPS5, there are also interface-support routines for determining the standard data type of an OPS5 atom (Table 8.2). These data-typing routines indicate whether an atom is of a particular type: integer, symbol, or floating-point number. The routines return a 1 if their argument is of the type being tested, and a 0 if it is not. Once the type of the atom has been determined, then the appropriate conversion routine can be used.

Figure 8.5 shows a VAX BASIC routine that tests the type of an argument that is passed from the OPS5 program using the `call` action. When the `select` statement determines the atom's type, the appropriate conversion routine is used to convert it in a print statement.

It is not always necessary to convert atoms that are passed to an external routine. Sometimes, the atom can be manipulated as it is. If the atom is used only as a key value, for example, or just to determine its type, then conversion is not necessary. Atom representations remain meaningful and unique throughout

Table 8.2 Type predicates in VAX OPS5.

Routine	Argument	Return Value
OPS$SYMBOL	(atom)	1 if atom is symbolic, else 0
OPS$INTEGER	(atom)	1 if atom is integer, else 0
OPS$FLOATING	(atom)	1 if atom is floating-point, else 0

the program execution, so they can be stored in external data structures for use later in the run.

8.4 Subroutines

A subroutine is used primarily for its side effects, such as creating WMEs, rather than for its return value. In this section, we discuss first how arguments are passed to a subroutine, and then how WMEs are created and returned from them.

8.4.1 Passing Arguments to a Subroutine

Passing arguments to a subroutine from an OPS5 rule uses the result element as an intermediate step. The arguments in a subroutine call are placed directly into the result element. The external subroutine must then "fetch" each argument from the result element using the interface-support routines shown in Table 8.3. (Remember that the LISP versions of these routines are normally prefixed with $ and the VAX OPS5 versions are prefixed with OPS$.)

The routine parametercount returns the position of the last value placed in the result element. This number usually corresponds to the number of arguments passed to the external routine. The routine parameter retrieves a value from a specified position in the result element.

Figure 8.6 shows how the interface-support routines OPS$PARAMETERCOUNT and OPS$PARAMETER can be used to fetch all the arguments of a subroutine written in VAX PASCAL. First, the routine OPS$PARAMETERCOUNT returns the number of values stored in the result element and stores this value in the variable wme_size. Then, each element of the array argument_list is filled with the value returned by the interface-support routine OPS$PARAMETER.

As an example of using the values in the result element, Figure 8.7 contains the routine debug-msg that prints all the arguments that are passed through the result element when debugging features are enabled. This routine can be used to control the printing or suppression of a set of helpful run-time messages, so that they print during program development, but it can be easily turned off when the program is in production use. The debug-msg subroutine can be used, for

```
100     SUB Write_Atom
        !+
        ! Description: (CALL WRITE_ATOM <atom>)
        !   Called from OPS5 as a subroutine with 1 argument.
        !   Write_Atom converts its argument and prints it.
        !   Note: Symbolic atoms are enclosed in
        !   quotation marks.
        !-
        %INCLUDE "OPS$LIBRARY:OPSDEF.BAS"
        COMMON (SYMB_ATOM) STRING atom_buffer = 256%
        DECLARE INTEGER arg_size    ! Used if it is symbolic
        DECLARE LONG param          ! To get the atom value.

        PARAM = OPS$PARAMETER(1)    ! Fetch argument from OPS5.

        ! Find out what type of atom param is and report it.
        SELECT 1
            CASE OPS$INTEGER (param)
                PRINT OPS$CVAN (param);
            CASE OPS$FLOATING (param)
                PRINT OPS$CVAF (param);
            CASE OPS$SYMBOL (param)
                arg_size = OPS$PNAME (param, atom_buffer, 128%)
                PRINT '"'; SEG$(atom_buffer, 1%, arg_size); '"';
            CASE ELSE
                PRINT "??";
        END SELECT
        END SUB ! Write_Atom
```

Figure 8.5 Converting a VAX OPS5 atom from VAX BASIC.

```
    :
VAR wme_size, i : INTEGER;
    argument_list : ARRAY [1..Max_Param] OF INTEGER;

BEGIN
wme_size := OPS$PARAMETERCOUNT;

(* Copy the result element into argument_list *)
FOR i := 1 to wme_size DO
    argument_list[i] := OPS$PARAMETER (i);
    :
```

Figure 8.6 Retrieving arguments from the result element (VAX PASCAL).

Table 8.3 Interface-support routines for reading from the result element.

Routine	Arguments	Return Value
parametercount	—	Position of last value placed in the result element
parameter	(integer-position)	The atom in the result element at this position
litbind	(atomic-attribute)	The position to which the attribute points

instance, in the pop-subtask rule from Chapter 5 to print the name of a subtask as it is being removed:

```
(p  pop-subtask
   { <Subtask>
      (subtask ^name <exhausted>) }
   -->
      (remove <Subtask>)
      (call debug-msg Popping <exhausted>))
```

In the COMMON LISP version of the debug-msg subroutine in Figure 8.7, the subroutine first calls another function to determine whether debugging messages should be printed (the function debug-mode-p). If they should, then the $parametercount routine determines the number of arguments, and each is retrieved from the result element with the $parameter routine. Each argument is printed with the princ function. If debug-msg is called from the pop-subtask rule as shown previously, the atom Popping and the name of a subtask that is bound to the variable <exhausted> are printed. If the debug-mode-p flag is not set, debug-msg does not produce any output.

```
(defun debug-msg ()
  "(CALL DEBUG-MSG atom...)
   An OPS5 subroutine that acts as a conditional WRITE action."
  (if (debug-mode-p)
      (let ((num-atoms ($parametercount)))
        (do ((position 1 (1+ position)))
            ((> position num-atoms) (terpri))
          (princ ($parameter position))
          (princ " ")))))
```

Figure 8.7 The debug-msg subroutine (COMMON LISP).

```
(let ((part-name ($parameter ($litbind 'name)))
      (supplier-code ($parameter ($litbind 'supplier))))
 ...)
```

Figure 8.8 LISP code fragment to retrieve values from the result element.

Sometimes, the arguments with a call to a subroutine are placed in specific locations in the result element using attribute names, as follows:

```
(call retrieve_component
    ^name <part-name> ^supplier <code>
    ^fields name stock price)
```

In this case, the parameter routine must be used after the position of each argument is determined. The litbind routine is the external routine's version of the OPS5 function litval. Litbind converts an attribute name into the numeric index that attribute uses to place values in a WME. The litbind routine can be used as an argument to the parameter routine to retrieve values from specific indices in the result element.

In the previous call to the subroutine retrieve_component, the values bound to the variables <part-name> and <code> were bound earlier in the rule. The values name, stock and price are constants. The attributes ^name, ^supplier and ^fields are used to position the values in the result element.

The fragment of LISP code in Figure 8.8 can be used to retrieve the value of the attributes ^name and ^supplier. The $litbind routine returns the index OPS5 has assigned to the ^name or ^supplier attribute, which is then used as the position from which the $parameter routine retrieves its value. The result of the $parameter routine is assigned to the LISP variable part-name or supplier-code.

8.4.2 Making WMEs From a Subroutine

The process of creating a WME from an external subroutine is similar to the process used by the make action. First, the subroutine places values in the result element, usually with each value placed in a position that corresponds to an attribute's index, and then copies the entire pattern into working memory. To accomplish these steps, the external subroutine must use a set of interface-support routines to construct the pattern in the result element. These routines are used to clear the result element of non-nil values, to move to positions of the result element, and to deposit values in those positions. There is also an interface-support routine that copies the contents of the result element into working memory, thereby actually creating the WME.

Table 8.4 lists the interface-support routines used to create WMEs from a subroutine. These routines are used in the following steps:

1. Initialize the result element. Calling the `reset` routine initializes all values in the result element to `nil` and resets the current position to the first position in the result element. If you are modifying a WME that is already in the result element, this step is omitted.
2. Deposit values in the result element. Fill the result element with atoms using calls to the `tab` routine to find the position for a value, and the `value` routine to place the atomic value in its correct position.
3. Copy the contents of the result element into working memory. The `assert` routine copies the contents of the result element into working memory as a new WME. Copying the result element to working memory has no effect on the values in the result element, so the `assert` routine can be called as many times as desired on the same result element producing multiple WMEs with the same values.

Figure 8.9 illustrates an external subroutine that creates a WME, and the related components of the rule base. The important features of this example are the following:

- The rule base contains declarations of the element class (`retrieve_component`) that is used for positioning the subroutine's arguments in the result element, the component retrieved from the database that is returned from the external subroutine as a WME (`component`), and also the name of the external subroutine, `retrieve_component`.
- The rule base contains a call to the external subroutine, `retrieve_component`. The arguments to this subroutine are placed in the result element at the positions specified by the attributes `^name`, `^supplier`, and `^fields`.
- The `retrieve_component` subroutine uses the function `make-component-wme` to find the item in the database and to create a WME of that item.

Table 8.4 Interface-support routines for writing to the result element.

Routine	Arguments	Returns
`reset`	—	Initializes the result element (all values `nil`)
`tab`	(atomic-position)	Moves to atomic-position in the result element
`value`	(atom-to-deposit)	Deposits atom-to-deposit at the current position in the result element and increments the position by one
`assert`	—	Copies current contents of result element into working memory as a new WME

In the OPS5 program:

```
;; A part description from the database
(literalize component
      name     ; Standardized part name
      stock    ; Quantity in stock
      price    ; Retail price
      ...)

;; Declaration of arguments to the subroutine
(literalize retrieve_component
      name     ; Part name
      supplier ; Supplier code
      fields)  ; Fields to return

(vector-attribute fields)

;; The external routine
(external
      retrieve_component)

;; A sample call to the subroutine retrieve_component
    ...
   -->
     (call retrieve_component
          ^name <part-name> ^supplier <code>
          ^fields name stock price))
```

The LISP function make-component-wme within the external module containing retrieve_component:

```
(defun make-component-wme (db-key fields)
  "(MAKE-COMPONENT-WME db-key list-of-field-names)
   Make a WME of element class COMPONENT, placing at each
   attribute field the value returned from the function
   fetch-db-attribute."
  ($reset)              ; Clear the result element.
  ($value 'component)   ; Deposit the wme class at ^1.
  (dolist (field fields); For each field requested
    ($tab field)        ; Set current position & deposit
    ($value (fetch-db-attribute db-key field)))
  ($assert))            ; Make a WME out of the RE.
```

Figure 8.9 Calling a subroutine that creates a WME (COMMON LISP).

- The function make-component-wme initializes the result element with $reset to set the current position in the result element to the first position and to set all the values to nil. The element class name, component, is placed in the first position. For each field requested, the $tab routine moves to the position of that attribute, then puts the value returned by the application function fetch-db-attribute in that position with the $value routine. Finally, the entire result element is copied into working memory as a new WME.

Figure 8.10 contains another version of the make-component-wme subroutine written in VAX C™ to illustrate data conversion when making a WME. In this version of the routine, the field names are passed from another C routine as a pointer to an array of C character pointers. The field names are converted to atoms to be used with OPS$TAB, and values returned from the call to fetch_db_field are converted and deposited into the result element

```
/* For each of the field names in the argument_list, fetch
 * a value from a database (using the function fetch_db_field)
 * and place it in the result element. When all values (up to
 * the number "fields") are in the result element, copy it into
 * working memory.
 */
void make_component_wme (db_key, fields, field_count)
unsigned long db_key;    /* A database key for this component */
char *fields[];          /* Vector of field name strings */
int field_count;         /* Length of fields vector */
{
    int i;
    char *field_name, *field_value;

    OPS$RESET();
    OPS$VALUE(OPS$INTERN("COMPONENT",9));
    for (i=0, i < field_count, ++i)
        {
        field_name = fields[i];
        field_value = fetch_db_field(db_key, field_name);
        OPS$TAB(OPS$INTERN(field_name, strlen(field_name)));
        OPS$VALUE(OPS$INTERN(field_value, strlen(field_value)));
        }
    OPS$ASSERT();
}
```

Figure 8.10 Creating a WME from a subroutine called from VAX OPS5 (VAX C).

```
(defun concat2 (atl at2)
  "(CONCAT2 <sym-atl> <sym-at2>)
   An RHS function that deposits the concatenation of these
   atoms into the result element."
  ($value (intern (concatenate 'string
                               (symbol-name atl)
                               (symbol-name at2)))))
```

Figure 8.11 COMMON LISP implementation of concat2.

by OPS$VALUE. After all fields are processed, OPS$ASSERT is called to create the WME.

8.5 Functions

External routines that are written as functions are used to return values. They are called from within actions or, in some OPS5 implementations, from within condition elements. There are few differences between functions called from the LHS and those called from the RHS, so this section first considers topics that are shared by both.

The method of passing arguments to functions differs from that of subroutines. In subroutines, the arguments are placed in the result element and are retrieved one at a time by the subroutine. In functions, the arguments listed in the function call are mapped directly onto the external function's parameter list.

For example, the function concat2 in Figures 8.11 and 8.12 is called with two symbolic atom arguments to be concatenated to form a new atom.* The following call to concat2, embedded in the make action, passes the values bound to the variables <file-name> and <file-type> as arguments.

```
(make file ^name (concat2 <file-name> <file-type>)
           ^status closed)
```

In both the LISP (Figure 8.11) and the VAX C (Figure 8.12) version of this function, the routine parameters atl and at2 are assigned the values bound to the OPS5 variables <file-name> and <file-type>.

Notice that, in the COMMON LISP code for this example (Figure 8.11), it is not necessary for the values assigned to atl and at2 to be converted from atoms. In the C version of concat2 (Figure 8.12) the symbolic atoms are converted to character strings with the conversion interface-support routine OPS$PNAME.

*Error checking is left out of concat2 to keep it simple.

```
/* RHS function that concatenates 2 arguments
 *   and places them in the result element.
 */
void concat2 (at1, at2)
int at1, at2;
{
    char pname_buf[MAX_ATOM_SIZE];
    int at1_size, at2_size;

    /* First get the strings into a single buffer */
    at1_size = OPS$PNAME(at1, pname_buf, MAX_ATOM_SIZE);
    at2_size = OPS$PNAME(at2, pname_buf + at1_size,
                         MAX_ATOM_SIZE - at1_size);

    /* Convert it to a symbolic atom and deposit it
       in the result element. */
    OPS$VALUE(OPS$INTERN(pname_buf, at1_size + at2_size));
}
```

Figure 8.12 C implementation of concat2 for VAX OPS5.

An RHS function is expected to put a value in the result element, but it must use an OPS5 interface-support routine to do so. In a typical OPS5 implementation, the external function calls the `value` interface-support routine to place a function's return value in the result element. The `value` support routine deposits one value in the result element in the position that the function appeared in the RHS pattern. The standard function return value is ignored.

This gives you the option of writing a function that has no return value at all. If no value is to be deposited, then the external function simply does not call `value`.

To illustrate how values are returned from an RHS function, we use the `gint` function shown in Figures 8.13 and 8.14. The `gint` function returns a unique integer atom that is incremented each time `gint` is called. The integers are usually used to distinguish between WMEs, and are assigned when the WME is created.

Although OPS5 provides a function called `genatom` that returns a unique atomic symbol each time it is called, the `gint` function is often preferred. Integer identifications have the advantage that they can be compared in magnitude. When the integer is assigned at the time of the WME's creation, it can represent the WME's recency like a time tag. Unlike a time tag, however, the integers can be compared for recency from within a rule. An integer identifier also does not take up much memory, since it does not require a position in the OPS5 symbol table; this might be an important consideration in a large application.

```
(defvar *gint-val* 0
  "Unique incremented integer for GINT routine")

(defun gint ()
  "(GINT)
   OPS5 RHS function to deposit an incremented integer into the RE."
  ($value (incf *gint-val*)))       ; Increment and deposit
```

Figure 8.13 COMMON LISP implementation of gint.

An example of a call from OPS5 to the `gint` function is the following:

```
(make distance ^from <x> ^to <y> ^at-time (gint)
               ^value-is <computed-distance>)
```

The `make` action first creates a `distance` WME in the result element. The function `gint` is called from the position in the WME pointed to by the attribute `^at-time`.

Figure 8.13 shows a COMMON LISP implementation of the `gint` function, and Figure 8.14 shows the same function written in VAX C. Note that in both versions a state variable is kept and incremented as a side effect of the call. In the LISP version, the variable is called `*gint-val*`; in the VAX C version, the variable is `gint-val`. Both versions of `gint` use the interface-support routine `$value` or `OPS$VALUE` to return the integer. The VAX C version must first call the routine `OPS$CVNA` to convert the integer into an OPS5 atom before depositing it in the result element.

In addition to depositing the value in the result element, the `value` routine also increments the current position in the result element by 1. Thus, an RHS function can return a vector of values by repeatedly calling `value`.

OPS5 does not allow "nesting" of RHS function calls. Because a call to the `value` routine always moves from the position at which it deposits a value, it is

```
/* Unique incremented integer for GINT routine*/
int gint_val = 0;

/* OPS5 RHS function to deposit an incremented integer into the RE. */
void gint ()
{
    OPS$VALUE(OPS$CVNA(++gint_val));  /* Increment and deposit */
}
```

Figure 8.14 C implementation of gint for VAX OPS5.

not possible to use one function call as an argument to another. When function calls are nested, each call to the `value` routine deposits a value *and* increments the position, leaving the final return value somewhere in the result element other than at the position from which the function was originally called.

8.5.1 LHS Functions

LHS functions are not a necessary feature of the OPS5 language. The original OPS5 implementation [Forgy 1981] and other more recent implementations do not have this feature, and do not lack computational power because of that omission. Furthermore, LHS functions can slow down program execution considerably if they are used inappropriately. When used carefully, however, LHS functions offer a computational convenience that is valuable to OPS5 programmers. This section introduces LHS functions as provided by VAX OPS5.

LHS functions can be used anywhere on the LHS where a variable can be evaluated. They can be used in place of any value in a condition element except within a disjunction. The value returned from the function is used in the match to a WME value.

Consider the following calls to LHS functions. The first two examples use the OPS5-provided `compute` function,* and the third is a user-written external function, `match_wild`.

1. Equality test

```
^line-number (compute <last> + 1)
```

2. Inequality test

```
^area >= (compute <width> * <depth>)
```

3. Bind and test

```
^reply { <participle> <=> word
         (match_wild |*ING| <participle>) }
```

The first example simply specifies that the value pointed to by the attribute `^line-number` must be greater by 1 than the value bound to the variable `<last>`.

In the second example, the value for the attribute `^area` is calculated by the `compute` function, which is then matched to a value in a WME that is greater than or equal to the returned value.

---

*The syntax of the `compute` function when used on the LHS in VAX OPS5 is the same as its use on the RHS.

In the third case, a value that is a symbolic atom (<=> word) is matched, and is bound to the variable <participle>, which is then passed to the external function match_wild. The function match_wild returns the atom bound to <participle> if it matched to the pattern *ING, but returns some other value—perhaps the integer 0—if the match is unsuccessful. Since the value pointed to by the attribute ^reply must always match a symbolic atom (<=> word), to ensure that the match to that instance of <participle> will fail, match_wild returns 0.

Like RHS functions, the arguments with the function call are mapped directly to the parameters of the user-written LHS function. *Unlike* RHS functions, however, the return value of the LHS function is the standard function return value. LHS functions, therefore, do not have to use the OPS$VALUE routine, although a call to OPS$VALUE may be used in the cases in which the function is called from both the LHS and the RHS.

Figure 8.15 is an example of a VAX C implementation of the match_wild function. The function is passed a symbol (as would be bound to the variable <participle> in the previous example) and a pattern (such as *ING). The pattern and symbol are converted to character strings by the interface-support routine OPS$PNAME. If the function str_match_wild finds that the converted pattern and symbol match, then the unconverted symbol held in the variable symbol is returned to the OPS5 program. If str_match_wild finds that the two do not match, then the integer 0 is converted to an atom and returned.

An LHS function is called for each make or remove of a WME that matches the condition element in which the function sits, and for each partial match involving this condition when an interelement variable used in this function call. This means that an LHS function may be called many times, especially if it is passed arguments that are variables bound in previous condition elements. For this reason, LHS functions should be purely functional. There should be no state information held between calls that affect return values of future calls. When using LHS functions in a program, you should estimate how many times each LHS function will be called during the match process, and how efficient a call to that function is. In general, you should use LHS functions in final applications only if you understand how they affect the efficiency of your program. The efficiency of LHS function calls is discussed in Chapter 10, *Efficiency*.

8.6 Debugging External Routines

Your first approach to debugging external routines should be to use the debugging facilities provided with the language of the external routine. Most LISP implementations have built-in debugging aids—such as single step, break points, and examination of the run-time stack—that all work as well with user-written OPS5 external routines as they do with other LISP programs. Since these features are specific to the LISP environment, we do not discuss them here.

```
/* LHS function matches a symbol to a pattern. Returns
 *    the original symbol if the two match, otherwise 0.
 */
int match_wild (pattern, symbol)
int pattern, symbol;    /* OPS5 symbolic atoms */
{
    char pattern_buf[MAX_ATOM_SIZE + 1],
         symbol_buf[MAX_ATOM_SIZE + 1];

    /* Convert symbolic arguments */
    pattern_buf[OPS$PNAME(pattern, pattern_buf, MAX_ATOM_SIZE)] = '\0';
    symbol_buf[OPS$PNAME(symbol,symbol_buf,MAX_ATOM_SIZE)] = '\0';

    /* if they match, return the original symbolic atom,
     * otherwise return 0 */
    if (str_match_wild(pattern_buf,symbol_buf))
       return symbol;
    else
       return OPS$CVNA(0);
}
```

Figure 8.15 An LHS function in VAX C.

Likewise, in a non-LISP programming environment, you can usually use existing debugging tools with your OPS5 external routines. For example, routines written for VAX OPS5 can be debugged using the VAX/VMS™ Debugger, which also provides symbolic debugging through source code stepping, break points, and data examination.*

In addition to the standard debugging utilities provided by the language of the external routine, you can use the OPS5 command interface to test external subroutines. Specifically, you can use the `call` command to invoke the subroutine directly from the command interface, with full control over the arguments used in the call. This capability is especially important to OPS5 systems not implemented in LISP, in which functions cannot usually be tested interactively without additional programming.

In Figure 8.16 we use the `call` command to invoke the subroutine `retrieve_component` with a set of arguments. We can see the result of calling the subroutine by examining the WMEs that were created.

*To use the VAX/VMS Debugger with VAX OPS5, you must compile and link your modules with the `/DEBUG` qualifier. When you run your OPS5 program, you first interact with the debugger, where you can set up your debugging session. See the *VAX/VMS Debugger Reference Manual*.

```
OPS5>(watch 2)

OPS5>(call retrieve_component
_OPS5>      ^name widget1 ^supplier amd
_OPS5>      ^fields name stock price)

=>WM: 42 [NIL] (COMPONENT ^NAME WIDGET1 ^STOCK 459 ^PRICE 30.0)
OPS5>
```

Figure 8.16 Testing an external subroutine with the call command.

The OPS5 command interface cannot usually serve as the only tool for external-routine testing. External routines should be written such that code that interacts directly with the OPS5 interface-support routines is minimized and is isolated from the larger portion of procedural code. This maximizes the potential for reuse of the code in non-rule-based applications, and facilitates testing that is separate from OPS5. Chapter 12, *Building and Testing OPS5 Systems*, discusses testing techniques in more detail.

8.7 Handling Real-time Interrupts

Real-time systems require immediate action on unsolicited events. Operating systems must handle asynchronous events, resource requests, and other activities. Network and communications software depend heavily on real-time capabilities. Process- and machine-control systems must react immediately to feedback from their environments. Forgy's original OPS5 implementation did not provide for the processing of real-time events, but this capability is becoming increasingly important as more real-time applications are finding a use for simple and efficient rule-based processing.

LISP-based OPS5 implementations can simulate a capability for handling real-time interrupts by regularly polling an external routine that checks for specific changes in the environment. A natural point for polling to take place is between subtasks. The `pop-subtask` rule, or other control rules, can contain a call to a polling subroutine.

VAX OPS5 provides a special mechanism for handling real-time interrupts. VAX OPS5 defines a "window" in the recognize-act cycle in which user routines can be invoked to make WMEs. That window is the moment at which matching is complete and the system is ready to choose the next instantiation from the conflict set. An asynchronous user-written routine can create new WMEs only in this window. Since the new WMEs are the most recent in working memory, they can invoke rules that take precedence in the conflict set during that cycle.*

The part of the recognize-act cycle that happens outside of the window is a *critical section*, meaning that attempts to make WMEs asynchronously during this time result in run-time errors. Therefore, to create WMEs asynchronously, you must wait until the end of a rule firing to do so.

The VAX OPS5 interface-support routine `OPS$COMPLETION` provides a simple interrupt-handling scheme. To make an asynchronous event known in working memory, a user-written routine that handles the interrupt calls the `OPS$COMPLETION` routine to synchronize with the recognize-act cycle. The `OPS$COMPLETION` routine does not create any WMEs; the argument to the `OPS$COMPLETION` routine is the address of another user-written routine that will make the WMEs reflecting the event. The `OPS$COMPLETION` routine makes sure that the interrupt happens at the end of the current rule firing and after the match is complete.

Handling an interrupt, then, requires two external routines. One is the AST (asynchronous system trap) routine that waits for a specific event to occur and calls the `OPS$COMPLETION` routine when it does. The second is called by `OPS$COMPLETION` to create the WMEs that describe the event to the OPS5 program at the appropriate time. The second routine is also responsible for "informing" the `OPS$COMPLETION` routine that the interrupt has in fact occurred (so that it is not called again during the next window). It does this by calling the `OPS$COMPLETION` routine with the argument 0.

The steps of handling an interrupt from VAX OPS5 are summarized below:

1. An AST routine, which we call routine A, is written to execute when an asynchronous event occurs external to the OPS5 program.

2. When the event occurs, the routine A is invoked. It does not make any WMEs for the OPS5 program, but it contains a call to the `OPS$COMPLETION` routine with the address of another user-written routine, which we call routine B, that should be called at the next interrupt "window."

3. When the OPS5 rule interpreter has finished executing the current instantiation, it calls the interrupt-notification routine, routine B.

4. When routine B is called, it makes the WMEs necessary to describe the event to the OPS5 program. To prevent routine A from calling routine B again at the next interrupt window, routine B also calls the `OPS$COMPLETION` routine with a 0 argument.

Figure 8.17 contains a diagram of the interaction between an OPS5 rule base, its external routines, and a VMS™ system service in the handling of an

---

*If the system is running with the MEA conflict resolution strategy, the rules that look for the new WMEs must match them to the first condition element in order to guarantee that they immediately dominate in the conflict set. This restriction does not hold for the LEX strategy.

asynchronous event. The event is an alarm that sounds to indicate the passing of a specified amount of time. The alarm is set from within the OPS5 program by a call to the external subroutine SET_ALARM. This subroutine calls a VMS system service (SYS$SETIMR) to start a timer. The timer is also given the name of a routine to call, TIMER_DONE (analogous to routine A), when the specified time has elapsed. The OPS5 program and the VMS "clock" run simultaneously once the timer is set.

When the amount of time on the clock has elapsed, the VMS system service calls the subroutine TIMER_DONE. The TIMER_DONE subroutine calls OPS$COMPLETION with the name of the subroutine ALARM-RANG (the same as routine B) as its argument. This tells the OPS$COMPLETION routine to schedule the execution of ALARM-RANG at the next window. The ALARM-RANG routine interrupts OPS5 at the appropriate time and creates the WME (ALARM-RANG). Presumably,

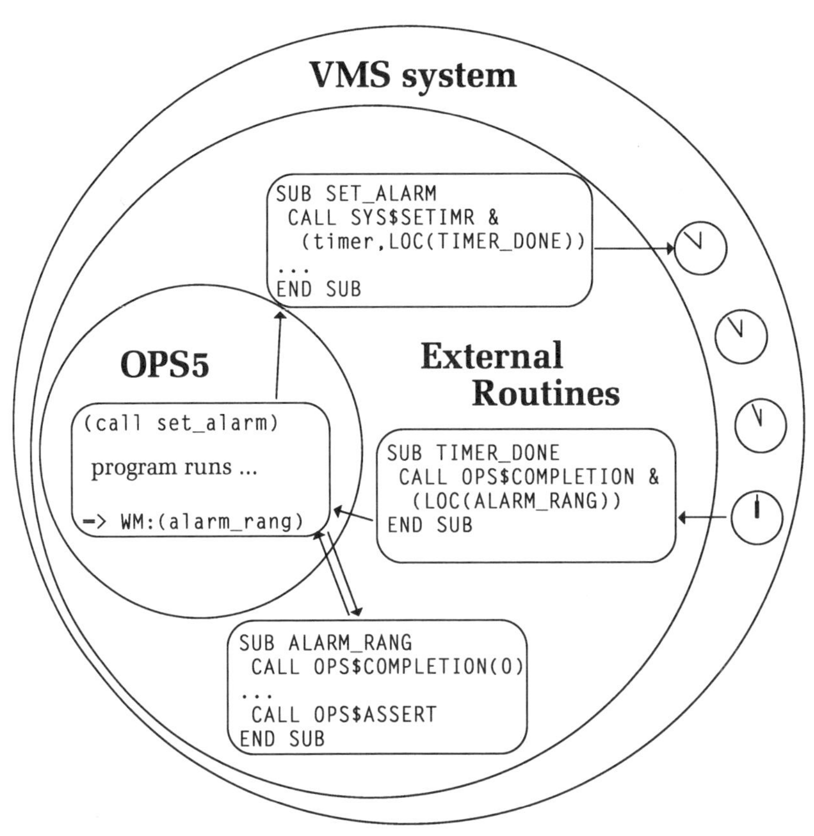

Figure 8.17 The interaction of routines in an asynchronous interrupt.

a rule in the rule base matches to this new, most recent WME, and that rule fires immediately to take the appropriate action.

If interrupts occur at intervals shorter than one recognize-act cycle, the `OPS$COMPLETION` routine alone cannot react to each interrupt. For example, continuous data from a real-time process, or mouse input from an interactive workstation environment, may occur in short, continuous spurts rather than at regular intervals. For each of these interrupts to be processed, you must write an event-queue handler (see Exercise 8.6).

Real-time interrupt-handling capability opens up an increasingly wide area of applications that rule-based languages previously could not handle.

Summary

- In all rule-based applications, there are tasks that are more appropriately performed in a procedural language. Tasks such as numerical calculations, well-understood algorithms, and sophisticated input-output processing are better written in a language other than OPS5.

- OPS5 allows for interaction with procedural code by providing a set of interface-support routines that can communicate with routines written in languages other than OPS5.

- There are two types of external routines: functions and subroutines. Functions are called to return a value to an action or a condition element. Subroutines are called as a separate RHS action, and are called purely for their side effects, such as creating WMEs or displaying output.

- The names of all external routines called from your OPS5 program must be declared with the `external` declaration.

- All OPS5 values are represented as atoms. For data to be passed between a non-LISP-based OPS5 program and its external routines, atoms must be converted into data types meaningful to the external routines. OPS5 provides the interface-support routines for data conversion.

- The result element is used by external subroutines for holding arguments to the `call` action and for creating WMEs.

- The arguments to an RHS function are mapped directly onto the arguments of the external function's parameter list. An RHS function returns a value to the position in the result element from which it was called with the OPS5 interface-support routine `value`.

- An LHS function returns a value to be used during match. LHS functions are useful to the experienced programmer, but are not computationally necessary for the language. Not all implementations of OPS5 allow function calls on the LHS.

- Debugging external routines is a combination of traditional testing techniques of the language of the external routine and of using the `call` command for interactive testing.
- Real-time interrupts can be handled with the VAX OPS5 interface routine `OPS$COMPLETION`.

Exercises

1. Explain how the `bind` action works in terms of the result-element model presented in this chapter. How could you make use of this feature in an OPS5 program?
2. Write a VAX C routine called `atom_to_string` that is passed a VAX OPS5 atom and an empty character buffer. The routine fills the buffer with a character-string representation of the atom, and returns the number of significant characters used.
3. Write an external function `OPS_SQRT` for computing the square root of two numerical atoms. Include the mechanisms for both LHS and RHS value returns for a VAX OPS5 program.
4. We discussed how subroutines can be tested at the command interface with the `call` command. In non-LISP implementions, however, only subroutines may be called this way. How might an RHS function be interactively tested in an environment other than LISP? How might an LHS function be tested?
5. It is sometimes useful to have debugging messages of varying levels of detail produced by rules in an OPS5 program. A programmer can then select the level of detail of debugging messages appropriate for the particular debugging problems at hand. For example, when little or no debugging information is desired, the programmer may call an external subroutine to set the debug level to a low value or to 0. When more detail is required, a higher debug level may be set, which will turn on all debug messages at that detail or lower.

   Modify the `debug-msg` routine in Figure 8.7 to handle debug-message detail "levels." This requires that you write an RHS subroutine `set-debug-detail-level` that, when given a debug level, causes to be printed all messages that are of that level or lower. Also modify the `debug-msg` routine in the following ways:

   a. Read the debug-message detail level as the first value in the call, and write the message only if it is not too detailed for the current setting.

   b. Change the message by supplying a "`DEBUG: `" prompt before all debug-message lines.
6. How might you use `OPS$COMPLETION` to process interrupts that may arrive at intervals shorter than the time between recognize-act cycles?

CHAPTER 9

Demons

THIS BOOK HAS EMPHASIZED the need to provide high-level control of the rules that compete for execution in the conflict set. Techniques have been presented that give us control over large, many-rule systems that could otherwise be chaotic.

But must every rule be a member of one and only one rule cluster? Can we have rules that are members of more than one cluster? All clusters? None? When and why might you want to step out of the bounds of the conventions established for control? Rules that are exceptions to the MEA strategy control technique form the basis of many useful OPS5 programming techniques.

We have already seen several exceptions to the convention that each rule belongs to one cluster. For example, the `pop-subtask` rule from Chapter 5 is a rule that belongs to *all* rule clusters. Because the first condition element does not include a specific subtask name, the `pop-subtask` rule is instantiated with all `subtask` WMEs. It is the last rule to execute in every subtask, and it competes as a full member of all rule clusters.

Less extreme than `pop-subtask`, a rule can be a member of more than one rule cluster when the names of the subtasks to which it belongs are included in a disjunction in the control element. For example, if a rule should be enabled during any of the subtasks named `initialize`, `data-collect` or `filter`, its first condition element may be

```
(subtask ^name << initialize data-collect filter >>)
```

Although this disjunction works—the rule with this condition element can be instantiated when any of the three subtasks are enabled—it is difficult to maintain. When a rule is shared among several rule clusters, with which cluster is it written? If you are looking for all the rules of a subtask, they may be scattered throughout the rule base. If your rule base is stored in multiple text files, it may be easier to repeat the rule for each subtask with which it is associated than it is to search for rules with disjunctive subtask names. Of course, making a rule for each subtask may create maintenance problems. If the rules are to be kept consistent, for instance, each of them must be documented with pointers to the others.

Rules that do not belong to *any* rule cluster are a third exception to the control technique and are the subject of this chapter. They may be considered independently from any and all subtasks. The LHSs of these rules specify conditions that can occur at *any* time during program execution. The first condition element of these rules does not match a control WME. We call these rules *demons.*

9.1 Definition and Characteristics of a Demon Rule

A demon, by common definition, is an attendant power or spirit, one who is unusually skillful or zealous. This name has been aptly used to denote a type of OPS5 rule that is an exception to the program's control method. Demon rules are watchful attendants; they wait for a certain condition to occur during an OPS5 program's execution. The zeal and skill of an OPS5 demon comes into play because the rule executes immediately when matched, so it is often used for high-priority situations.

In implementation, demons are *not* an OPS5 language feature; rather, they are a programming technique used in conjunction with the MEA-based control techniques discussed in Chapter 5. A demon rule is one that *by convention* does not contain a control element as its first condition element. Instead, the first condition element of a demon matches a WME that, when created or modified, signals the need for immediate action. We refer to the demon's first condition element as the demon's *trigger.* When a WME matches to this condition element, the demon is said to be *triggered.*

The most important characteristic of a demon is its high priority in relation to all other rules in the program. A demon rule is chosen to fire with high priority because its trigger, the first condition element, matches a WME that is newer in working memory than is the most recent control WME. Using the MEA conflict resolution strategy, OPS5 guarantees that the demon rule with its first condition element matched to the most recent WME will be chosen over any instantiation of a rule that matches an older control element.

As an example, consider a system that manages the processing of customer orders and maintains a warehouse inventory for the items in stock. As those items are shipped to customers, the demon rule in Figure 9.1 watches over the inventory to determine when to reorder materials from suppliers. When necessary, the rule must interrupt the regular processing of subtasks, since

```
(p  demon!reorder-supplies
;
; When we run low on an item, order more.
;
   { <Inventory>
      (supply ^in-stock <available> ^status <> reorder
              ^reorder-limit > <available>) }
   -->
      (modify <Inventory> ^status reorder)
      (make subtask ^name reorder-supplies))
```

Figure 9.1 Simple demon rule.

action should be taken as soon as the current stock drops below a certain threshold, no matter when or why the program is using the stock quantities.

The demon rule in Figure 9.1 is clearly not a member of any rule cluster—it does not have a control element. It may be necessary for this rule's action to be performed at any time when items are allocated. This demon alleviates the need for each subtask to check inventory levels explicitly for reordering each time that the subtask allocates items for orders.

Demon rules restore a high level of flexibility and responsiveness in an OPS5 program that is partitioned and regulated by a control technique. Although within each subtask there is complete data-driven behavior, the control techniques place a rather rigid, procedural control over the program. With the addition of a small number of demon rules, however, the program can still react to situations that may occur at any time and in any subtask. This gives the OPS5 program a control technique that makes it maintainable, while remaining responsive to situations that need immediate attention.

9.2 Uses of Demons

Demons may play an important role in large OPS5 programs, and serve as the basis of useful programming techniques. This section describes a few of those techniques.

9.2.1 Maintaining Relationships Among WMEs

One interesting use of demons is in maintaining relationships among WMEs. Most OPS5 programs make extensive use of the relationships that exist between different element classes. In some cases, changes in one of the element classes make it necessary to update values that maintain the relationship.

As an example, we use a program that arranges objects such as pieces of computer equipment in a room. The shape of each piece is unimportant;

placement of a piece is represented simply by an ordered pair (x, y) in relation to an x,y axis. The program arranges the pieces according to a set of constraints, such as the parts that should be placed in proximity to each other, the distance of parts from doors and windows, and the weight load on the floor.

For our OPS5 representation of this problem we use the element class `piece` to represent each piece of equipment in the system. Each piece has a name (`^name`), and a location on an x,y axis (`^x` and `^y`). We use the programming technique of attribute-value shadowing from Chapter 7 to keep track of changes of position, by repeating the x,y position values in the attributes `^x-shadow` and `^y-shadow`. The attribute `^moved` keeps track of whether a piece has moved.

```
;; An object to be placed in the room
(literalize piece
    name        ; Name of the piece of equipment
    x           ; Position on x axis
    y           ; Position on y axis
    x-shadow    ; Repeated x axis position
    y-shadow    ; Repeated y axis position
    moved)      ; << t nil >> whether a move is detected
                ;    by difference between x,y and their
                ;    shadows
```

In addition to other constraints, the program must maintain the appropriate distance between pieces. For example, line printers should not be placed near certain disk or tape drives, and noisy components should be as far as possible from terminals. This constraint requires that the program keep track of not only the placement of each piece, but also of the distance between a piece and every other piece in the system. We represent the distance between the two pieces with the following element class:

```
;; Records the distance between 2 pieces
(literalize distance
    from     ; FROM one piece
    to       ; TO another piece
    value    ; Value of the distance between them,
             ;   computed by an external routine
    time)    ; A unique integer representing relative
             ;   time of creation of distance WMEs
```

The `^time` attribute has a value that is a unique integer assigned to the WME when it is created. The time values on different `distance` WMEs can be compared to determine the relative time of creation of distance information between two pieces. Since a distance WME is created each time a piece is moved, the newest distance WME between two pieces is the one that is correct. The value for the `^time` attribute is generated by the user-written, external function called `gint` (see Chapter 8, *External Routines*).

	p1	p2	p3	p4
p1	–	2	6	9
p2	2	–	3	12
p3	6	3	–	1
p4	9	12	1	–

Figure 9.2 A piece-to-piece distance matrix.

For any two pieces, there are two distance WMEs. If there are two pieces named q and z, it is necessary to represent both the distance between q and z, and the distance between z and q (see Exercise 9.1):

```
(DISTANCE ^FROM Q ^TO Z ^VALUE 10...)
(DISTANCE ^FROM Z ^TO Q ^VALUE 10...)
```

The distances between N pieces can be represented by the N × N distance matrix shown in Figure 9.2. Each cell contains the distance between the pieces represented by its row and column. This matrix is, of course, symmetric with respect to the diagonal.

The role for demons in this problem is to maintain the correct distances between every two pieces in the system. The distance WMEs are initially created at the outset of the program. Whenever a piece is moved, the demon triggers on the moved position and creates new `distance` WMEs.

Since demons will be used to update distances from pieces as they are moved, subtask rules do not have to invoke any special subtask to maintain these distances. The person writing the rules that move pieces can assume that distances are maintained while remaining naive as to *how* they are maintained. Here the demons are enforcing modularity by isolating the maintenance of distance WMEs from any subtask that may move pieces.

There are two demons that are responsible for reacting to a moved piece: one that triggers when there has been a change in an *x* coordinate, and one that triggers on a change in a *y* coordinate. If both coordinates change, it does not matter which of the demons executes.

The demons are shown in Figure 9.3. The condition element in the first demon matches a piece WME whose value for the `^x` attribute (or, in the other demon, for the `^y` attribute) is not the same as for the corresponding shadow attribute. The `^x-shadow` value is set to the `^x` value when the distance WME is made, so a discrepancy between the values of these two attributes indicates that the piece has been moved but new distance WMEs have not been created.

The demons' first action is to invoke a new subtask, called `recompute-distances`, to update the distances. We shall see more examples of demons like these that do little work in actions on the RHS, but that invoke a subtask to take some action immediately.

```
(p  demon!note-x-location-change
;
; When the x coordinate changes in a piece, recompute its
; distance to other pieces.
;
   { <Piece>
      (piece ^x <changed> ^x-shadow <> <changed> ^y <y>) }
   -->
      (make subtask ^name recompute-distances)
      (modify <Piece> ^x-shadow <changed> ^y-shadow <y>
          ^moved t))

(p  demon!note-y-location-change
;
; When the y coordinate changes in a piece, recompute its
; distance to other pieces.
;
   { <Piece>
      (piece ^y <changed> ^y-shadow <> <changed> ^x <x>) }
   -->
      (make subtask ^name recompute-distances)
      (modify <Piece> ^y-shadow <changed> ^x-shadow <y>
          ^moved t))
```

Figure 9.3 Demons that watch for changes in *x* or *y* locations.

Next, the demons set the shadow values to be the same as the new *x* or *y* positions, and to set the value on the `^moved` attribute to be `t` (for `true`). The `^moved` attribute is used to mark the piece that has just been moved.

The subtask `recompute-distances` that is called from the demons has three rules: one to create new distance WMEs, one to remove the old distance WMEs, and one to reset the `^moved` attribute on the moved piece back to `nil`. These rules are shown in Figure 9.4.

The first rule creates two new distance WMEs between the piece that was moved (`^moved t`) and every other piece in the program. Due to refraction, no pair of pieces will have more than two distance WMEs made for them. The distance is calculated by an external function we have called `compute_distance`. The second rule finds two distance WMEs for a pair of pieces and removes the obsolete distance. The third rule resets the piece by changing the value of the attribute `^moved` back to `nil`.

In this example, a relationship exists between the location of pieces and the distances between them. The subtasks are primarily concerned with placing and moving pieces. The distances between pieces are necessary to have avail-

```
(p  recompute-distances!make-distance-wme
;
; Find a stationary piece and compute its distance to
; the one just moved.
;
      (subtask ^name recompute-distances)
      (piece ^name <moved> ^moved t ^x <mx> ^y <my>)
      (piece ^name <other> ^moved nil ^x <ox> ^y <oy>)
   -->
      (bind <dist> (compute_distance <mx> <my> <ox> <oy>))
      (make distance ^from <moved> ^to <other>
            ^value <dist> ^time (gint))
      (make distance ^from <other> ^to <moved>
            ^value <dist> ^time (gint)))

(p  recompute-distances!remove-obsolete-distance
;
; When two distance WMEs are present between the same
; pieces, remove the older one.
;
      (subtask ^name recompute-distances)
      (distance ^from <f> ^to <t> ^time <new>)
   { <Old-distance>
      (distance ^from <f> ^to <t> ^time < <new>) }
   -->
      (remove <Old-distance>))

(p  recompute-distances!moved
;
; Mark the moved piece as stationary (^moved nil).
;
      (subtask ^name recompute-distances)
   { <Moved-piece>
      (piece ^moved t) }
   -->
      (modify <Moved-piece> ^moved nil))
```

Figure 9.4 The subtask that creates new distance WMEs.

able, but their maintenance is not tightly knit into the main problem-solving task. Demons, therefore, maintain the distance relationship between pieces without including that maintenance as part of the control strategy. The programmer can concentrate on the domain-specific rules in subtasks, and can depend on demons to keep the relationship between element classes up-to-date.

9.2.2 Recognizing High Priority Exceptions

Among the most important purposes of demons is to react with high priority to exception cases that require immediate action. If we are arranging pieces of equipment on a computer room floor, for example, we need immediate notification if we have made the mistake of putting too much weight on a section of floor. The demon in Figure 9.5 watches for this situation, and creates a control WME for a subtask that makes the necessary corrections. Demons are often used in this way in exception-driven programs (see Chapter 7, *Programming Techniques*).

Demons that create a control WME on their RHS, such as those in Figures 9.3 and 9.5, are called *demon scouts*. A demon scout matches a particular problem situation and, rather than take action on it directly, invokes a subtask that does what is necessary to rectify that situation. The subtask invoked is essentially slipped into the control flow and is instantiated immediately after the demon fires. It is common for a demon to be a scout, since it is relatively easy to detect a situation, but the complexity of the action to be taken may require several rules.

The subtask that is invoked from a demon scout is usually not part of the normal control flow, but rather is accessible only from the demon. The demon's subtask interrupts the program's current processing, since all of its instantiations match the most recent control WME. When all of the subtask's instantiations have executed, the control WME is usually removed with one of the program's control rules, such as `pop-subtask`, and the interrupted subtask resumes.

A demon scout should disable its own rematch to avoid an infinite firing loop. Notice that, in Figure 9.5, the attribute `^overloaded` is set to the value t to indicate that the event has taken place. If this value had not been set, when

```
(p  demon!breaking-floor
;
; If the floor load is over the maximum rating, dispatch
; to a subtask to resolve the problem.
;
   { <Floor>
      (floor-load ^max <allowed> ^current > <allowed>
           ^overloaded nil) }
  -->
     (write CRASH!)
     (make subtask ^name floor-overloaded)
     (modify <Floor> ^overloaded t))
```

Figure 9.5 Example of a demon scout.

the floor-load WME is modified in any way except to change the situation on which the demon fired, the demon scout can fire again, create another subtask floor-overloaded, and repeat that cycle indefinitely. Only after the problem has been corrected is the value of ^overloaded reset to nil.

9.2.3 Simulating a Virtual Resource

Demons can also be used to simulate an unlimited resource. For example, an OPS5 application that performs optimizations as part of a compiler may need a resource of register or memory addresses that are available for data storage and manipulation. Another OPS5 application may manage a database, requiring a virtual resource of database locks. In reality, resources are allocated only when needed. However, it is convenient to use a vector representation for already allocated resources, and to do the actual allocations via demons only when required.

Demons are useful for monitoring the need for allocation of new resources. A demon can look for a resource that is depleted and invoke a subtask or call an external routine to allocate more resources. For example, the last value in a vector might be the symbol *empty*. A demon watches for that value to appear as the next allocated resource, and then allocates more into the vector. Any resource vector generated in the program must obey this convention and terminate with the *empty* symbol.

The demon that creates new resources can be written generally enough so that it can extend the resources of any type in the application. Each resource to be extended must have an identifying name that is stored with it. To generate more of that resource, the external function allocate_next allocates one or more new items; the type of resource is passed as an argument to the function.

```
(p  demon!allocate-next-item
;
; When a resource allocation runs out, call out to
; allocate more, and follow the new resource vector
; with another empty symbol.
;
   { <The-resource>
      (resource ^type <type> ^allocated *empty*) }
   -->
      (modify <The-resource>
          ^allocated (allocate_next <type>) *empty*))
```

Figure 9.6 Demon that keeps an allocation vector filled.

In Figure 9.6, the variable <type> is bound to the identifier of the type of extendable resource. The value for the next item in that resource is the symbol `*empty*`, indicating that the resource needs replenishing. The subtask rules that use the resource assume that there is an unlimited supply.

The rules that use one of the values of the resource take the value off the front of the vector and move all other values forward one position. We used this same set of actions in the control rule for an agenda (see Chapter 5, *Control of OPS5 Programs*), as in the following:

```
    :
{ <Resource>
    (resource ^type register ^allocated <register>) }
-->
    (bind <allocated> (litval allocated))
    (bind <allocated+1> (compute <allocated> + 1))
    (modify <Resource>
      ^allocated (substr <Resource> <allocated+1> inf) nil)
    :
```

When the value for the attribute `^next` is `*empty*`, the demon, `demon!allocate-next-item` fires again and replenishes the resource.

9.2.4 Maintaining Data Structures

There is seldom a need in OPS5 to construct abstract data types, such as queues and linked lists. These are the building materials of procedural programs. Since OPS5's strength is matching, usually the best representations are different from those of procedural programs.

Sometimes, however, abstract data types are useful metaphors for the relationships between element classes in an OPS5 program. We used the concept of a stack, for example, to implement the priority of control WMEs based on their order of creation. A directed graph with nodes and arcs between nodes is another data structure that is useful for representing relationships in a symbolic domain. Demons are often essential components in building and maintaining these data structures.

Let us use a directed graph to represent a lattice. The lattice defines a partial ordering of nodes via arcs. An arc originates at one node and points to a successor node.

To represent the lattice in OPS5, we can use the two element classes `node` and `arc`. The representation of each of these element classes can be embellished for the needs of specific applications, but for this example we use only the essential attributes. A node must have a unique identifier, such as the attribute `^name`.

An arc must specify the node from which it originates (the attribute ^from), and the one on which it terminates (the attribute ^to).

```
(literalize node
    name      ; Identifier of the node
    :)

(literalize arc
    from      ; The node on which the arc originates
    to        ; The node on which the arc terminates
    :)
```

Suppose we are writing a project-planning tool in which a lattice representing a plan is stored in an external database. Nodes represent the individual steps in the plan and arcs represent dependencies between tasks. Furthermore, suppose that our program is interested in only a relatively few nodes and their successors. Rather than load the entire lattice into working memory, we want only as much of the lattice in working memory as is necessary at any time. When a node is fetched, we want all successor nodes that are not yet in working memory to be pulled in as well, since changes to one node may affect these tasks also.

By using demons to retrieve and even to update parts of this lattice, the programmer can write rules in any subtask in the application without concern for the integrity of the lattice or the fetching of related nodes.

When a subtask rule fetches a node from the external database, the routine creates the node WME and all arc WMEs that point to this node's successors. If the successor node named by an arc is already in working memory from a previous fetch, then there is no need to fetch it again. If an arc names a successor node that is not present in working memory, then a demon rule calls the routine to fetch that node and the arcs to its successor nodes from the external database. This demon rule will fire over and over again until all successors are read into working memory. This technique brings into working memory only the nodes of interest, and not the entire lattice.

Figure 9.7 shows a demon rule that will bring into working memory all successors of a fetched node. The subroutine fetch_node creates the node for <successor>, and the arcs to all successor nodes. The lattice is filled in depth-first, since the newest (and most recent arc) is always extended, if necessary, before older arcs are. The order of extending the lattice is irrelevant, of course, since the demon will eventually fire with all arcs that instantiate it.

There are many uses of this representation of a lattice in an OPS5 program. In addition to modeling complex planning tasks, a lattice can be used in solving a containership problem, in which an arc represents the *is-contained-in* relation between two entities represented as nodes. Rules can then use this lattice to

```
(p  demon!fetch-successor
;
; When an arc points to a successor node that does not yet
;  exist, call fetch_node to bring in that node
;  and its successor arcs.
;
     (arc ^to <successor>)
     - (node ^name <successor>)
  -->
     (call fetch_node <successor>))
```

Figure 9.7 Expanding a lattice representation.

suggest ways of combining many items into a small set of larger ones under various constraints.

The arc can also represent the *can-be-connected-to* relation between two objects. The configuration task can use a representation such as this to specify how components can be assembled.* A lattice can be used to represent inheritance, where an arc signifies an *is-a* relation. Dataflow-analysis systems can also make good use of lattice structures.

9.2.5 "Subtask-scoped" WMEs

Since working memory is global to the entire rule base, you may want to designate certain pieces of information that should be removed immediately after a subtask ends. Demons can be used to implement the deletion of WMEs that hold information pertaining to only a single subtask. WMEs that are used in this way include a designation of the subtask of which they are a part. These WMEs are often called *locals*, or *subtask-scoped WMEs*. They usually have their own element class, are created for the execution of a subtask, and are then deleted when the rules in the subtask have all executed. Local WMEs help to minimize the number of WMEs in working memory, particularly the WMEs that currently serve no purpose or that may be used inappropriately in subtasks other than that for which they were intended. Local WMEs serve as "local variables," and are particularly useful in preventing loops in subtasks.

An example of an element class declaration for a subtask-scoped WME is the following:

```
;; Subtask-scoped WME class
(literalize local
```

*DEC's XSEL eXpert SELLing assistant program uses this as its primary model of computer hardware configuration.

```
content    ; A name for the information this WME holds
value      ; The value for this specific WME
scope)     ; The subtask with which this local is associated
```

Within the subtask, there may be more than one use for a local WME. The attribute `^content` holds a name for the information to which this WME refers. The `^value` attribute holds the named value. The `^scope` attribute is used to designate the subtask in which this piece of information is used. An example of a local WME is the following:

```
(LOCAL ^CONTENT NEW-BLOCK-COUNT ^VALUE 0 ^SCOPE OBJECT-ENTRY)
```

Usually, a local WME is created from within the subtask that uses it. Often, the other rules in the subtask depend on the creation of local WMEs, so the first rule to be instantiated in the subtask checks whether the necessary local WME is missing, and creates it if appropriate. See Figure 9.8.

When the subtask finishes executing and its control WME is removed, a demon is used to "clean up" after the subtask by removing all local WMEs. The demon in Figure 9.9 removes all local WMEs scoped to a subtask immediately after the control WME is removed with the `pop-subtask` rule and before a new control WME is created or dominates in the conflict set. The local WME that matches the demon's first condition element is more recent than are any of the other control WMEs.

The idea of a special element class that is used for temporary data that are specific to a subtask, and that can be controlled by a demon is an extension of the idea of global control rules. These WMEs are used in many OPS5 applications because they isolate the creation and use of data (which is efficient and easy to maintain), while not burdening the programmer with worrying about deleting obsolete WMEs.

```
(p  object-entry!initialize-new-block-count
;
; If we do not yet have a new-block-count,
; create one and initialize it to 0.
;
      (subtask ^name object-entry)
      - (local ^content new-block-count)
   -->
      (make local ^content new-block-count ^value 0
          ^scope object-entry))
```

Figure 9.8 Creating a local WME.

```
(p  demon!remove-local
;
; If the scope of a local has expired, remove the local.
;
   { <Local>
      (local ^scope <gone>) }
      - (subtask ^name <gone>)
   -->
      (remove <Local>))
```

Figure 9.9 Removing a local WME.

9.3 The Dangers of Using Demons

Demons are frequently used incorrectly, and thus fail to produce the desired results. Problems occur in determining the appropriate triggers, in maintaining a proper mix of demons and subtask rules, and in avoiding demons that are indefinitely postponed. This section discusses these situations so that you can avoid them. Chapter 10 discusses situations in which demons are correctly written but are extremely inefficient.

A demon is effective only if it is reliably triggered each time the situation requiring the demon occurs. Although a demon may have more than one condition element, the situation must be described by the creation or modification of *one* WME—the WME that matches the first condition element. Unfortunately, when the situation must be described by two or more WMEs, you may not be able to determine beforehand which WME should trigger the demon.

For example, in a nuclear-power-plant application, you may want a demon that detects an impending meltdown. The demon must detect two conditions: that radiation is detected, and that the temperature is rising. But which condition should be listed as the first condition element in the rule to be the trigger for the demon to fire? Clearly, the program needs to detect either condition. One solution is to write two demons, each with a different first condition element, like the location-change demons in Figure 9.3. But what if the situation is actually described by three condition elements? What if it requires four?

Since a demon is triggered by only its first condition element, there is no general solution that is practical in all cases. You could create a subtask to check for the situation and to invoke the subtask explicitly from each rule that could trigger it. Or, possibly, you could define a more reliable trigger, such as by altering your representation of the situation to encode either situation in one condition element.

It is important to maintain a workable ratio between demons and subtask rules in a program. Demons are so useful in most programs that there is a

```
(p  demon!catch-credit-overrun
;
; If the credit balance exceeds the credit limit in an account
; that is not being resolved, mark the account as over credit
; limit and dispatch to a subtask to handle the situation.
;
   { <Account>
      (account ^credit-limit <max-credit> ^balance > <max-credit>
               ^status <> over-credit-limit) }
   -->
      (make subtask ^name resolve-credit-overrun)
      (modify <Account> ^status over-credit-limit))
```

Figure 9.10 Demon to watch for credit overruns.

temptation to create too many of them. If there are too many demons, however, they may compete in the conflict set, increasing the chance that one of them will not execute as soon as it is needed. Furthermore, if too many demons compete for execution in the conflict set, there may be a need for arbitrating the order of demon execution. Controlling the order of execution of demons defeats the primary advantage of the demon, however, which is to act as an *exception* to the program's control strategy.

A large number of demons also increases the effort required in maintenance and debugging activities. Each demon is another candidate for firing in any subtask. Demons also restrict the possibilities for using refraction as a programming technique.

Demons can destroy the effects of refraction by modifying a WME involved in the refraction during a subtask. This occurs most frequently when demons fire often. However, you can minimize this danger by isolating the rules that rely on refraction into a separate subtask that is invoked and fired immediately before the invoking subtask is popped. If the rules make no changes to working memory, and there is no possibility of receiving asynchronous inputs, you can be sure that the demons cannot interrupt in the middle of their firings.

A demon may be indefinitely postponed if a control WME is created in the same rule but *after* the creation or modification of the WME that triggers the instantiation of a demon. The control WME is then more recent than is the demon's triggering WME, and all associated instantiations of subtasks are chosen from the conflict set before the demon's instantiation. Since it is difficult to keep track of each WME that instantiates a demon, it is easy to create a control WME without realizing its effect on the instantiation of demons.

To illustrate the problem, we use the demon in Figure 9.10, which watches for credit overruns in customer accounts. This demon is instantiated whenever an `account` WME has a balance (value for the attribute `^balance`) that is greater

```
(p  process-purchase!add-to-credit
;
; Add a credit transaction to the account,
; increasing the account's balance.
;
      (subtask ^name process-purchase)
   { <Request>
      (credit-request ^account <account> ^amount <to-credit>) }
   { <Account>
      (account ^number <account> ^balance <current-balance>) }
   -->
      (remove <Request>)
      (modify <Account>
         ^balance (compute <to-credit> + <current-balance>))
      (make subtask ^name update-accounts))
```

Figure 9.11 Candidate for indefinite postponement.

than the allowed credit limit (`^credit-limit`). Another rule in the program, such as one in Figure 9.11, may create the WME that instantiates this demon.

The `account` WME in the rule in Figure 9.11 is modified by adding the current credit request (`<to-credit>`) to the current balance (`<current-balance>`). When the value for the balance exceeds the credit limit, the demon is instantiated. However, after the creation of the new `account` WME, a new control WME is also created. Since the control WME is the last created, it is more recent than the `account` WME, so instantiations of the subtask `update-accounts` have priority over the demon. The `update-accounts` subtask, and other subtasks invoked from within the subtask, run to completion before the demon can execute, heedless of the problem that should have been solved by the demon before the program continued execution. When and if the demon is finally able to execute, there may have been more activity on the overdrawn account, all of which is now in error.

An easy and reliable solution to this type of problem is routinely to create subtask WMEs on the RHS before making any other changes to working memory, as shown in the rule in Figure 9.12. This practice requires some acclimation, since it is common for RHS actions to culminate in the creation of a new subtask. However, in a large system, this is one way to ensure that a demon somewhere in the system is not postponed by a more recent control WME.

9.4 Effects of Demons on Program Efficiency

Demons often degrade system performance, primarily because of the amount of matching that is performed on them. Rules in subtasks are restricted from most

```
(p  process-purchase!add-to-credit
;
; Add a credit transaction to the account,
; increasing the account's balance.
;
      (subtask ^name process-purchase)
   { <Request>
      (credit-request ^account <account> ^amount <to-credit>) }
   { <Account>
      (account ^number <account> ^balance <current-balance>) }
   -->
      (make subtask ^name update-accounts)
      (remove <Request>)
      (modify <Account>
         ^balance (compute <to-credit> + <current-balance>)))
```

Figure 9.12 No longer a candidate for postponement.

unnecessary matching either whenever their control WME is not in working memory, or when it has a value altered to restrict matching (such as when the attribute `^status` has the value `pending`). Since demons do not have a control WME, there is no way to "turn off" the matching anytime during program execution.

In the lattice example from Figure 9.7, for instance, there are two condition elements on the LHS—one from the element class `arc`, and the other from the `node` element class. Whenever there is a change to an `arc` WME, this rule makes a comparison between that `arc` WME and every other `node` WME in working memory. Likewise, changes to a `node` WME cause this rule to test each `arc` WME against that node. If the program uses 40 `arc` WMEs and 10 `node` WMEs, roughly 40 comparisons are made each time a node is changed, and 10 are made each time an arc changes. These numbers can become prohibitive if the number of arcs and nodes grows very large, or if arcs and nodes are changed often.

However, there are situations in which demons are far more efficient than are subtask rules. Whereas a subtask rule must be effectively rematched each time its corresponding control WME is created, a demon, having no control element, may maintain its matched state much more effectively. Partial matches to condition elements in subtask rules are removed from memory every time their control WME is removed with `pop-subtask`.

For example, although the demon `demon!fetch-successor` makes roughly 400 comparisons when the initial 40 arcs and 10 nodes are created, it makes only 10 extra comparisons when one arc is added. If `demon!fetch-successor` is written as part of a subtask, however, each time the control WME for that subtask is created, all 400 comparisons must be remade. This could slow down the application considerably if the subtask was enabled many times during the program's execution.

See Chapter 10, *Efficiency*, for a complete discussion of rule matching and the reasons for rule inefficiencies.

9.5 Design Considerations

Programs containing demons are best designed such that only a small proportion of rules in the system are demons. If there are no demons, then development may be complex and inflexible, as there may be a need for many explicit calls to subtasks. In addition, run-time may be slow due to the amount of rematching caused by the creation of certain control WMEs. The lack of demons also unnecessarily restricts a data-driven system from doing what it does best—spontaneously reacting to changes in data.

At the other extreme, however, a system that has a very high demon-to-subtask-rule ratio is beset with different problems, the most obvious being the control among demons. When will demons compete? How can you ensure that a more important demon executes immediately even if another, less important demon is also in the conflict set? The control problems among demons are similar to those that we faced when we were looking for some way to control rule clusters in our programs.

A system with many demons is also inevitably complex because the branching factor is very high. If every possible firing is a branch point, control WMEs limit the number of rules that are instantiated and therefore the number of possible branches. Every demon instantiated, however, increases the amount of branching. A demon scout adds even more branching by creating one or more control WMEs. For this reason, a system with many demons may become overwhelmingly difficult to understand and debug.

We cannot give a number that represents the "correct" ratio between demons and other rules in the program. The guideline for finding this ratio in your application is that a proper mix of demons and subtask rules results in demons that fire immediately when they are instantiated, and that do not compete with other demons.

Summary

- A demon is a rule that does not conform to the conventions established in cluster control techniques using the MEA strategy. A demon's first condition element is not from the control element class.

- Demon rules add global responsiveness to programs using a rule cluster control technique. Demons respond immediately to high-priority situations that occur at any time during the execution of an OPS5 program.

- Demons can be used to maintain relationships between WMEs, to recognize and act on critical situations, and to simulate virtual resources. Demons are also useful in creating and maintaining data structures.
- Demons help in the implementation of WMEs that are specific to one subtask, called subtask-scoped WMEs.
- Demons are not without their drawbacks. A demon may fail to execute immediately when matched due to inappropriate triggers, competition with other demons, or indefinite postponement.
- Demons generally degrade system performance, except in certain cases in which they are more efficient because they do not have to rematch all WMEs to condition elements when a control WME is created or removed.
- A proper balance between demons and subtask rules results in a maintainable application capable of responding quickly to various situations regardless of when those situations occur.

Exercises

1. Recall the `distance` WMEs presented in Section 9.2.1. Why do we represent the distance between two pieces with two WMEs rather than with just one?
2. Section 9.2.3 described a representation for virtual resource management using a vector attribute. Could you use a scalar attribute to store virtual resources? If so, explain how. If not, discuss why not.
3. A major feature of subtask-scoped WMEs is that they are automatically removed when the associated subtask WME is removed.
   a. Besides the efficiency concerns, why should these WMEs be removed at all?
   b. Why is it important to remove local WMEs *after* the subtask WME is removed, rather than *before*?
   c. Suppose you did not use a demon to remove locals when a subtask ends. Discuss alternative ways to remove locals. How do these techniques compare with the demon solution?
4. Examine the following demon:

```
(p  demon!unpriced-transmission
   { <Transmission>
      (transmission ^name <name> ^price nil) }
   -->
      (write (crlf) |Oops - a| <name>
             |has no price!  Enter price:|)
      (modify <Transmission> ^price (accept)))
```

a. How might you make this demon rule apply in only the subtask named `select-transmission`?

b. Describe the behavior of this modified demon compared to the rules in the subtask `select-transmission`.

c. What is the danger in using this technique?

5. At the end of Section 9.3, a solution was proposed for avoiding demon starvation: Rules that make subtask WMEs do so before making any other changes to working memory. How will this ensure that demons will not be postponed by rules of the subtask that is made?

CHAPTER 10
Efficiency

FOR A NEW OPS5 PROGRAMMER, many development goals are more important than run-time efficiency is.* It is important that a program have a representation of domain knowledge that is easy to understand, modify, and augment. The program should also have a control technique that is separate from the domain knowledge and is clear to the reader, while it does not sacrifice data-driven behavior by being overly restrictive on the order of rule firings. And, of course, the program should do what it was intended to do—it should work. These concerns are more important to the long-term success of a program than is the program's efficiency.

At some point before going into production, however, the program must be reviewed to determine whether it meets execution speed requirements. If not, greater attention must be paid to making the program more efficient before the step from prototype to production is taken.

This chapter discusses how OPS5 matches WMEs to rules, and what makes some rules faster than others. To write efficient rules, you must have some knowledge of the inner workings of the OPS5 match process. This knowledge gives programmers an ability to design and tune an OPS5 program to run efficiently. Just as important, it serves as the basis for good programming style. It helps the programmer distinguish between efficient rules and inefficient ones, and between what is natural to OPS5 and what is not.

*When we talk about efficiency in this chapter, we are referring to the CPU time required to complete an average run.

10.1 Efficiency of the Recognize-act Cycle

To speed up the execution of an OPS5 program, we focus on the activity that takes the most CPU time. As you recall from Chapter 3, the OPS5 recognize-act cycle comprises three phases: match, conflict resolution, and act. Of these three phases, the match phase is by far the most expensive, accounting for more than 90 percent of execution time in some programs [Gupta 1985]. Therefore, to maximize the efficiency of an OPS5 program, you should understand how OPS5 matches WMEs to rules, and what programming practices make this phase more efficient.

The fact that the recognize-act cycle spends so much time in the match phase should not be surprising. Consider what takes place during that phase. Every WME is compared to every condition element in every rule. Imagine a program with 100 WMEs, and 100 rules that each have approximately five condition elements—not a large program. During the match phase, this program would make 50,000 comparisons between WMEs and condition elements! An OPS5 implementation that computed all these matches each cycle would obviously spend most of its time in the match phase.

OPS5 is based on an efficient match algorithm called the *RETE match algorithm.** A basic understanding of the RETE match algorithm is essential to an understanding of efficiency in OPS5.

In the next section we provide a basic sketch of how the algorithm works. In Sections 10.3 and 10.4 we suggest a few maxims and programming practices for writing rules that use the algorithm most efficiently. We then discuss common efficiency problems and suggest ways to avoid them.

10.2 The RETE Match Algorithm

The RETE match algorithm trades space for time by saving the match state between recognize-act cycles. When a WME is created, it is compared with all condition elements in the program, and it is stored with each condition element to which it matches. Therefore, only *incremental* changes to working memory are matched on each cycle.

For this approach to be efficient, we must assume that most of working memory remains unchanged from one rule firing to the next—a reasonable assumption given that a typical OPS5 rule makes few changes to working memory.†

*For a detailed explanation of this algorithm and its implementation, see [Forgy 1982].

†Based on an informal analysis by the authors of over 16,000 OPS5 rules from various applications at DEC, a typical OPS5 rule contains only two actions that affect working memory.

10.2.1 Rule Compilation

To match WMEs efficiently, we compile the condition elements of all the OPS5 rules into a network of test nodes. Each node represents one of the tests in a condition element. A test is a predicate operator with a constant, bound variable, or a disjunction. For example, one node might represent the test that the value for the attribute `^type` is the symbol `or`.

```
^type = or
```

The nodes are connected in the order in which the tests occur in the condition elements. So, the condition element

```
(gate ^type or ^value <> true)
```

is compiled into the string of nodes in Figure 10.1.

If another condition element, such as

```
(gate ^type or ^value <> false)
```

is also compiled, it will share the first two test nodes in the network (Figure 10.2). When condition elements share nodes in the network (*node sharing*), this reduces the number of redundant tests and, therefore, the number of nodes in the network. This is one factor in the algorithm's efficiency.

The match process takes place when a WME is created or removed.* A pointer to the new WME is passed to the network *root node*, which forwards a copy to all the top nodes in the network. Each node acts like a switch. When

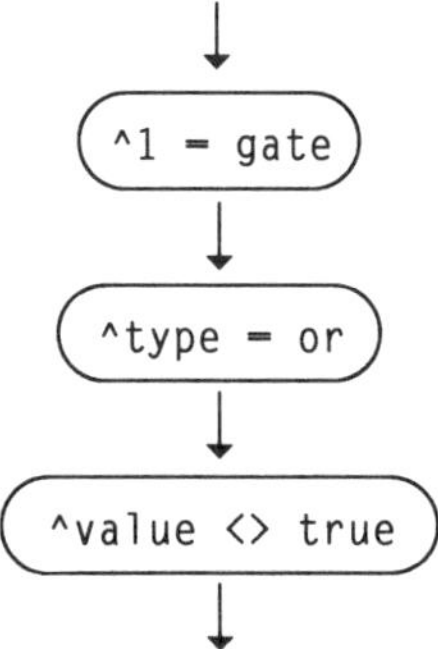

Figure 10.1 Nodes connected in the order of condition element tests.

*Since a `modify` is performed by a `remove` and a `make`, `modify` is not specifically mentioned in this discussion about match activity.

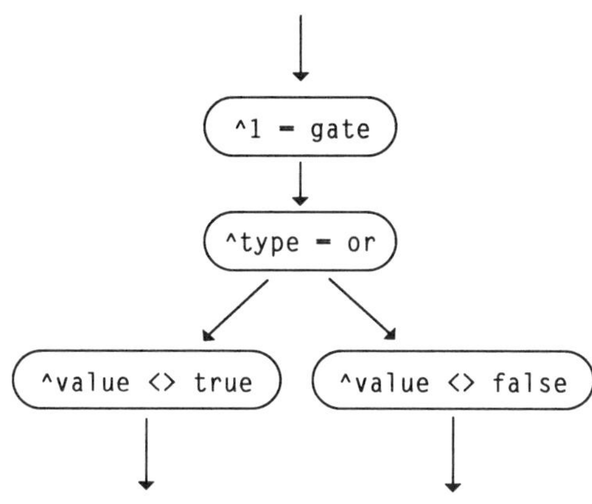

Figure 10.2 Node sharing between two condition elements.

a node receives the WME pointer, it performs its test on the associated WME. If the WME passes the test at that node, the switch opens and the pointer drops through to the next nodes. If the WME value fails the test, the switch does not open and the WME cannot go further along that path. If the WME proceeds far enough, it will be combined with WMEs matching other condition elements to form complete instantiations in the conflict set.

WME pointers are sent through the match network as *tokens*. A token contains pointers to one or more WMEs, and a status that indicates that the token originated from either a `make` or a `remove` action.* Tokens that have a `make` status are stored with condition elements they match; tokens with a `remove` status are deleted from condition elements with which they are stored.

10.2.2 One- and Two-input Nodes

In Chapter 3, we discussed the two types of match: intraelement and interelement. Intraelement match is the comparison between WME values and the tests *within* the condition element—for example, a check to see whether a WME has the attribute and value `^type or` is an intraelement test. Interelement match is the comparison between entire WMEs that match the condition elements of the same rule. Interelement match ensures that variables with the same name in different condition elements refer to the same values.

The two types of match are represented by different types of nodes in the match network. Intraelement matches are performed by *one-input nodes*, like

*A `modify` action causes a `remove` token and a `make` token to be sent through the match network.

those shown in Figure 10.1. Each node performs one of the tests specified in a condition element; a string of one-input nodes represents all the tests in the condition element. The name "one-input" refers to the fact that the work done in that node depends on one input into the node: a single token.

Variable consistency is handled by one-input nodes only when the variable is used twice in the same condition element; the one-input node tests that these values are consistent within the condition element. For example, the condition element

```
(customer ^balance <huge> ^credit-limit < <huge>)
```

would be compiled into the one-input nodes

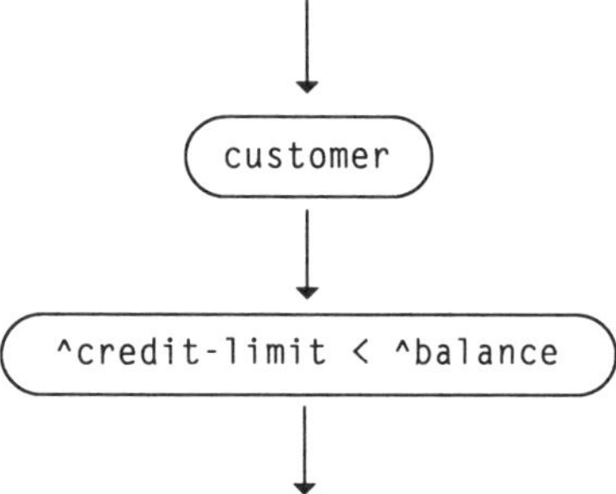

Interelement matches are performed by *two-input nodes*. Two-input nodes combine the output of two one-input nodes, performing interelement tests and producing consistent partial or full instantiations.

Consider the rule in Figure 10.3 and its compiled network form in Figure 10.4. The three condition elements from the element classes `task`, `gate`, and `line` each compile into a string of one-input nodes. Notice that there is no one-input node for testing the values of the variable `<id>` in the second and third condition elements' tests.

Two-input nodes check variable consistency across condition elements. The two-input node labeled `1&2` in Figure 10.4 forms every combination of WMEs that match the first condition element and those that match the second. Since there are no variables in common between these condition elements, the two-input node forms a cross-product of the two, and passes each of these pairs to the next two-input node. Each token emitted from `1&2` contains a pair of WMEs and a `make` or `remove` status.

The two-input node labeled `(1&2)&3` receives tokens from node `1&2`, and from the last one-input node compiled from the third condition element. A token from this one-input node contains a pointer to a WME that successfully matched the third condition element. In node `(1&2)&3`, pointers to the WMEs matching the first two condition elements are combined with the pointer to the WME matching the third to form a token containing pointers to the three WMEs.

```
(p  propagate!or-true
;
; If an OR gate is found with a TRUE line input, set the gate
; value to TRUE as well.
;
      (task ^name propagate)
   { <The-OR-gate>
      (gate ^type or ^id <id> ^value <> true) }
      (line ^to <id> ^value true)
   -->
      (modify <The-OR-gate> ^value true))
```

Figure 10.3 Example rule for compilation.

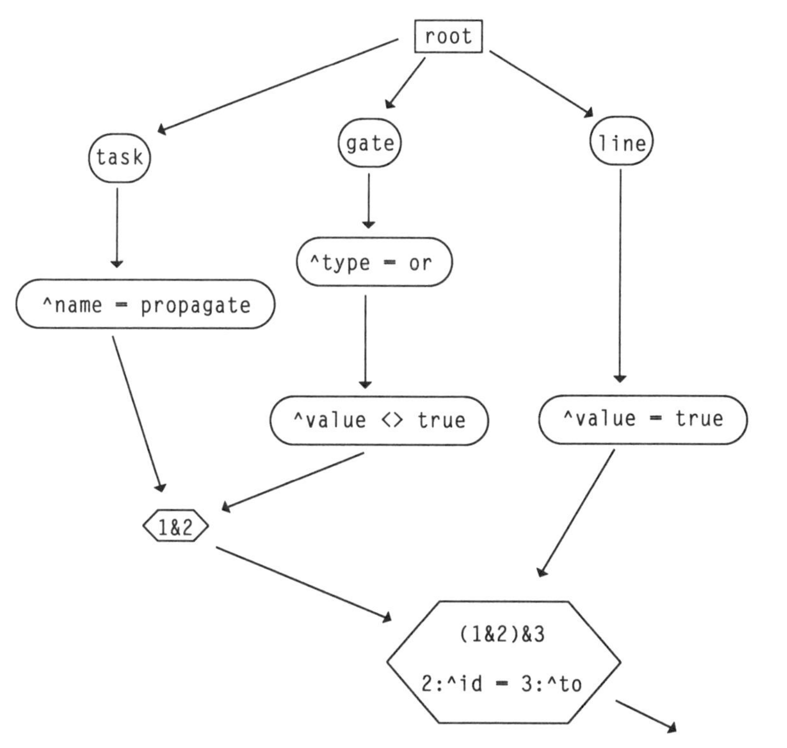

Figure 10.4 A simple network of one- and two-input nodes.

This token represents an instantiation of the rule. To form a new token, node (1&2)&3 must determine that the value for the attribute ^id in the second WME is the same as the value for the attribute ^to in the third WME. This constraint, which comes from the use of the variable <id> in the second and third condition elements, limits the number of triplets formed.

Since there are no more condition elements, the resulting set of tokens becomes an instantiation and is placed in the conflict set. If there had been a fourth condition element in our example rule, the token emitted from node (1&2)&3 would have been the input to another two-input node, (1&2&3)&4, which would try to combine the partial matches from the first three condition elements with every WME that matched the fourth condition element.

10.2.3 Alpha and Beta Memories

Each two-input node has two memories—one each for storing tokens from its two inputs. An *alpha memory* holds tokens received from its one-input node. Each token contains a pointer to a WME that successfully matched the condition element. A *beta memory* holds sets of tokens that were the result of the work of a previous two-input node. These tokens contain pointers to WMEs that together form a consistent match to a group of condition elements earlier in the rule.*

Two-input nodes that join positive condition element matches to previous condition element matches are called AND nodes. Figure 10.5 shows an AND node and its associated token memories. Notice that, in the figure, the tokens represented coming into the right side of the node are always stored in alpha memory. The tokens represented entering the left side of the AND node are alpha memory when this AND node is the first two-input node in the network (because the input to the node at that time can be the result of only a one-input node), but are beta memory at all other positions in the network (when their input is from the result of a previous two-input node). We sometimes refer to "right memory" and "left memory," to account for the fact that the left memory may be either alpha or beta.

In Figure 10.6, the first two condition elements in the rule propagate!or-true (Figure 10.3) compile into two strings of one-input nodes. The two-input AND node labeled 1&2 accepts tokens from these two strings and stores them in two corresponding alpha memories. The third condition element compiles into another string of one-input nodes. The two-input node (1&2)&3 then accepts tokens from this string from the right and stores them in its alpha memory. Node (1&2)&3 accepts tokens emitted from node 1&2 and stores them in the beta memory.

A two-input node is activated whenever a token arrives from the right or from the left. When a token with a make status arrives, it is stored in the node's corresponding memory and then is compared with all tokens stored in the

*The OPS5 interpreter matches command shows the contents of these memories.

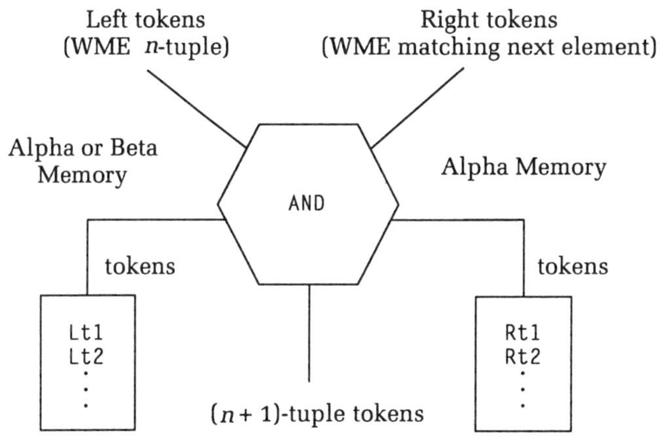

Figure 10.5 AND two-input node for positive conditions.

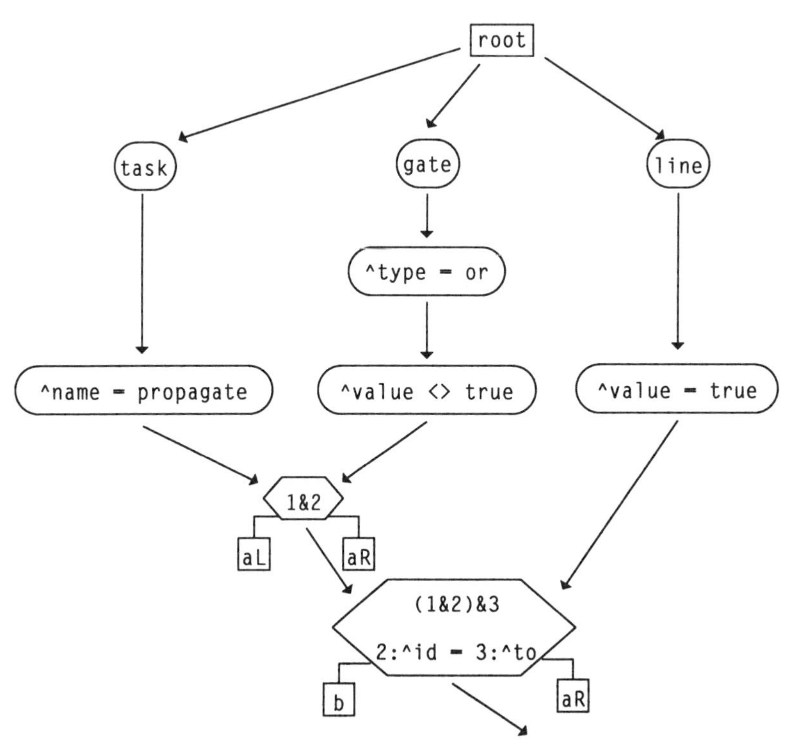

Figure 10.6 Alpha and beta memories on two-input nodes.

node's other memory. Each consistent match that occurs causes the node to combine the WME pointers in both tokens to form a new one, which is then passed to all successor nodes. If the original token arrives with a `remove` status, it goes through the same matching process as does a token with a `make` status, except that, rather than the token being stored in the token memory, it must be located and removed from the memory. The tokens emitted from a two-input node are given the same status as the token that just arrived.

10.2.4 Negated Condition Elements

Up to this point, we have been discussing the joining of positive condition elements. Negated condition elements require another type of two-input node. The compilation of a negated condition element creates a NOT two-input node, illustrated in Figure 10.7.

The WMEs that match the string of one-input nodes representing a negated condition element are represented by tokens stored in the NOT two-input node's alpha memory. If a negated condition element does not contain any variables bound in other condition elements, the mere presence of a token in this memory ensures that no tokens from the left will pass through that two-input node. If the negated condition element refers to variables bound in previous condition elements, however, the tokens stored in the alpha memory must be matched against the tokens in the left memory to see whether the negated element is consistently matched.

In Figure 10.7, the memory on the left (either alpha or beta) contains a *negation count* with each token. This is a count of the number of tokens in the memory on the right that successfully match the left token, inhibiting that token

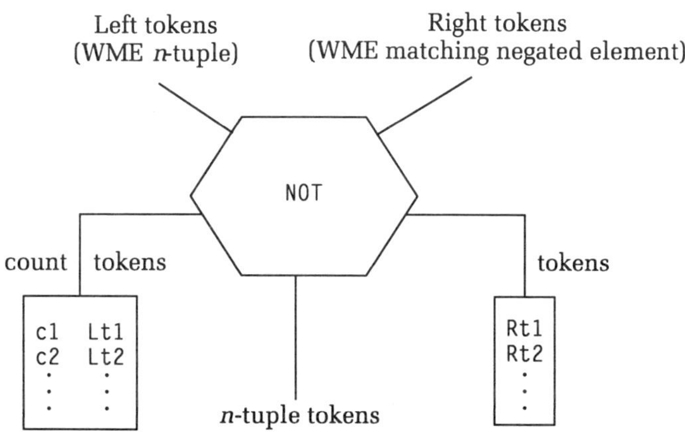

Figure 10.7 NOT two-input node for negated conditions.

```
(p  propagate!or-true
;
; If an OR gate is found with a TRUE line input, set the gate
; value to TRUE as well.
;
      (task ^name propagate)
      (line ^to <or-gate> ^value true)
   { <The-OR-gate>
      (gate ^id <or-gate> ^type or ^value <> true) }
   -->
      (modify <The-OR-gate> ^value true))

(p  propagate!not-false
;
; If a NOT gate is found with a TRUE line input, set the gate
; value to FALSE if it is not already FALSE.
;
      (task ^name propagate)
      (line ^to <not-gate> ^value true)
   { <The-NOT-gate>
      (gate ^id <not-gate> ^type not ^value <> false) }
   -->
      (modify <The-NOT-gate> ^value false))
```

Figure 10.8 Two example rules that can share two-input nodes.

from proceeding further in the network. The right memory contains tokens that successfully matched the string of one-input nodes representing the negated condition element.

When a new token arrives from the left, it is compared to all the tokens on the right. The number of consistent matches found is that token's negation count. The token and its negation count are then stored in the left memory. If the negation count is 0, then a copy of the token is emitted from the NOT node, representing a match of previous condition elements that was not inhibited by the negated condition element. If the negation count is greater than 0, then the token is not emitted. A token arriving from the left with a `remove` status will remove its corresponding `make` token from the left memory and will be emitted only if the negation count was 0.

Coming from the right, a token is stored (or removed if it has a `remove` status) and then is compared against all tokens in the left memory. Tokens that match have their negation count incremented if the right token has a `make` status, or decremented if the right token is being removed. If a negation count is incremented to 1, then the corresponding left tuple is emitted with a `remove` status since it is now being inhibited. If a negation count is decremented to 0,

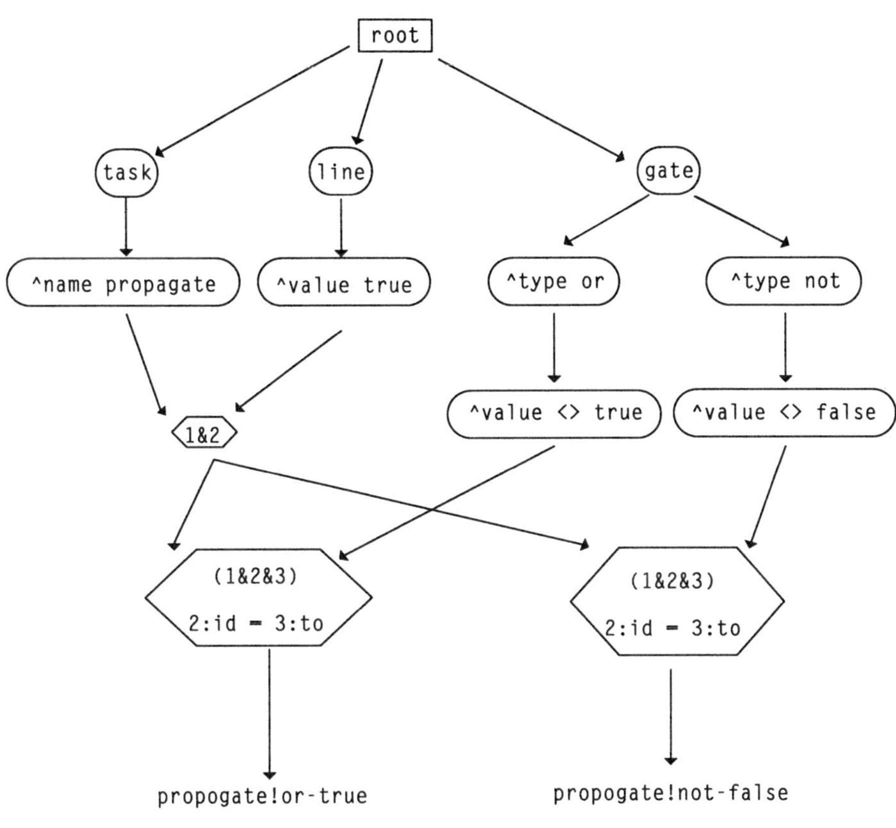

Figure 10.9 The match network with two-input node sharing.

then the corresponding left tuple is emitted with a make status, since it is no longer being inhibited by a token on the right.

10.2.5 Two-input Node Sharing

The picture of the RETE network we have presented here is not yet complete. We saw earlier how one-input nodes can be shared by two or more condition elements. Likewise, two-input nodes can also be shared by two or more rules. As an example, let us use the two rules in Figure 10.8, and the compiled RETE network for the rules in Figure 10.9.

These rules share both one-input and two-input nodes. Since both rules share intraelement tests on the first two condition elements, they also share one-input nodes in the match network. The third condition element in each rule differs after the WME class is tested, so only one one-input node can be shared—the one that tests that the WME class is `gate`. Each rule, having three conditions, should normally have two two-input nodes. However, since the first two conditions in both rules share interelement tests (there are none), they can also share a two-input node that combines tokens from these two conditions. Although the final two-input node does the same work for both rules—that is, it checks that the values bound to the attributes `^id` and `^to` are the same—separate two-input nodes are necessary, since they receive inputs from different one-input nodes on the right.

10.3 Using the Network Efficiently

We can use the simplified picture of the match network presented in the previous section to discuss efficient OPS5 programming practices.

First, we focus on the most time-consuming activity in the match network. The tests in one-input nodes are very fast. A WME is checked by one-input nodes only when it is created and when it is removed. Two-input nodes, on the other hand, may take much more time combining tokens. When a token enters one memory, a two-input node must compare it against every element in the other memory, possibly making many more tokens propagate in the network. Therefore, a good way to begin writing efficient rules is to minimize the time spent in two-input nodes.

The programming practices described in the following sections help you to minimize the work in two-input nodes.

10.3.1 Minimize the Number of Two-Input Nodes

The most obvious way of minimizing the work in two-input nodes is to create fewer of these nodes. Although you can create fewer two-input nodes by writing fewer rules, there are other ways to minimize two-input nodes that do not restrict the number of rules. For example, you can write smaller rules, or you can compose sets of rules with similar structure.

As we saw in the previous section, a rule with N condition elements compiles into a network with $N-1$ two-input nodes. So fewer two-input nodes will be created if you write rules with fewer conditions.

To write smaller rules, design large element classes rather than many more small ones. WMEs with many attributes can allow working-memory state to be matched concisely without referring to many WMEs. A more compact representation usually involves some redundancy of data in working memory, but the management of that redundancy may require less execution time than would matching rules with many more condition elements.

Consider an OPS5 program that solves simple geometry problems. Triangles may be represented by matching three angles that share endpoints:

```
(angle ^end1 <p1> ^end2 <p2>)
(angle ^end1 <p2> ^end2 <p3>)
(angle ^end1 <p3> ^end2 <p1>)
```

If angles must be represented explicitly, this may be a convenient and adequate representation of triangles. However, an additional specific triangle representation may be more efficient. The three-angle condition representation adds three two-input nodes in rules that match triangles. A better representation would use a separate WME class for a triangle.

```
(triangle ^corner1 <p1> ^corner2 <p2> ^corner3 <p3>)
```

If both the angle and triangle element classes exist, they will encode information redundantly. Rules must then be written to maintain consistency of the redundant information as these representations are manipulated in the program. This adds some complexity and run-time overhead, but the time saved by fewer two-input nodes may be greater than the overhead of maintaining the redundancy, depending on the requirements of the application.

Another way to create fewer two-input nodes is to write several rules that share two-input nodes. As a rule is compiled, before creating each new node, the compiler looks to see whether the needed node is already connected to the present node. If it is, that node is used again; if it does not already exist, a new node and therefore a new path in the network is created. Two-input nodes are shared when all preceding nodes are shared and the interelement tests are the same. In other words, ignoring specific variable names, two rules will share two-input nodes up to the point at which their condition elements differ. The two rules in Figure 10.8 share their first two-input node because their first two conditions are equivalent.

The implication for rule writing of this compilation process is that similar rules should be written similarly. That is, when two condition elements are equivalent in either the same rule or another one, the tests within should be written in the same order, so that one-input nodes are shared. When rules have equivalent, shared condition elements, they should be written in the same order, thereby sharing two-input nodes as well.

Program designs that use the idea of general and special case rules are particularly good at node sharing. A general case rule covers the most common, or least specific, case. Special case rules handle specialized cases of the general rule. For example, a general case rule may have five condition elements, and the specific case rules have those five condition elements plus a few extra condition elements or additional tests within a condition element. This technique is efficient because it maximizes two-input node sharing. All the matches for the tests shared with more than one rule are performed only once. It is also convenient for adding more special case rules at a later time.

```
(p  configure-device!fetch-controller
;
; If we are out of controllers, pick up another one of the required
; type.  This is a general case rule.
;
      (subtask ^name configure-device)
      (component ^class device ^configured no
                 ^controller-type <ctype>)
      - (component ^class controller ^configured yes ^type <ctype>)
   -->
      (call retrieve_component ^class controller ^type <ctype>))

(p  configure-device!reject-component
;
;   If we are out of controllers, and we have reached our maximum on
;   this type of controller, reject the device as well.
;   Note: This is a special case of configure-device!fetch-controller
;
      (subtask ^name configure-device)
   { <Device>
      (component ^class device ^configured no
                 ^controller-type <ctype>) }
      - (component ^class controller ^configured yes ^type <ctype>)
      (order-constraint ^class controller ^type <ctype>
                        ^limit <max> ^current <max>)
   -->
      (modify <Device> ^configured reject
         ^reason |Cannot have any more than|
                 <max> <ctype> |controllers.|))
```

Figure 10.10 General and special case rules sharing two-input nodes.

In the example in Figure 10.10 from a hypothetical configuration program, a computer device requires a controller that must be fetched from an external database by the routine `retrieve_component`. The general case rule simply fetches the component. A special case rule notices that a limit on the number of this type of controller has been reached, and instead rejects the device. These rules share an AND and a NOT two-input node, and eight one-input nodes.

10.3.2 Minimize the Frequency of Tokens Arriving at Two-input Nodes

Recall that, in the RETE network, tokens are passed from one AND two-input node to another, each one combining the results of the previous two-input node with tokens from matches to the incoming condition element. Each string of one-input nodes acts as a control to a two-input node. If all tokens are removed from an AND node's alpha memory, all beta memories below that AND two-input node are also emptied. This can be quite expensive if the beta memories are very full. Likewise, a very large alpha memory can explode the size of beta memories below it in the network, since the AND two-input node combines these with all tokens in its other memory. This can cause substantial work in two-input nodes, combining memories or removing tokens from memories.

Placement of Frequently Matched Condition Elements

Due to the domino effect from earlier nodes to their successors, matching is more expensive on earlier condition elements than on later ones. When a change is made to a WME, match time is spent at the two-input node whose alpha memory contains that WME. If that two-input node is early in the network, its new output causes token matching in all the two-input nodes following in the network. If the two-input node is at the end, or near the end, of the network, there is not the same domino effect on other two-input nodes—most of the rule match remains unchanged.

Note that, in the rules in Figure 10.10, if WMEs of class `component` are being changed often, the matcher spends significant time undoing and then redoing the match action in all two-input nodes associated with these rules. The time is spent even if the changes to the `component` WME are not relevant to the rules shown.

The programming practice related to this domino effect in the network is that condition elements that are matched by frequently changing WMEs should be placed near the end of the LHS to avoid wasting time in two-input nodes.

Effect of Rule Clusters on Efficiency

Clustering rules into subtasks and using control rules to activate subtasks and to remove control WMEs when a subtask finishes can increase efficiency by limiting two-input node action. Since the condition element matching the control WME is the first condition element in the rule, the lack of a match to that condition element "turns off" the two-input matching for the rest of the network. So when a subtask is not enabled, the partial matching for that rule is restricted to intraelement match, and does not do any interelement match.

A great deal of two-input node matching time may be spent when a control WME is created and when it is removed. When a new subtask is invoked, there is an initial flood of two-input node action as the rules associated with the new subtask "catch up." The time spent instantiating these rules will depend on the efficiency of each rule of the subtask. (Any subtask that is already instantiated when a new subtask is invoked continues to be fully instantiated while the new one is in effect.) Removing a control WME may also incur significant matching time, since all beta memories in the associated rules must be emptied when the subtask WME is removed.

To maximize the efficiency of changing the subtask name, tune your rule clusters such that many rules fire between switching subtasks. You can accomplish this by increasing the work done in a single subtask, or by postponing subtask invocations until absolutely necessary.

Demons

Because their two-input nodes are not protected by a control element, demon rules can be a major source of inefficiency. Regardless of whether it ever fires, a demon rule may maintain a large partial match that is affected by many subtasks. Special care should be taken to be sure that demon rules do not form unnecessarily large token memories.

The fact that a demon rule preserves its partial matches, however, may make it *more* efficient than rewriting it in a subtask would be. For example, suppose one subtask maintains consistency in a large graph structure represented in working memory. It may be invoked many times during the course of a program execution, once for each modification of the graph. Each time the subtask is entered, the rules must rematch the entire graph structure, looking for inconsistencies. Clearly, a more efficient design would be to use demon rules for graph maintenance.* In addition to the efficiency gains from avoiding the redundant rematching, this would also avoid the need to invoke a subtask each time the graph is modified.

Refraction

In Chapter 7, we discussed the uses of refraction for programming techniques that count or iterate through a set of WMEs in which there are no changes to the WMEs involved. We called this *nonmodifying iteration*, and stressed that the advantage of this technique is its speed of execution. Now that we have a model of the RETE network, we can understand why, in fact, refraction is efficient.

Suppose we have a rule that is part of a two-rule process of counting WMEs that contain a particular pattern: These WMEs have the element class `request` and the attribute-value `^status waiting`:

```
(p  monitor!count-waiting-requests
;
; Increment the waiting-requests counter for each waiting
```

*This situation occurred in the development of XSEL, DEC's eXpert SELling assistant. After being converted to demons, several of the rules incurred less than 10 percent of the previous matching time.

```
;  request.
;
      (subtask ^name count-waiting-requests)
      (request ^status waiting)
   -->
      (call increment_count waiting-requests 1))
```

As soon as the request WMEs are created, they match and are stored in the alpha memory associated with the second condition element. When the subtask WME that matches the first condition element is made, an instantiation is formed for each of the request WMEs. As each of these instantiations fires, the WMEs involved no longer form instantiations, but there are *no changes to* the node network. The routine increment_count simply increments a value associated with the atom waiting-requests in some external data structure.

If we had modified the WMEs as we counted them, the network would spend time matching each of the WMEs as they were removed, and then again as the modified WMEs were made again. A rule that depends on refraction to avoid looping does not modify its matching WMEs or make new WMEs that match, so it does not affect the token memories associated with this rule. The rule monitor!count-waiting-requests is even more efficient than is simple rule refraction since it makes no changes to working memory when it fires. No changes are made to *any* token memories. Use of refraction is in keeping with the principle that changes in token memories should be minimized.

10.3.3 Minimize Token Memory Sizes

Each two-input node has two associated token memories. The larger the size of the memories, the more time spent in the two-input node to combine the contents of one memory with the other. When a two-input node has new elements to work with, it passes on new work to the next two-input node. Any memory that changes early in the network of a rule affects all the two-input nodes later in the network to which it passes output. Removing a WME from the network involves the extra work of searching the saved tokens to find one to delete. Since the token memories are typically linear structures, the average time to remove a token is the time required to search one half of the token memory.

Since large token memories cause more work for the two-input nodes and longer search times for token removal, it is a good idea to minimize the size of token memories as much as possible. There are at least two programming practices that work toward this end: rearranging condition elements and adding restrictive tests.

The first practice is to arrange condition elements such that more restrictive conditions are placed earlier in the LHS. This causes partial matches to be rejected as early as possible, before they can cause combinatorial problems for two-input nodes. The earlier a WME can be rejected, the fewer token memories it will fill for no reason.

The second practice is to add more restrictive tests within condition elements to keep alpha memories small. A *restrictive test* is one that matches to a small number of values. Constant-value tests such as `^status current`, or `^initialized true` can help to restrict the number of WMEs that can match, thus minimizing the size of the token memory associated with this condition element. Not all tests are restrictive. For example, a variable binding is not at all restrictive because it can match to any value. A predicate with a constant, such as `^status active`, may be restrictive if there are few WMEs of that element class with that value, or may not be restrictive if the test can be passed by a large set of WMEs. A condition element that contains only a class name, such as `(item)` is unrestrictive if there are many WMEs with the element class name `item`, but is restrictive if there is only one such WME.

In short, whether or not a test or condition element is restrictive can be determined only by the contents of working memory. Therefore, rules that are matched by many WMEs and are key rules to the program should be analyzed for the approximate numbers of WMEs matching each condition element. The condition elements matched by fewer WMEs should be placed earlier in the rule; the tests within a condition element that reduce the number of possible matches should be placed earlier in the condition element.

Unfortunately, sometimes our two techniques for the proper ordering of condition elements in a rule conflict with each other by suggesting the opposite ordering. We have suggested that the most restrictive condition elements should appear early in LHS and that the condition elements matching the most frequently changing WMEs should be placed at the end of the LHS. But when the most restrictive condition element is also the most frequently modified, where do you place that condition element? Unfortunately, there is no simple answer. In these cases, a more detailed examination of the rule base and timing results is required to see which ordering will minimize the match time of the rule.

10.3.4 Minimize Cost of Two-Input Tests

In reducing the amount of time spent in two-input nodes, we have discussed reducing the number of two-input nodes and the number of tokens they must process. Another way to increase efficiency is to minimize the time a two-input node takes to combine tokens. This can be accomplished only if you understand the relative costs of interelement tests.

In a condition element, each reference to a variable in an earlier condition creates a test in a two-input node. If a condition element refers to none of the variables bound in earlier condition elements, it creates a two-input node that performs no tests; it emits all tokens formed from the cross-product of its two inputs. Although this makes the two-input node fast, the resulting tokens may create problems by making a large beta memory in the successor node.

Interelement tests with equal-to (=) and not-equal-to (<>) predicates can be optimized by good compilers. But other predicates may require a scan through an entire token memory in order to find every match. Your OPS5 documentation may tell you the relative costs of these predicates.

In implementations that allow LHS function calls, there is another potential source of performance bottlenecks. LHS functions differ greatly in how they affect the performance of a program, depending on whether they are compiled as one-input or as two-input tests.

When the arguments to an LHS function are only constants or variables bound in the current condition element, the LHS function can be performed by a one-input node. The function is called once when a matching WME is made, and once when it is removed. This situation is not likely to cause serious performance problems.

An LHS function requires a two-input node, however, if one of its arguments is a variable that first appeared in an earlier condition element. The two-input node is necessary because it receives as input the partial instantiations of the previous condition elements. If the node memories are very large, or if the number of tokens moving through this node is large, then the LHS function will be called many times.

When it is necessary to call an LHS function such that it is performed by a two-input node, you should take care to make the function fast, and to limit the number of times it is called. Since it may be called many times, even as a result of a single `make` or `remove`, the function should execute as quickly as possible. You can limit the calls to it by placing the most restrictive elements earlier in the rule to cut off the match before this condition element. Placing this element early in the rule may also reduce the sizes of the token memories that must be combined by the two-input node that calls the LHS function. These two suggestions should help you to minimize the token traffic and the node memory sizes, thus minimizing the number of calls to your LHS function.

As an alternative, if the result of the function does not change frequently given a particular WME, consider computing the result of the function once on the RHS and storing that result in some WME to be matched in place of the LHS function call.

10.4 Rule Decomposition

When two or more condition elements, particularly those with shared variables, are matched by many or frequently modified WMEs, the formation of every consistent combination of the two can be very inefficient. This section discusses *rule decomposition*, a useful and simple technique for eliminating these combinatorial matching problems.

Figure 10.11 contains a rule from a program that configures peripherals to computer systems. In one of the subtasks in this program, terminals must be fitted with cables to be plugged into terminal ports of the appropriate line type. The rule in this figure associates a suitable data cable with each terminal.

```
(p  cable-terminals!match-terminal-to-power-cable
;
; Cable together all terminals and compatible cables.
;
      (subtask ^name cable-terminals)
   { <Uncabled-terminal>
      (component ^class terminal ^status unconfigured
                 ^line-type <line>) }
   { <Unused-cable>
      (component ^class cable ^status unconfigured
                 ^line-type <line> ^name <cable>) }
   -->
      (modify <Uncabled-terminal> ^status cabled ^data-cable <cable>)
      (modify <Unused-cable> ^status used))
```

Figure 10.11 A pairwise-matching problem.

```
(p  cable-terminals!choose-terminal-to-cable
;
; Choose a single terminal to cable.
;
      (subtask ^name cable-terminals)
   { <Uncabled-terminal>
      (component ^class terminal ^status unconfigured) }
   -->
      (modify <Uncabled-terminal> ^status needs-cable))

(p  cable-terminal!cable-chosen-terminal
;
; Choose a cable for this terminal.
;
      (subtask ^name cable-terminals)
   { <Uncabled-terminal>
      (component ^status needs-cable ^line-type <line>) }
   { <Unused-cable>
      (component ^class cable ^status unconfigured
                 ^line-type <line> ^name <cable>) }
   -->
      (modify <Uncabled-terminal> ^status cabled ^data-cable <cable>)
      (modify <Unused-cable> ^status used))
```

Figure 10.12 An improvement over the pairwise-matching in Figure 10.11.

If there are many terminals and many cable components, the rule in Figure 10.11 is likely to be inefficient, because all WMEs representing a terminal `(component ^class terminal)` must be tested against all those that match the cables `(component ^class cable)`. If there are 50 terminals and 50 cables, there will be 50 × 50 = 2500 combinations of terminals and cables tested for the same value for the attribute `^line-type`. As a result, as many as 2500 instantiations are inserted into the conflict set to be sorted and executed. Each time a rule fires and modifies either a `terminal` or a `cable` component so that it no longer has the attribute-value `^status unconfigured`, as many as 50 instantiations are removed from the conflict set. We have discussed in Section 10.3.3 why removing WMEs from large memories is expensive.

Rules that exhibit this combinatorial behavior can often be decomposed into more than one rule, each one handling a subset of the matching problem.

For example, Figure 10.12 shows the rule in Figure 10.11 decomposed into two smaller rules. In the first rule, all the WMEs representing terminals match, but they do not combine with the WMEs representing cables. As soon as one terminal WME has the value `needs-cable`, the second rule is matched and fires. The condition element matching to terminals in this second rule, however, is matched by only one WME at a time—the one that is modified to have the value `needs-cable`. The size of a token memory in this case never exceeds 50 × 1, or 50 tokens. Depending on the number of WMEs involved, rule decomposition may result in a vast improvement in run time.

10.5 Efficiency Myths

Over the years that we have used OPS5 for rule-based programming, certain myths about what makes an OPS5 program efficient have enjoyed unwarranted popularity. Because of network analysis and empirical studies with timing packages, we can now confidently dispel some of these myths for most implementations of OPS5. We include them here, with descriptions of why they are inaccurate, so that you can avoid similar misconceptions.

10.5.1 Myth: More Rule Firings Means Lower Efficiency

In our experience, OPS5 developers have placed too much emphasis on the correlation between the number of rule firings and efficiency. Application design decisions that were "based on efficiency" were often made by comparing the number of rule firings expected in two designs. Although the number of rule firings gives an indication of efficiency, it is significant only when we are speaking in terms of orders of magnitude, or are comparing two designs that are similar in the structure of rules and working-memory content.

The problem with equating rule firings with efficiency is that it does not take into account partial matching and the time spent in two-input nodes. These two components of the match cycle take up a significant portion of the match time, and yet are not reflected in instantiations or rule firings. As in our rule-decomposition example, it is frequently the case that, when a program is made more efficient, the number of rule firings increases, rather than decreases.

10.5.2 Myth: Negated Conditions are More Expensive than Positive Ones are

Another myth suggests that negated condition elements should be avoided because of their inherent inefficiency. The fact is that negated condition elements are not significantly more expensive than are positive condition elements. The perception that they are slow is probably due to the fact that negated condition elements often contain more interelement tests, causing more matching time at two-input nodes. However, avoiding these negated conditions may prove to be even more expensive. Two-input nodes are the slow part of match, whether from a positive or a negated condition element.

10.5.3 Myth: All Variables are Expensive

The first occurrence of a variable on the LHS does not require any match time. It is a declaration to the compiler that the value represented by that variable can be found in a particular location. If a variable is bound on the LHS and is used on only the RHS, there is no matching expense. Subsequent use of the variable in the same condition element is an intraelement test, performed by an efficient one-input node. It is the use of the variable in subsequent condition elements that causes work in a two-input node. As we mentioned in Section 10.3.4, some implementations optimize interelement tests on particular predicates, so even these may not be very costly. But predicates such as less-than (<), greater-than (>), less-than-or-equal-to (<=), and greater-than-or-equal-to (>=), used with previously bound variables, are likely to be expensive, especially when the token memories are large or very active.

Cut-and-paste editing styles often leave unnecessary bindings in rules. Although an LHS variable binding is treated as a declaration and not as a test, it should be avoided unless the variable will be used later in the rule. It is not good programming style to bind a variable that is never referred to again in the rule—either in the RHS or in the LHS. As in any language, unnecessary declarations make the code harder to understand and serve no useful purpose.

10.5.4 Myth: The Number of Rules has a Significant Effect on Run Time

It is generally true that adding rules to an OPS5 program will increase execution time. However, as it is inaccurate to judge a program by the number of rule firings, it is misleading to count the number of rules as a measure of a program's efficiency. This is primarily because of the amount of node sharing that a many-rule system may have, and the nonuniformity in rule efficiency. Forgy [Forgy 1982] reported that the time for one rule firing is proportional to the number of rules in only the worst case.* In the best case, it is logarithmic. Aside from limits inherent in a particular OPS5 implementation, you should have few practical efficiency concerns about the size of your rule base.

10.5.5 Myth: The Number of Distinct Element Classes has a Predictable Effect on Efficiency

It is a common myth that a large number of distinct element classes match more efficiently than do few classes, presumably because each element class is more specific to a purpose and so there will be fewer WMEs of each class. Unfortunately, neither this nor its opposite is necessarily true. The match network with many, very specific element classes looks very broad, because it contains many short strings of one-input nodes. The network with few element classes is "deeper"; more attributes are compacted into each element class, so there tend to be longer strings of one-input nodes. Both designs will activate approximately the same number of nodes; each carries possible disadvantages.

If a program has many element classes, there are probably fewer WMEs per element class. Rules have more condition elements, and each condition element is matched by a smaller set of WMEs. The advantage in terms of efficiency is that the token memories for the condition elements are not as large, and do not overfill. The disadvantage of using many smaller element classes, however, is that combining the larger number of condition elements causes there to be more interelement tests. The culprits of program inefficiency, two-input nodes, are then responsible for more of the work.†

Using a few element classes with more attributes per class, on the other hand, is efficient because more intraelement matches are taken care of by one-input nodes. We have discussed in Section 10.3 the relative efficiency of this work done in one-input nodes. The disadvantage of compacting information into

---

*It is difficult to write an OPS5 program that demonstrates the worst case.

†A less obvious disadvantage of using many element classes is that it is sometimes difficult to express interelement variable relationships in negated condition elements. Sometimes it is necessary for all information to be in one element class in order for a concept to be expressed in a negated condition element, rather than to be dispersed over many condition elements.

fewer element classes is that it is easy to forget to specify condition elements completely enough to restrict matching as much as you should. This may lead to large token memories, and may increase the amount of unnecessary matching.

10.6 Rule Timing in VAX OPS5

The VAX OPS5 implementation includes a rule-timing feature called the Performance Measurement and Evaluation (PME) package. The PME tracks timing data on the LHS and RHS of rules, the number of times each rule fires, and the set of rules that made or removed WMEs that allowed each rule to be instantiated. The following sections discuss the use and interpretation of those timing data.

10.6.1 Using the PME

Since collecting timing information takes time itself, the PME feature is disabled by default. It is activated by the `enable` command before the execution of the rules to be timed:

```
OPS5>(enable timing)
```

Once the PME is enabled, it collects timing data on any rules executed. Once you have executed all the rules you want timed, you can generate the timing reports with the `report timing` command:

```
OPS5>(report timing)
```

The `report timing` command generates two files of reports: `timingcpu.txt` (the timing report), and `timingcau.txt` (the cause report). After exiting from OPS5, you can access these files.

You can reset the timing data collected before or after generating the report using the `clear timing` command.

```
OPS5>(clear timing)
```

You may need this if you have run rules on which you did not want data collected, or have generated one report and want to collect timing data on another set of rules. The second set of reports are written to the same files, but to later versions of them.

If you have generated a report and want to stay within the OPS5 environment, you can turn off the collection of timing information with the `disable` command:

```
OPS5>(disable timing)
```

```
Timing CPU report on 21-JUN-1987 14:51:35.25

PRODUCTION NAME                         # FIRINGS  LHS TIME    RHS TIME

PLACEMENT!DONE-MOVING-GROUPS               12          0          15
PLACEMENT!NEW-ROOM                         16        284         871
PLACEMENT!CONDENSE-COMPATIBLE-ROOM          4        204         501
PLACEMENT!MOVE-STUDENT                     17         53         138
PLACEMENT!OLD-ROOM                          9         91         493
```

Figure 10.13 Sample CPU report from the VAX OPS5 PME.

10.6.2 Contents of the Reports

Examples of the `timingcpu.txt` and `timingcau.txt` files are shown in Figures 10.13 and 10.14.

The `timingcpu.txt` file contains the amount of time spent on the LHS, the amount of time spent on the RHS, and the number of times each rule fires.

The timing on the LHS is determined by measuring the amount of CPU time spent at each two-input node that leads to that rule's instantiation, regardless of how many times the rule has fired. When reviewing LHS times, therefore, you should not take into account how many times that rule fires. A high LHS time may mean that the rule does efficient matching to produce instantiations, or may indicate that a large amount of partial, perhaps unnecessary, matching is taking place.

The RHS time for a rule is the sum of the CPU time spent for all firings of that rule. The time spent on the RHS is measured by the total matching time incurred from the actions on the RHS of the rule. The RHS time divided by the number of times the rule has fired gives the average time to fire this rule.

The `timingcau.txt` file lists each rule along the left column, and in the corresponding right column it lists the rules that create or delete WMEs that caused the rule on the left to be instantiated. This report can be used to find the source of WMEs that instantiate a rule, either for debugging or for determining the set of rules that are causing another rule to have a high LHS time.

10.6.3 How to Use the Reports

Using the reports generated by the PME requires more art than science. There are no guaranteed methods of using the PME to enhance program efficiency. The following is a set of steps for applying the results of the PME. These steps, in combination with the rules of thumb for writing efficient rules in Sections 10.3 and 10.4, should give you a basis for tuning a program.

```
Cause report on 21-JUN-1987 14:51:36.21

PRODUCTION NAME                        EFFECTING PRODUCTION NAME


PLACEMENT!NEW-ROOM                     PLACEMENT!NEW-ROOM
PLACEMENT!NEW-ROOM                     PLACEMENT!OLD-ROOM
PLACEMENT!NEW-ROOM                     PLACEMENT!CONDENSE-COMPATIBLE-ROOM
PLACEMENT!NEW-ROOM                     PLACEMENT!MOVE-STUDENT

PLACEMENT!CONDENSE-COMPATIBLE-ROOM     PLACEMENT!NEW-ROOM
PLACEMENT!CONDENSE-COMPATIBLE-ROOM     PLACEMENT!OLD-ROOM
PLACEMENT!CONDENSE-COMPATIBLE-ROOM     PLACEMENT!CONDENSE-COMPATIBLE-ROOM

PLACEMENT!MOVE-STUDENT                 PLACEMENT!NEW-ROOM
PLACEMENT!MOVE-STUDENT                 PLACEMENT!OLD-ROOM
PLACEMENT!MOVE-STUDENT                 PLACEMENT!CONDENSE-COMPATIBLE-ROOM
PLACEMENT!MOVE-STUDENT                 PLACEMENT!MOVE-STUDENT

PLACEMENT!OLD-ROOM                     PLACEMENT!NEW-ROOM
PLACEMENT!OLD-ROOM                     PLACEMENT!OLD-ROOM
PLACEMENT!OLD-ROOM                     PLACEMENT!CONDENSE-COMPATIBLE-ROOM
PLACEMENT!OLD-ROOM                     PLACEMENT!MOVE-STUDENT
```

Figure 10.14 Sample cause report from the VAX OPS5 PME.

1. Order the rules based on their LHS times, and consider those with the highest LHS times first. The definition of a "high" LHS time is an LHS time that is notably larger than the other LHS times in the program. If many rules have relatively high LHS times, look at what they may have in common, such as how they are controlled or invoked. You may decide that changes are required in control technique or representation. Rather than working on each rule, you may want to rewrite the subtask to execute more efficiently.

2. To improve the efficiency of a rule with a relatively high LHS matching time, use the guidelines for writing efficient rules to modify the LHSs or the element class representations. Try adding restrictive tests, reordering condition elements, applying rule decomposition, or making representation changes as necessary on the rules with outstanding LHS times. Remember, it may be appropriate to convert a rule with a very high LHS time into a demon.

3. When LHS times for most rules are comparable, try minimizing the number of firings of rules with the highest RHS times. Focus initially

on rules that fire frequently and have large RHS times. High RHS times may indicate unnecessary changes are being made to working memory, such as removing WMEs that should just be left alone. You may want to try changing a proactive strategy to a more reactive, demand-driven approach.

4. You can use the cause report to find rules that are affected by rules with very high RHS times. To address the high RHS time, try to lower the LHS times of the affected rules.
5. If your attempts to make a rule or group of rules more efficient seem fruitless, consider writing an external routine to replace inefficent rules.

Summary

- Efficiency concerns should be addressed only after a program is correct and maintainable.
- To improve the efficiency of an OPS5 program, we focus on the match phase of the recognize-act cycle, which may account for more than 90 percent of the CPU time in some programs.
- The match phase is implemented by use of the RETE match algorithm, which efficiently matches changes to working memory into changes in the conflict set.
- The OPS5 compiler compiles rules into a match network by first compiling condition elements into one-input nodes, and then joining them together with two-input nodes to form complete instantiations. One-input nodes perform intraelement tests in condition elements, and execute very quickly. Two-input nodes perform interelement tests, and are a potential source of combinatorial problems.
- Match is the process of passing WMEs through the nodes of the network, where they combine to form instantiations of rules.
- Given a picture of the RETE network, we can make inferences about what programming practices make the network efficient, such as how to minimize the time spent in two-input nodes, and how to restrict the size of node memories.
- Decomposition is a valuable technique in solving performance bottlenecks due to combinatorial explosions in rule matching.
- Various myths surround the efficiency implications of the number of rule firings, the use of negated condition elements and variables, the number of rules, and the number of element classes.
- VAX OPS5 provides a rule-timing package called the Performance Management and Evaluation Package (PME). This package enables programmers to identify and understand performance bottlenecks in a VAX OPS5 program.

Exercises

1. Draw the entire match network resulting from the compilation of the following rules.

```
(p  color-regions!tell-neighbor-about-color-change
;
; Use attribute shadowing to propogate a region's
; color to all its neighbor links.
;
      (subtask ^name color-regions)
      (region ^name <changed> ^color <new>)
   { <Neighbor-link>
      (neighbor ^is <changed> ^color <> <new>) }
   -->
      (modify <Neighbor-link> ^color <new>))


(p  color-regions!assign-new-color
;
; Find an uncolored region with the highest
; border count, and color it with a new color.
; Note: This is a general case of assign-unused-color.
;
      (subtask ^name color-regions)
   { <Region>
      (region ^color nil ^border-count <max>
              ^name <next-region>) }
      - (region ^color nil ^border-count > <max>)
   -->
      (bind <new-color>)
      (make color ^name <new-color>)
      (modify <Region> ^color <new-color>))


(p  color-regions!assign-unused-color
;
; Find an uncolored region with the highest
; border count, and a color not used by any of
; its neighbors.  Use that color for this region.
;
      (subtask ^name color-regions)
   { <Region>
      (region ^color nil ^border-count <max>
              ^name <next-region>) }
```

```
    - (region ^color nil ^border-count > <max>)
    (color ^name <free>)
    - (neighbor ^of <next-region> ^color <free>)
-->
    (modify <Region> ^color <free>))
```

If we could assume that there were enough `color` WMEs in working memory to color all regions, how much execution time could we save by removing the rule `color-regions!assign-new-color`?

2. Given the match network in Exercise 10.1, show the contents of the token memories after each of the following rule actions.
   a. `(make subtask ^name color-regions)`
   b. `(make region ^border-count 2)`
   c. `(make region ^name crowded ^border-count 5)`
   d. Fire the instantiation for `color-regions!assign-new-color`
   e. Remove `(SUBTASK ^NAME COLOR-REGIONS)`
3. Refer to the two rules in Figure 10.10:
   a. Show a RETE match network for the two rules.
   b. What would the RETE network look like without node sharing?
   c. How many two-input nodes are added when the second rule is compiled?
4. Knowing that the efficiency of subtask changes, why should you prefer a subtask agenda control strategy over an approach that simply makes several subtask WMEs simultaneously?
5. Suppose that, in tuning a manufacturing-scheduling application, you determine that significant LHS time is spent in the many rules that match `line-item` WMEs. On further investigation, you discover that much of this time is spent unnecessarily, since a few rules are frequently changing the value for the `^status` attribute in ways that are irrelevant to most of the rules matching `line-item` WMEs. How might you change the representation of the `line-item` WME to avoid this problem? What are the potential drawbacks of the technique you suggest?
6. Consider the positioning of condition elements and tests within condition elements in the rule in Figure 10.15.

   Assume we know that

   - There are many more `part` WMEs than there are `line-item` WMEs at any time
   - Only a small number of the `line-item` WMEs have the value `to-be-scheduled` for the `^status` attribute at any time

```
(p  area-schedule!temporarily-assign
;
; Schedule any unscheduled parts of a to-be-scheduled
; line item to their assigned build areas, if there is room.
;
      (subtask ^name area-schedule)
   { <Part-to-assign>
      (part ^area-assignment <area> ^name <part-name>
            ^scheduled nil ^parent-line-item <item>
            ^quantity <to-schedule>) }
   { <Build-area>
      (build-area ^name <area> ^assigned <some>
                  ^max < (compute <to-schedule> + <some>)) }
      (line-item ^status to-be-scheduled ^name <item>)
   -->
      (modify <Part-to-assign> ^scheduled t)
      (modify <Build-area>
            ^assigned (compute <to-schedule> + <some>)))
```

Figure 10.15 Rule for Exercise 6.

Timing CPU report on 15-JAN-1988 13:12:17.87

PRODUCTION NAME	# FIRINGS	LHS TIME	RHS TIME
STARTUP!INITIALIZE	1	3	1
CREATE-OBJECTS!QUEEN	8	4	2
CREATE-OBJECTS!SQUARE	64	3	33
CREATE-OBJECTS!SQUARE-NEW-COLUMN	8	0	2
PLACE-QUEENS!NEXT-UNPROTECTED-SQUARE	113	364	623
PLACE-QUEENS!UNDO-LAST-QUEEN	105	189	551
PLACEMENT!DONE-MOVING-GROUPS	12	0	15
UPDATE-SQUARES!PROTECT-SQUARES-ON-ROW	554	243	385
UPDATE-SQUARES!PROTECT-SQUARES-ON-UP-	303	407	191
UPDATE-SQUARES!PROTECT-SQUARES-ON-DOW	387	463	234
UPDATE-SQUARES!UNPROTECT-SQUARE	740	115	248
EVALUATE-PLACEMENT!SUCCESS	1	3	0
EVALUATE-PLACEMENT!ILLEGAL-PLACEMENT	0	1617	0

Figure 10.16 VAX OPS5 timing report.

- There are more than three `build-area` WMEs
- The `part` WMEs are modified frequently during this subtask

a. Draw a match network for this rule and explain why the rule is inefficient

b. Modify the rule to make it more efficient

7. Given the VAX OPS5 timing results in Figure 10.16, describe a rational approach to making the system more efficient.

CHAPTER 11

Designing an OPS5 Application

IN THESE FINAL CHAPTERS, we discuss the methodology of OPS5 program development: program design, the evolution from a program to a production-level system, and testing. We limit this discussion to the concerns that are unique to OPS5 programs, except when more general topics are necessary to establish a context.

Until this point, we have not distinguished between the different *types* of applications for which OPS5 may be used. We have not stipulated, for example, that an OPS5 program be a knowledge-based or expert system or that it be an algorithmic program of more traditional scope. Since this distinction is relevant in a discussion of programming methodology, we narrow our focus for these chapters. In these chapters, we are concerned with developing programs for the class of problems that have one or more of the following characteristics:

- A large amount of ill-defined knowledge
- A rapidly changing or growing set of constraints
- An algorithmic solution for part of the problem, but a significant number of exception cases
- An algorithmic solution that is too complicated or inefficient to be practical

For problems with these characteristics, the structured design approach to software development is usually inappropriate and is replaced with a rapid-prototyping methodology. Rapid prototyping is an experimental method of arriving at a program design, the user and expert requirements, and an understanding of the domain. A prototype is developed iteratively, starting with limited functionality that is then incrementally refined and increased.

In this and the following chapter, we discuss OPS5 program development using a rapid-prototyping methodology. We do not claim that this is the *only* methodology that can be used to develop an OPS5 program, but we have found that it is a successful one. These chapters point out the principal steps involved in the methodology, and the techniques we have found useful in this process.

11.1 The Order-Scheduling Problem

In this chapter we use a simplified order-scheduling problem to illustrate design and development points. The problem is to schedule a company's customers' orders based on the availability of parts as forecasted by manufacturing. The input to the program is a customer order and a forecast of the number of each of the parts of the order that will be manufactured each month. The output is the assignment of a delivery date for each part on the order, and an updated forecast of part availability (see Figure 11.1).

Customer orders like the one in Figure 11.2 are stored in a database. The order consists of header information and line items. The header information lists the order number, the customer name and address, the date on which the customer requests that the order be shipped, the actual order schedule date, if any, and information about whether the customer will accept delivery of the order in several shipments. The rest of the order consists of a number of *line items*, each specifying the name of the ordered part, the quantity, the parent line item, if any, and the part's schedule date (the date `nil` indicates that the order has not been scheduled). There may be any number of line items on an order, but there is not more than one line item for the same part.

The fourth column of each line item indicates whether the part is a component of a group of parts (called a *bundle*). If the part is a component of a bundle, the fourth column specifies the number of the line that contains the part that names the entire bundle (the *parent*). For example, the order in Figure 11.2 has a bundle in parts on lines 4 through 11, indicated by the fact that the final column for all those parts have line 3 as their parent part.

```
Input: Customer order containing named parts and
          specified quantities of each part.
       A listing of the quantity of each part on the
          order made each month.

Output: An order with delivery dates assigned to
          each part, and for the entire order.
        An updated parts-availability forecast.
```

Figure 11.1 The input to and output from the order-scheduling program.

ORDER#	CUSTOMER	ADDRESS	REQUESTED	SCHEDULED	PARTIALS
1	P&P-INC	BOSTON-MA	JUL87	NIL	NO

LI#	LINE-ITEM	QTY	PARENT	SCHEDULED
1	I884-000-000H	1	0	NIL
2	B187-20010	1	0	NIL
3	I884801-SVH	1	0	NIL
4	I884-005-000H-1	1	3	NIL
5	I884-006-000H-2	1	3	NIL
6	I884-007-000H-3	2	3	NIL
7	I884-008-00NH-5	1	3	NIL
8	I884-009-00NH-6	1	3	NIL
9	I884-010-00NH-7	3	3	NIL
10	I884-011-00NH-8	1	3	NIL
11	I884-012-00H-13	1	3	NIL
12	B187-20009	2	0	NIL
13	B187815-SVH	3	0	NIL

Figure 11.2 An example of a customer order.

A second input to the scheduling process is the data on part availability; these consist of a list of the quantity of each part that will be manufactured each month (Figure 11.3). Each record of this database is called an *allocation*; the entire database contains forecasts of manufacturing allocations for each part for 6 months or more.

Let us suppose that the current scheduling process is performed manually. Past attempts at automating this task have failed because the methods have not been able to incorporate irregular procedures based on customer priorities, rush orders, and special time limits, and because the business processes are constantly changing. The task is to build a system that solves the problem the way the human schedulers do so.

Four heuristics used by the human schedulers are presented in Figure 11.4. The first heuristic applies to a majority of the orders:

1. If there are sufficient allocations, schedule a line item for the requested month.

If the allocation for a part in the month that the customer has requested is not sufficient, then there are two techniques for handling the problem: *partialing* and *moving out.* First the part that is short of allocations is partialed. If partialing is not successful, or if the order-header information specifies no

PART#	MONTH	QTY
I884-000-000H	JUL87	158
B187-20010	JUL87	48
I884-005-000H-1	JUL87	957
I884-006-000H-2	JUL87	99
I884-007-000H-3	JUL87	905
I884-008-00NH-5	JUL87	77
I884-009-00NH-6	JUL87	196
I884-010-00NH-7	JUL87	94
I884-011-00NH-8	JUL87	965
I884-012-00H-13	JUL87	99
B187-20009	JUL87	96
B187815-SVH	JUL87	117

Figure 11.3 Example of allocation records.

partials, the entire order is moved out. Both of these techniques are described in the next sections.

11.1.1 Partialing

A partialed order is one that is delivered to the customer in more than one shipment. The customer must agree that partial shipments are permissible; this

1. If there are sufficient allocations, schedule a line item for the month requested.
2. If you cannot schedule a line item for the requested month, then try partialing that part to the successive month (do this no more than three times).
3. If the customer has not allowed partialing, or if partialing has not been successful within 3 months, then move out the order to the next month (do this no more than three times).
4. Schedule all the items in a bundle in the same month, since the items are assembled before being shipped. To schedule a bundle whose parent is named A and that is made up of parts B, C, and D, schedule the line items B, C, and D, but not A (there are no allocations in the allocations database for a parent part). A is assigned the schedule month of all its components after they have all been scheduled.

Figure 11.4 Scheduling heuristics.

information is recorded in the header information of the order (see Figure 11.2). It is usually easier to fill an order from several months of inventory than it is to do so from 1 month, so the customer receives the completed order sooner if it is partialed. The company has set a limit of three on the number of partial-order shipments (one per consecutive month) that can be made from a single order.

11.1.2 Moving Out

If partialing the order is unsuccessful, or if the customer does not approve partial orders, and there is a part with insufficient allocations in the requested month, then the entire order must be scheduled in a later month. When the date on the entire order is changed to 1 month later, we call this moving out the order. The order can be moved out three times before it is necessary to explain to the customer the delay in receiving the order, and agree on a later request date.

When all the parts on an order have been assigned a schedule date, the order itself is given a final schedule date that corresponds to the last part scheduled on the order. The quantity of each part ordered is then deducted from the allocation in the month in which that part was scheduled.

We have presented a simplified version of the problem. There are several additional scheduling techniques for "problem" orders. There are exceptions and special cases in all the techniques. There are also constraints on how certain parts can be scheduled in relation to other parts. The scheduling problem as described here is useful, however, for the purposes of this chapter.

11.2 Bounding the Problem

A first step in program design is to define your system's boundaries. *Bounding* a problem means performing an analysis that results in limits on your system's capabilities: You consciously decide for or against implementing certain aspects of the problem. Bounding defines a realistic starting point, helps you to manage the complexity of a large problem, and is used for setting the expectations of other people interested in your progress.

Bounding sets limits not only on what the program does, but also on how well it does it. You may choose to implement a program with broad but shallow knowledge, or one that is specialized, with a high level of expertise in a specific area. This distinction is an important aspect of setting user and management expectations, early in the development process, on what the program will be able to do when it is fully functional.

It is important to start with a fairly simple and well-understood aspect of the larger problem; as from there, you can later expand. Bounding the problem defines that perfect kernel within the problem that is small, contained, and amenable to implementation, but that is still meaningful to users and is representative of the larger system.

The scheduling problem has three natural levels of functionality. At the simplest level, the program can schedule orders for which all the parts are available from manufacturing in the month requested. This is a schedulable order without exceptions, and represents the scheduling process for the majority of the orders. Another level handles exception orders—those that cannot be filled in the month that they are requested by the customer. The third level handles problem orders and customer priorities; it is the most complex and difficult to define.

Having defined these levels, we can assess how important each is to the overall functionality, and can then define a reasonable first milestone. How far above and beyond the basic scheduling process—the simplest case—should we first attempt to travel? The use of scripts is one method for bounding the initial functionality of the program.

The *script* is a mock program interaction or program output. You can use a script to illustrate your view of the program's interaction with a user or to show the program's results. A script is a tangible item that can be used to solicit information from a domain expert; a script may stimulate an expert into thinking of situations and countersituations related to the actual or hypothetical cases of the system's proposed actions. It also teaches experts and users about what to expect from the prototype and initial systems. The script is for information gathering and expectation setting; it is only a guide, however, to the final program interface.

A sample script of the scheduling system is shown in Figure 11.5. In this script, the system is proposed to be a batch program that runs nightly, reading new customer orders from an order-processing database, and scheduling each order against an allocations database from manufacturing. The resulting schedule is stored back in the order database and is summarized in the form of the report shown in Figure 11.5.

Scripts are proposed before any code has been designed or written. Revisions to the scripts are made after feedback from the experts or users. Scripts are used during the phase in which the programmer is learning about the domain and the problem, and is defining the entities and relationships to be represented in the program.

```
ORDER 831K-403B
  Customer: AJAX Liquor Store          Request Month:     JUN87
  Address:  111 Main St.               Schedule Month:    JUL87 *
            Armadale, IL               Partials allowed:  NO
  Notes:
Not enough allocations for line item 3 ( 4 VT240-B ) in JUN87
```

Figure 11.5 A sample script for the order-scheduling problem.

11.3 Rapid Prototyping

Several characteristics of OPS5 make it a good language for prototyping. The data structure is simple; all information is mapped into element classes with attributes. OPS5's built-in inference mechanism, the recognize-act cycle, determines how the program executes based on the data; the program code does not have to dictate the control flow. In well-designed OPS5 programs, the rules are independent nuggets of information that are minimally interdependent. You can add and delete rules without disrupting the control flow. For these two reasons, it is possible to write an OPS5 program before you understand the full complexity of a domain, before you recognize an algorithm, and without a complete picture of how the objects in a domain are interrelated and should therefore be represented.

Prototyping is used to test and experiment with both technical and organizational aspects of a program. Technically, a prototype is used to determine feasibility. Is the problem solvable through rule-based technology? Is there an algorithm? Is OPS5 the right language? How much of the problem is it reasonable to expect to automate? How should the problem be bounded? How should the knowledge and control be represented? Prototype development provides answers to many of these questions.

The prototype also starts the often complex process of establishing the role of a new system in an organization. By being involved in the system's early stages of development, the people who will play important roles in the success of the system are identified, and influence the direction of the prototype by their attitudes, opinions and expectations. The prototype is an excellent means of demonstrating to management that a program is feasible and worthwhile, and it can therefore be used to obtain full funding or commitment. Perhaps most important, the prototype serves as a medium through which to set expectations, both of users and of management, about what the program will and will not be able to do.

As a result of bounding the problem, the first step in writing a prototype is the implementation of the problem's simplest significant case. This case should include the crux of the problem, but with as much of the complexity removed as possible. You can demonstrate the overall flow of the program at the same time by building a program *skeleton*. The skeleton is the framework for the system; it contains the control and module structures into which the knowledge can be added later, and it demonstrates how individual modules interact. It contains little or no real expertise, but it provides the structure in which to add expertise.

In our scheduling example, the crux of the problem is scheduling orders using the exception order-scheduling techniques of partialing and moving out. Rules that schedule orders using these techniques could demonstrate the usefulness and feasibility of such a system. The skeleton of the system can "dummy" the subtask that reads orders and allocations from the database by creating sample allocations and orders from `make` actions at the start of the program. Although you will eventually write routines that extract orders from a database, it is not necessary to do so for a skeleton system. Similarly, the subtasks for output can be dummied to produce a simple report, rather than to write these results back to a database.

The life of a prototype can follow one of two paths. Either the prototype provides the basis for and is extended into the final system, or it is abandoned and the lessons learned from its development are used to implement another program, possibly in another language. On the former path, you may refine the design in your prototype until it stabilizes, converging on a model that allows you to integrate the prototype into a real setting. On the latter one, you may find that your overall design is too awkward to extend easily, and that the usefulness of adding new knowledge is outweighed by the difficulty of adding that knowledge. In redesigning the program, you benefit from the experiments with the prototype that have provided a more complete understanding of the domain.

Whatever development path your prototype takes, you should have answered certain questions by the end of the prototyping phase. You should have decided how the problem can be bounded, and how the knowledge and control should be represented in the final system.* The representation of knowledge and control into an architecture is the specific concern of the rest of this chapter.

11.4 Designing an Architecture

The goal of the design of an OPS5 program is to arrive at an *architecture* that can support the program functionality, and, more important, can be later extended for program modifications and additions. We use *architecture* to mean the representation of knowledge, the representation of control information, and the reasoning mechanism used.

When you choose OPS5 as a programming language, one level of architecture decisions have been made for you. You are using rules for representation of knowledge. The reasoning mechanism is the forward-chaining recognize-act cycle.†

Despite the design aspects that OPS5 provides, you as programmer still have a significant task in designing a program. There has been a tendency to oversimplify the design task because a data-driven rule interpreter is *supposed* to be able to arbitrate among rules on its own. But, as Gruber observes,

> Some sources have given the impression that building an expert system is a simple matter of forming IF–THEN rules and giving them

---

*An equally important result of the prototyping phase is the procurement of management commitment if necessary, and of a more thorough specification of the user's requirements.

†Of course, you have chosen forward chaining in only the formal sense of the language. Backward inferencing is still possible by goal-directed forward-chaining rules. See Chapter 1.

> to an interpreter. This is true, in the same way that programming in FORTRAN is a simple matter of writing down lines of code and giving them to a compiler [?].

It is exactly *because* rules are so easy to write and put together in a rule base that careful design and an explicit architecture are necessary. In defining an architecture, you make choices about *how* the knowledge is represented in rules, and *how* the interpreter controls the choice of rules from the rule base. On top of the unrestrictive OPS5 syntax, you devise domain representations, and establish a set of program conventions that organize the data and control in your program.

There are two, sometimes competing, purposes behind the design decisions in an architecture. The first is to make the OPS5 program sound from a software-engineering perspective—to make sure that the system is as fully functional, maintainable, and verifiable as possible. The second, particularly for expert systems, is to create a program whose knowledge base can be augmented easily. The first purpose suggests engineering decisions that stress program modularity and defined data structures and dataflow. The second purpose is concerned with the level of abstraction and generality of the program entities, so that reasoning is done at the level of domain concepts rather than at that of computer implementation. When you keep the internal representation similar to physical reality, it is easier to make incremental additions to expertise and to explain the system's reasoning to a user.

For example, one domain concept is a bundle—a group of line items that are assembled together into a single unit. We can represent a bundle in several ways. We can add a special attribute to each line item that indicates that the line item is a part or a parent of a bundle (`^bundle?`). We can also define a unique element class that redundantly stores which line items on an order work together as a bundle. Or, we could not represent a bundle in any special way; we can just remember that a bundled line item is one that has a number other than 0 as a value for its parent line number. Of these three representations, the first two contain a more explicit representation of the concept of a bundle. If we were to write rules that referred to bundles, these two representations might make those rules more accessible to experts, to developers, and to maintainers of the program.

11.4.1 Designing the Knowledge Representation

The initial design of knowledge representation involves two activities:

1. Defining and naming the important entities in the domain and mapping these entities onto OPS5 element classes
2. Defining the relationships and concepts involved in problem solving that require special programming constructs, and mapping these onto OPS5 element classes and rules

```
;; The number of a line items manufactured in a given month.
(literalize allocation
    item             ; Name of the line item
    month            ; Month of manufacture
    available)       ; Quantity available this month

;; A component or group (bundle) of components on the order.
(literalize line-item
    order-id         ; Identifier of order that owns this
    name             ; Name of line item
    number           ; Line number
    quantity)        ; Quantity ordered

;; A list of line items, request month, and some information on the
;;  customer (header information) that specifies a sale.
(literalize order
    id               ; Unique identifier of this order
    request-month)   ; Date when the customer requested the order
```

Figure 11.6 Initial working memory elements for order scheduling.

The first activity requires that you first begin to understand the relevant terminology of the domain. The terminology often maps directly onto element-class names or attributes. Yet this mapping is often problematic. Is the term a major entity that is independently manipulated, or is it part of the description of a more generalized concept? To answer this question, you must understand the relationship of these concepts during problem solving.

In the order-scheduling problem, for example, we can get a first approximation of the necessary element classes by extracting attribute-value pairs straight from the definitions in Section 11.1. This direct mapping from definitions of domain objects is only a starting point; most certainly it will require modification. Figure 11.6 presents a literal translation of our major terms into element classes. It is clear that an order is a central program entity. But what about each line item of the order? Should a line item be an attribute in the `order` element class or should it be represented by its own element class? The line item is represented as a separate element class here because the scheduling process sometimes requires that line items be manipulated individually.

The second activity in developing a knowledge representation is defining the structures necessary from a programming perspective. This step requires

1. Gaining insight into how problem-solving steps can be expressed in OPS5

2. Choosing which assumptions underlying problem solving should be made explicit in the implementation

In our order-scheduling example, we must somehow express that an order is made up of an ordered list of line items. We have an element class to represent an order, and an element class to represent a line item. How do we express the relationship between the two? An attribute in the `order` element class called `^id` contains a value to identify each order uniquely. Each WME in the `line-item` element class contains the attribute `^order-id` to identify the order of which it is a part. The `line-item` element class also contains an attribute (`^number`) to indicate on which line in the order that line item sits. Membership in an order is therefore established when orders and line items have the same order identifier. Ordering within the order is accomplished with the line number.

It is not always obvious or unambiguous even to the experienced programmer, however, what programming constructs are necessary to represent the relationships required of problem solving. All methods to arrive at these constructs use some amount of trial and error. We present two such methods here: pseudo-rule refinement and the use of decision tables.

Pseudo-rule Refinement

The method of *pseudo-rule refinement* is a way of developing a program's first set of rules. To start, we need a set of initial element-class definitions, such as those gleaned from the domain terminology, and a group of English IF–THEN rules. We call these English rules *pseudo-rules* after their counterpart, pseudo-code, in conventional languages. In pseudo-rule refinement, we repeatedly modify the English rules to reflect the structure of the element-class definitions, and modify the element-class definitions to reflect what is needed to express the conditions in the pseudo-rules. This process should result in an initial set of rules in OPS5 syntax, and in a more complete set of element- class definitions.

To illustrate this method, we use our simple set of "core" element classes from Figure 11.6 and the heuristics of the scheduling process listed in Figure 11.4. The most basic pseudo-rule we can write about the scheduling process is the following:

```
1. If there are sufficient allocations,
   then schedule a line item for the requested month.
```

This rule involves three of our defined element classes: the `line-item`, an `allocation`, and the `order`. We can restate rule 1 in terms of these element classes to make it clear from which class we get each piece of information:

```
1. If you have the order request month,
   and an unscheduled line item of that order with a certain
        quantity,
   and an allocation for that line item and month
        with at least the quantity requested on the order,
   then schedule a line item for its request month.
```

How do we know that a line-item has an unscheduled quantity? Since the entire quantity requested of an item must be scheduled entirely in 1 month, we can add just one attribute, `^schedule-month`, to the `line-item` element class to represent the month in which a line item is scheduled. When that line item has not been scheduled, the value of `^schedule-month` is `nil`.

Now we can convert our first pseudo-rule to OPS5 syntax:

```
(p  schedule-line-item-on-request-month
;
;  1. If there are sufficient allocations,
;     then schedule a line item for the request month.
;
    (order ^id <current> ^request-month <asked>)
 { <Line-item>
    (line-item ^order-id <current> ^name <item>
               ^quantity <qty-desired>
               ^schedule-month nil) }
 { <Allocation>
    (allocation ^item <item> ^month <asked>
                    ^available { <left> >= <qty-desired> }) }
   -->
    (modify <Line-item> ^schedule-month <asked>)
    (modify <Allocation>
                ^available (compute <left> - <qty-desired>)))
```

Assuming we have a suitable initial representation for rule 1, we now try to refine heuristics 2 and 3.

2. If you cannot schedule a line item for its request month,
   and the order can be partialed,
   then try to schedule just that line item in one of the
   3 subsequent months.

3. If you cannot schedule a line item for its request month,
   and the order header says the order cannot be partialed,
   or the line item has been partialed three times,
   then try to schedule the entire order 1 month later.

We consider these rules simultaneously because they are both concerned with the same point in problem solving—when a line item cannot be scheduled in the month in which it has been requested. The first scheduling strategy to try in this case is partialing—try to schedule the line item in consecutive months rather than in the month requested on the order. One rule (rule 2) covers the case in which partialing is allowed; the other (rule 3) covers that in which all the line items on the order have to be rescheduled 1 month later (moving out).

These two rules present concepts that are not yet represented in our element classes:

1. A representation of whether partials are allowed. In the header information in each incoming order, there is a field that indicates whether the customer has approved partial shipment. We can add the attribute `^partials` to the `order` element class.

2. A count of the number of times the schedule month of the line item changes. If partials are allowed, we can try to find allocations for that line item 1, 2, or 3 months later than the current date. An attribute to keep track of the count, such as `^month-offset`, can be added to the line item. The value of this attribute should be initialized to 0.

3. A representation for dates. So far, we have ignored the representation of dates, assuming that they are symbolic values as appear on the incoming data. At this stage in the problem, we discover that we have to change the given months, either the month on the line item or the requested ship month on the order header. For the prototype version of the program, we decide to convert all symbolic month names to integers, so that we can use addition to change to a later month. We can convert months back to their symbolic names for output. Later we may want to write RHS functions that can compare and increment dates, allowing us to revert back to the symbolic representation of dates.

Moving out an order and partialing a line item are two different ways that a month on an order is changed—either the month associated with a line item or the month in the order header. These two month changes must be represented by different OPS5 rules. Rule 2 must be split into three rules. The first rule increments the month offset. The second rule recognizes that the line item has been moved the maximum number of times (three in this case), so that it is necessary to move out the order. The third rule unschedules previously scheduled line items when an order is moved out.

With the necessary additions to element classes, we can make pseudo-rules 2 and 3 reflect the element classes and programming details discussed.

2a. If you cannot schedule a line item for the offset month,
    and the offset month is still less than 3,
    and the order can be partialed,
  then increment the line-item month offset by 1.

2b. If a line-item month offset is greater than 3,
    and the order schedule month has not been moved more
      than three times,
  then reset the line-item month offset to 0
    and increment the order schedule month by 1.

2c. If a line-item schedule month is less than the order schedule month
then mark the line item as unscheduled
and reset the month offset to 0.

3a. If you cannot schedule a line item for its request month,
and the order cannot be partialed
then increment the order schedule month by 1.

3b. If an order schedule month has been moved 3 months beyond the request-month,
then mark the order as a problem order and do not schedule it.

Notice that all these rules rely on our first, general scheduling rule to do the actual scheduling. If one of the exception scheduling rules is not instantiated, then the general scheduling rule does its job.

The scheduling prototype developed in this section, including the OPS5 rules for the rules presented, is listed in Appendix C. These initial rules completely ignore input, output, and control. These issues are treated separately, usually after the representation of the knowledge of the domain is mostly defined.

Decision Tables

Another approach to creating an initial representation and set of rules is to use *decision tables.* A decision table contains a list of program conditions or states and actions. Each rule in the system is represented by marking the states and actions necessary to express that rule.

An example of a decision table for the initial order-scheduling rules is shown in Table 11.1. In the top half of the table, each row represents a unique condition of the problem states in the domain. The rows in the bottom half of the table represent actions. The notations in each column represent the conditions and actions of the corresponding rule named at the top of the column. A Y or an N in the top half of the table signifies the presence or absence of the condition; when nothing appears in a space in the grid, this indicates that the condition is not relevant to the rule. An X in the lower half represents an action to be taken as a result of the existing conditions.

Decision tables are helpful because they force you to define all the relevant conditions and actions of a problem in one place. Decision tables impose a formality to the process of writing conditions that makes the information used in each rule thorough and explicit. They help you to think about all possible combinations of conditions. As a result, the initial rule base is uniform and more complete.

Table 11.1 Decision-table design for the order-scheduling problem.

Rules	1	2a	2b	2c	3a	3b
Conditions						
Sufficient allocations	Y	N			N	
Partials allowed		Y			N	
Line item > 3 later than order			Y			
Order > 3 later than requested						Y
Line item scheduled before order				Y		
Actions						
Schedule a line item	X					
Schedule a line item a month later		X				
Unschedule the line item			X	X		
Schedule order 1 month later			X		X	
Reject the order						X

Decision tables do not, however, provide a method of iterative refinement as pseudo-rules do. The final rules are written directly from the results of the decision tables, and become unwieldy when the number of rules grows larger than 20 or 30. Therefore, decision tables tend to be of limited use in expanding on the initial rules of the system.

It is also difficult to specify some relationships that exist *between conditions* in a decision table. The conditions in the domain must be independent such that relationships are expressed naturally in a single condition element.

Pseudo-rule refinement and decision tables are bottom-up approaches. They allow you to work on a case-by-case basis to grapple with the difficulties of representing specific problem-solving steps. You can share pseudo-rules and decision tables with users or domain experts to confirm your understanding of the problem and to double-check your approach.

Just as vital to the design, however, is the top-down organization of program functionality addressed in the next section. In the early stages of program development in particular, top-down and bottom-up refinement can be approached independent of each other.

11.4.2 Designing the Control Structure

Although we have stressed the importance of separating control from domain knowledge, realistically, this often is difficult to do. Each rule is itself an operator that changes the program from one state to another, and as such contains some inherent control. Many pieces of domain information in working memory also contain indicators used for control. When a line item has a schedule date, for example, that date indicates that it has *already been scheduled*, which is implicit control information. Despite the close connection between domain and control knowledge in OPS5, we can still define an abstract layer of control information. This is the purpose of the previously discussed OPS5 control techniques.

In our discussion of control techniques in OPS5, we have stressed that the control knowledge should be abstracted from other knowledge in the program, represented in as uniform a representation and as centralized a location as possible. When control information is separated from the domain-specific knowledge base and is represented in a declarative form, the way that the knowledge is used is more obvious to readers and to programmers. The flow of control can be determined easily. Ideally, when control information for one problem is separated from the knowledge base, the knowledge base can be used for more than one problem.

We approach the design of a representation for control in a top-down fashion; we consider the overall program, looking for the best ways to divide the large task into smaller functional units. Our top-down approach to program design starts with the most basic division of functional parts. For order scheduling, we first establish a very high-level description of the scheduling batch process, as shown in Figure 11.7. We know that, for most orders, we read the order from the order database (`read-order`), schedule all its line items (`schedule-order`), and then update the order and allocations databases, and write a report of the scheduled order (`write-order`). There is an occasional need to handle problems in an order (`problem`).

Let us review the steps we use to establish these tasks in an OPS5 control technique.

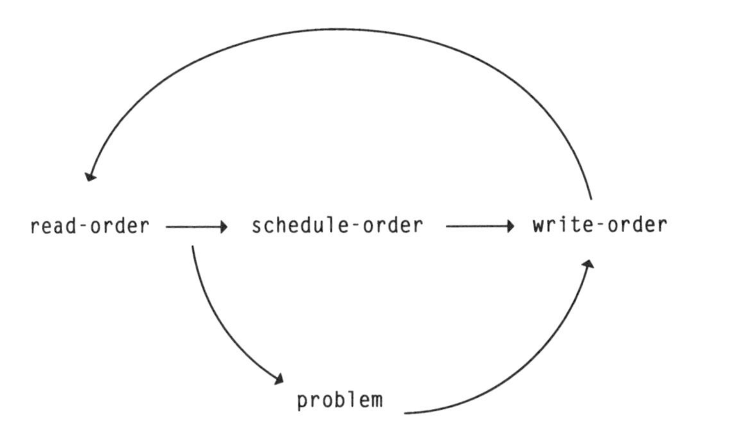

Figure 11.7 High-level control for order scheduling.

- Define and name clusters of rules that work together as complete functional units
- Represent those clusters in an element class
- Create the WME or WMEs for control
- Include rules that direct the flow of control (control rules)

We discuss each of these points as they apply to the order-scheduling problem, with particular concern for developing a technique that is flexible.

Define and Name Clusters

Our first attempt to define functional units may not map onto subtask names that we can use in an OPS5 control technique. The first set may be tasks that are too large to be represented by a single cluster of rules, or too small to merit a separate subtask. You can determine that your subtasks are at the right level of abstraction by concurrent bottom-up rule writing. If rules within a cluster become too numerous, or if they compete for execution when they should not do so, a separate subtask can be defined. Likewise, many single-rule subtasks indicate too fine a level of granularity in naming subtasks.

Let us assume that the modules defined in Figure 11.7 each have a corresponding subtask. Given the subtasks `read-order`, `schedule-order`, and `write-order`, our control technique must cycle through these subtasks for each order. The `problem-order` subtask must be invoked from within the `schedule-order` subtask when an order cannot be scheduled by the usual scheduling rules.

Represent Clusters in an Element Class

The element-class representation you choose for control is based on how subtasks are invoked. If the program uses a sequential list of subtasks, then a simple agenda or subtask stack is sufficient.

Since, in the scheduling problem, we know that certain subtasks are repeated cyclically (for the main `read-order`, `schedule-order`, and `write-order` loop) we represent control information in the following element class:

```
;; MEA control element class
(literalize subtask
        name            ; Name of currently active subtask
        cycle)          ; All subtask names in this cycle

(vector-attribute cycle)
```

The `^name` attribute represents the currently executing subtask, and the `^cycle` attribute holds the names of the rest of the subtasks in the cycle. Notice that this representation requires that the rules in a subtask contain a conditional element of the form (subtask ^name...). We are not writing a representation of a cycle into any of the subtask rules, because this is a structure we may change. All that is important to individual rules is the name of the currently active subtask.

Create Control WME

We create an initial WME for control at the start of the program:

```
(make subtask ^name read-order
              ^cycle schedule-order write-order)
```

Include Control Rules

Figure 11.8 shows a control rule that could loop through any set of subtasks indefinitely. The program ends when a rule in the read subtask detects that there are no more orders to schedule and uses the halt action to stop the program.

Note that this control technique is completely isolated from the subtask rules. This gives us the flexibility to switch easily to other techniques—such as an agenda-based technique—as the prototype matures, without modifying the control elements in all the subtask rules.

11.4.3 General Approaches to Designing an Architecture

It is infeasible to discuss many specific OPS5 architectures. We can, however, identify two common approaches to architecture design.

```
(p  demon!cycle-subtasks
;
;  In general, cycle into the next subtask.
;
   { <Subtask>
        (subtask ^name <done> ^cycle <next>) }
   -->
        (bind <cycle> (litval <cycle>))
        (bind <cycle+1> (compute <cycle> + 1))
        (modify <Subtask> ^name <next>
            ^cycle (substr <Subtask> <cycle+1> inf)
                   <done>))
```

Figure 11.8 Order-scheduling subtask control.

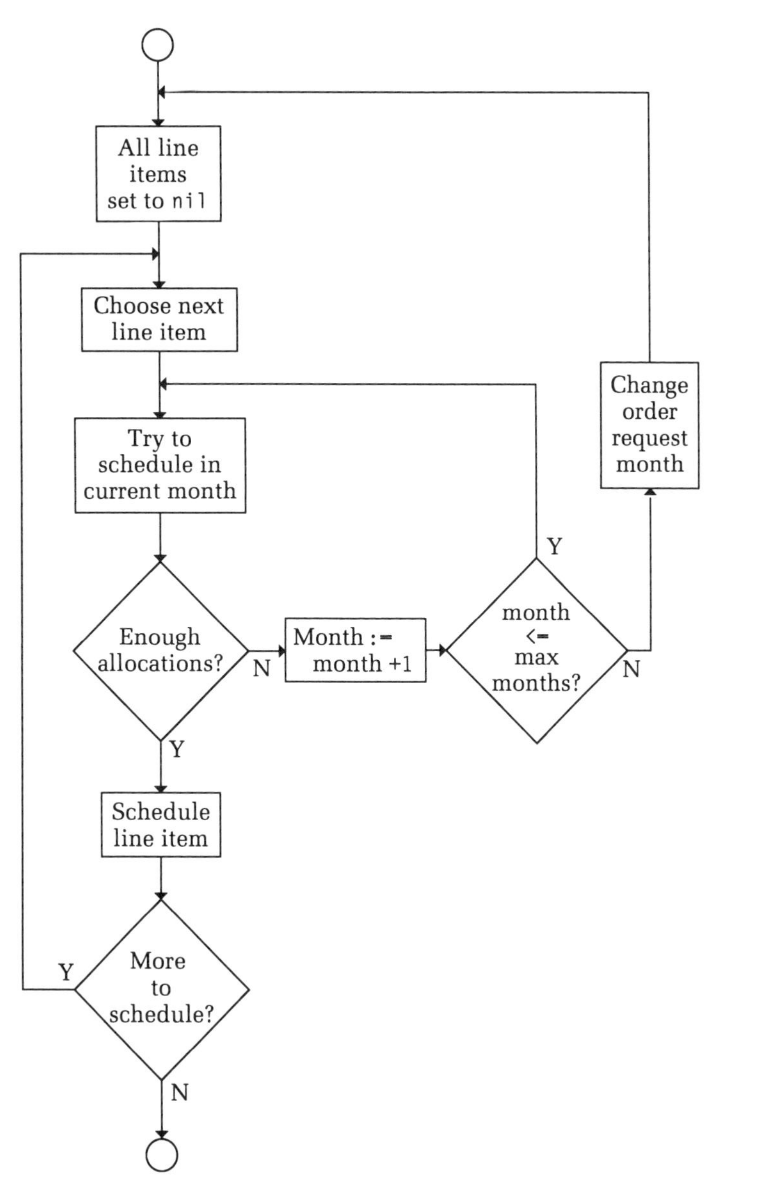

Figure 11.9 A flowchart for the order-scheduling problem.

The first approach is to think of the steps of a problem sequentially, in which each element of the domain or each part of the problem is processed in some order. This type of architecture can usually be represented by a flowchart. This approach applied to order scheduling is represented in the flowchart in Figure 11.9. We schedule each line item individually, choosing line items perhaps by the sequence in which they are written on the order. Each line item that cannot be scheduled in the request month is partialed. When partialing is not successful for some line item, it is necessary to move the entire order to a later schedule date, to reset all the line items to a schedule date `nil`, and to restart the entire process.

Another general approach to an OPS5 application architecture is to assume that the most common case holds, and to use the rules to identify exceptions to that assumption. The use of this approach for order scheduling is represented by the diagram in Figure 11.10. All line items are initialized to the schedule date that the customer requests. This subtask also contains rules that look for specific problems, and that dispatch control to a subtask (if necessary) to alleviate any problems with the schedule dates assigned.

For example, if a line item is scheduled in a month for which there are not sufficient allocations, one rule matches to that case and changes the date on that line item to 1 month later. Note that the program does not check whether this later date has sufficient allocations; it assumes that the date does, and it relies on another rule in the subtask to correct any problems. When the assignment is completed, and no exception-finding rules are instantiated, that task is popped, and the dates on the line items are valid schedule dates. The quantities for each line item can then be subtracted from allocations, and the final schedule date can be put on the top of the order.

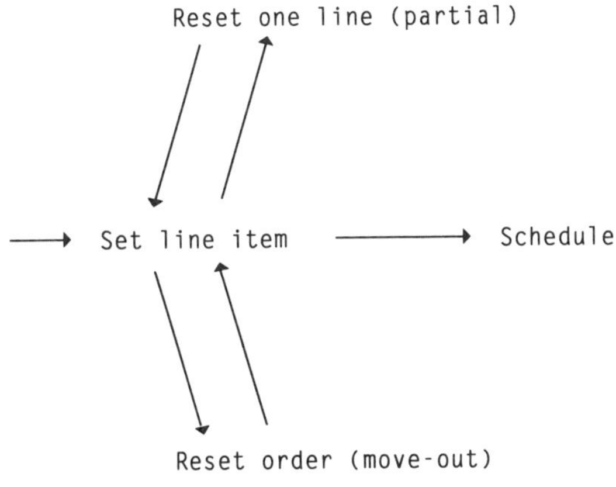

Figure 11.10 The exception-driven architecture for order scheduling.

The second architecture represents a *reactive* design; the first represents a *proactive* design. The reactive approach lends itself more readily to a prototyping paradigm. A flowchart is not necessary; not all elements of problem solving must be incorporated into the original design. The central task (`Set line item`) can be expanded easily by more rules that match to different exception cases. The solution in the reactive design, therefore, is easier to modify.

The reactive architecture also takes better advantage of the data-driven nature of OPS5. It makes use of the fact that OPS5 does not have to search through line items to find those that are not schedulable. The rules that look for scheduling problems are "eyes" onto the simpler scheduling process; they pick out the exception cases.

Summary

- OPS5 can be used successfully for rapid prototyping, which is the experimental method of arriving at a program design, user and expert requirements, and domain understanding.
- Bounding a problem to be coded in OPS5 is the process of deciding what is and is not to be included in the functionality of the program. Script writing is one method for bounding a problem.
- An architecture is a program's representation of knowledge and control, and of the reasoning mechanism used. Although, at one level, these decisions are made in advance for the OPS5 programmer, there are many decisions to be made in devising knowledge representations and control conventions that are essential to the ease of development and maintainability of the program.
- Design of an initial knowledge representation can be accomplished through techniques such as pseudo-rule refinement and decision tables.
- Designing a control structure requires that you define the functional modules that will be mapped onto OPS5 subtasks, and also define how the subtasks will be represented and manipulated.
- Application architectures based on reactive designs are often more natural to OPS5 and more easily extended than are those based on proactive designs.

CHAPTER 12

Building and Testing OPS5 Systems

CHAPTER 11 DISCUSSED the development of an OPS5 program from conception through design and prototyping. At the end of these stages, the system structure should have been solidified, representation issues should have been resolved, and the program should solve real problems within a bounded domain. This chapter addresses the next major step in development—the change from prototype *program* to production *system*. By our definition, this change occurs when the program has to be integrated with other programs or databases, and when it is put to work in the end-user environment.

Priorities and problems change as the program enters production use. The user community changes from a hand-picked group of prototype users who were chosen for their patience and perseverance, to users who require run-time performance, program intelligence, ease of use, and development team responsiveness to problems. The development team must establish a process to acquire knowledge to expand the knowledge base. The changes and additions to the program must be planned and executed smoothly.

This chapter discusses how effective system-evolution strategy, teamwork, tools, and testing can help organize and deploy an increasingly complex rule-based system. With these mechanisms in place, the system has a greater chance of being used for an extended duration, and of being developed and maintained in ways that continually meet users' changing requirements.

Note that the comments and suggestions offered in this chapter are drawn from our involvement in the development of highly complex and growing OPS5 systems consisting of hundreds or thousands of rules. Although this chapter is most applicable to groups developing systems of similar dimensions, all the topics in this chapter are also relevant to smaller systems.

12.1 System Evolution

The following sections discuss various aspects of system evolution to help you make intelligent decisions when planning or designing a potentially large OPS5 application.

12.1.1 Sources of Increasing Program Complexity

When you are planning the development of a large OPS5 system, program complexity is the limiting factor on successful system growth. What is the source of complexity? As the system becomes more expert at its task, the problem solving becomes more complex. The system's knowledge representation and control structure become more complex to support broader and deeper knowledge. The growth in size and scope of the system also introduces complexity into the management of the development task.

This section discusses three perspectives on the changes that take place in the ongoing development of a large OPS5 system—from the program's expertise, its design, and the development environment. These changes reflect the growing complexity of the application and its ongoing evolution.

Acquisition of Expertise

The OPS5 language defines a simple and efficient forward-chaining rule paradigm. A good system design keeps rule dependencies to a minimum, such that extensions are often a matter of simply "adding rules." Control is simple, explicit, and specific, making it easy to add rules in the right place to take effect at the proper time. Although the concept of totally independent rules is never fully realized, OPS5 applications can usually support rapid growth in size—more so than can many other languages. Because of the ease of extension of well-designed OPS5 programs, such programs tend to grow in size and complexity at a surprising rate.

Rapid growth in the rule base implies that there is a rapid acquisition of domain expertise. In knowledge-based systems, it is usually a requirement that the knowledge base grow and change for the system to remain expert, or knowledgeable. As a result, the system can easily outgrow the expertise of any single individual. The complexity of such a system makes it difficult to manage the program as a single entity.

Changes in the Design

When no single person knows the details of the entire system, it is difficult to maintain an accurate and consistent design. There are many modules, created by many different developers, and it is not always clear how they interact. This is especially true of applications written in OPS5 in which familiar software engineering techniques—such as data abstraction, information hiding, and structured programming—are foreign or impractical.

Inevitably, an OPS5 program, like any very large system, outgrows its design. At various times, either part or all of the system must be rewritten. The original design is replaced with new representations of knowledge and control that reflects greater understanding of the program's domain and the need for maintainability. The freedom of developers to create variations of control, representation and approach is traded for an agreed upon, defined structure. Control is made more explicit, and separated from domain knowledge as much as possible. Richer control methods emerge to integrate the components of the system.

Demands on the Development Environment

As the domain expertise increases and the system design becomes more complex, the development environment must grow in sophistication to handle the development complexity. Specifically, certain specialized tools are required to manage the complexity. As in any large application, one or more of the following tools is needed:

- *Source-code management tools* to handle concurrent development of the system by several developers

- *Testing tools* to ensure quality by facilitating the detection and correction of errors

- *Support tools*, such as on-line data dictionaries, specialized database systems or other tools specific to the application, to organize the information used during development

- *System-analysis tools* to track the structure and performance of a rapidly growing system

- *Navigation tools* to help guide developers through the system to points of interest

Explicit coding standards and conventions are also vital to the ongoing development of a large OPS5 application. If many rule writers are adding and modifying rules throughout the system, explicit coding standards for rule format, commenting, and naming are needed to ensure consistency. Conventions that define control mechanisms, attribute usage, and rule interactions help to guide newer rule writers to write well-designed and maintainable code (see Appendix B).

12.1.2 Dynamics of System Growth

One way you can judge how quickly and in what ways a large system will grow is to assess the problem domain's stability. Any domain can be placed somewhere on a continuum from a static, unchanging domain, to a rapidly changing, dynamic domain. Most domains have aspects of both types, but lean toward one extreme. It is important to know how stable your domain is, so that you can answer important development questions, such as how much effort should go into making a flexible design, how estimates of ongoing development costs can be made, and how experienced the development team should be.

When we talk about *domain stability*, we are referring to how quickly the real-world knowledge is changing, not to how quickly our understanding of a domain changes. The latter changes occur for almost all problems and can be accomodated, preferably during prototyping, by changes in the system's design. Only some problems, however, are dynamic in the sense that your most basic *model* of how the physical domain is structured and behaves changes over time. The model that you have of your domain, whether it is implicit or explicit, is expressed in the structures, relationships, and assumptions that have gone into creating a design.

If your domain is in chemistry, biology, or physics, for example, it is unlikely that your underlying model of that world will have to change during system development. In a business environment, however, it is highly likely that the model on which you have structured the problem will have to make significant changes, since it is predictable that business processes and requirements will change.

In this section, we discuss the extreme ends of the continuum of domain stability, which we call static and dynamic domains, and the implications of these types of domains for the development of large systems.

Static Domain

A *static domain* is one in which knowledge, once added to the system, never becomes invalid in the future. Newly acquired domain knowledge can be coded into rules that build on the existing rules. Systems with static domains most often have only a single, all-encompassing problem-solving method. Many diagnostic systems, for example, have static domains.

The number of rules in systems that solve problems in static domains tends to grow linearly. The number of rules continually increases, and the system gets proportionally more competent. Just as the domain is static, so is the system's underlying model of the domain. Such systems tend to have a well-defined structure that does not need much maintenance after full implementation.

Dynamic Domain

At the other extreme, a *dynamic domain* is one in which knowledge is time-dependent. Knowledge is added and then deleted from the rule base. Knowledge in dynamic domains can become obsolete.

The underlying model is constantly changing in a dynamic domain, and this affects the design process. The design of each section of the system is based on a model of the current state of the domain. When that model begins to grow obsolete, the section is often extended in the form of exception rules. Soon the original model becomes so out of date that the exception rules are exercised more than are the rules that implement the original model. The section gets hard enough to extend with exception rules that finally a developer decides to rewrite the section based on a new model of the current state of the domain, possibly using exception rules for handling past, infrequent cases.

The number of rules in a dynamic domain system grows sporadically. The growth of the rule set is periodically interrupted as aging portions are rewritten, since the portions of the system containing many exception rules can typically be replaced by smaller, more concise rule sets that handle the current model. This causes the system suddenly to have fewer rules, after which the number of rules begins to grow again. The goal is to maintain a design that will handle the most common situations by a concise model implemented by efficient rules, with exceptional cases handled by exception rules that may be less efficient and less elegant. Figure 12.1 contrasts the relative growth rates in numbers of rules of systems in static versus dynamic domains. This diagram is exaggerated to show the extreme cases; most real domains have characteristics of both of these extremes.

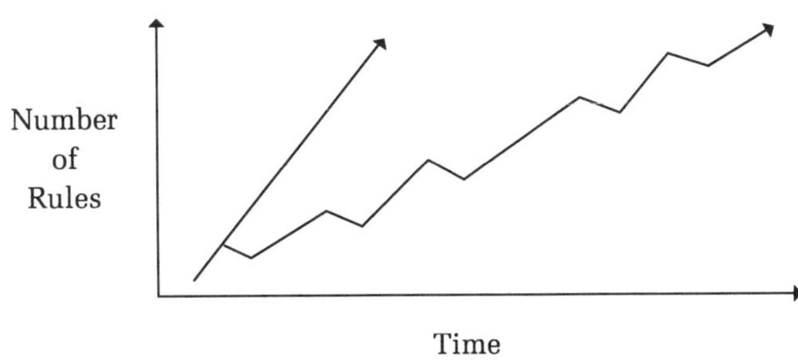

Figure 12.1 Growth of systems in static versus dynamic domains.

A dynamic domain poses a challenge to ongoing system maintenance and development. The main difficulty arises from the need to revise the solution model constantly in a system with a dynamic domain. The developers must attempt to keep the knowledge representation relatively independent of the solution model itself. Ideally, this separation allows the system's control flow to change when the model changes *without* necessitating a massive rewrite of the rules that contain domain knowledge. A development team that has well-developed design skills is needed to maintain systems in dynamic domains.

One good example of a system in a dynamic domain is DEC's XCON program. XCON validates customer orders of VAX™ and PDP-11™ systems by producing a configuration based on the ordered items. The domain is continually changing because of new VAX and PDP-11 system processors, peripherals, and software. Many engineering and manufacturing configuration rules change each time new hardware is introduced. For example, all early VAX system components were configured around the SBI™, UNIBUS™, and MASSBUS™ bus architectures. Newer machines are built around other buses, such as the BI™ and CI™. Since very few machines are sold today with the old bus architectures, the rules that supported configuration with the early bus models are now the exception rules.

The architectural changes required by the change in bus hardware, as well as many others of varying complexity, must be reflected in changes in the configuration models that XCON uses. In early 1985, a senior team member estimated that, each year, 50 percent of the rules in XCON either were new or were modified from the previous year. XCON already had nearly 4000 rules. By 1988 the number of rules in XCON had grown to over 9500.

12.1.3 Procedural Migration

It is common for functionality that is clearly algorithmic or procedural to migrate from rules to external, procedural languages. In the early stages of an OPS5 system's design and development, many design decisions are not resolved. The problem may not be well defined, and many attempts at a solution may be discarded. The flexibility of programming in a rule-based language such as OPS5 will lead developers to use the language occasionally to prototype functionality that, in the long run, is better suited to a procedural language. As the system matures and the problem and its implementation are better understood, however, pruning takes place. Certain subtasks or groups of rules are cut out of the system and are reimplemented in a procedural language to be called from the rules. As a result, the rule-based portion of the program does not waste time providing functionality that is not inherently rule based, and performance is improved. We refer to this process of moving portions of a program from rules into procedural languages as *procedural migration*.

A good example of this migration process took place in XSEL, DEC's eXpert SELling assistant. XSEL is a sister system to XCON. It interacts with the user, most often a DEC salesperson, to specify an initial customer order based on the user's full or partial knowledge of the parts required. XSEL knows what the capabilities of the major parts on an order are, and how to select parts based on the customer's requirements. It forms an abstract model of the customer configuration, ensures consistency of the parts in that model, and communicates with XCON to verify that its model of the configuration is technically correct. XSEL can be viewed as an intelligent front end to XCON for DEC salespeople.

One of XSEL's features is the determination of full part names based on an initially incomplete specification. This is a valuable feature since DEC sells thousands of parts, each with many variations, and each with a unique, and often cryptic, name. During an XSEL session, the user can enter a partial part name, and XSEL will help him to identify the exact, full part specification. For example, he can enter `VT220-BA`, which fully specifies a particular DEC terminal. Or he can simply enter `VT220`, which specifies any of the VT220 family of terminals. If the user is not sure of the family, he can even enter `VIDEO TERMINAL` or just `TERMINAL`, which indicates one of hundreds of terminals.

When given a partial or generic part name, XSEL invokes a rule module that we will call `further-specify`. This module determines the fully specified part name by asking the user discriminating questions. Each question is generated by comparing the candidate set of parts with respect to a distinguishing attribute, such as `screen-color`. When the user selects a preference—for example, `green`—then all VT220 terminals without a green screen are no longer considered. This questioning process continues to prune the candidate set, leaving only those that have the desired features.

Let us look at how parts of the functionality of the `further-specify` module were migrated to procedural code. We can divide the migration process into three steps:

1. Target the rules for which procedural migration should be considered
2. Determine the requirements of the rule base
3. Design and implement the procedural migration

Target the Rules for Procedural Migration

The first step of the migration process is to identify the rules or groups of rules to move into procedural code. There are at least three obvious signs that functionality should be considered for reimplementation in a procedural language:

- *Performance.* A run-time performance analysis, such as that provided by the VAX OPS5 timing facility, may indicate that a set of rules is obviously inefficient, and has an adverse effect on the overall efficiency of the system.
- *Design limitations.* Sometimes when rules begin to stretch their design limitations, it is clear that it is best to revise them in procedural code.

When a solution model becomes obsolete, it may be worth considering it for procedural migration before rewriting it again with rules.

- *Rules mimicking procedural code.* Some groups of rules are simply an awkward rule-based implementation of a procedural function. A set of rules that count certain WMEs from a database, for example, may be replaced by procedural code that counts those items of the database before they are created as WMEs.

The migrating functionality may not initially be implemented in OPS5 as a single subtask. The functionality may be part of a subtask, or may be strewn over more than one subtask in the system. It is best if there is a well-defined point of integration between the migrating functionality and the rest of the system, such as is provided by a subtask name. The more isolated the function, the easier it will be to design a procedural interface for that function.

In the original design of XSEL, the system's database of parts that could appear on an order comprised only a few hundred items. When the `further-specify` module provided a full specification of an under-specified part, the module had to consider only 10 or 20 parts at a time. XSEL read all of these parts from the external database into working memory. There it compared them to one another to determine the discriminating feature questions. Answers to these questions were used to narrow down the choices to the particular part the customer wanted.

As DEC's product set grew, and as XSEL's expertise expanded, XSEL's database of parts grew to comprise several thousand items. Now when XSEL needed to form a candidate set of parts from which to complete an under-specified terminal, for example, XSEL had to create between 50 and 100 WMEs. Because of the unacceptable performance and design limitations that the database retrieval was causing, the `further-specify` module became a candidate for migration to procedural code.

Determine the Rule Base Requirements

The next step in migrating functionality from the rules into procedural code is to determine the role the targeted rules play in the rule base. Before the functionality is moved from rules to procedural code, the following prerequisites must hold:

1. *The basic structure of the rules has been stable.* Whenever you move a section of rules into procedural code, you solidify an integration point that often requires that the problem-solving strategy not change significantly. Rules are almost always easier to change than is procedural code, so they should be at least stable enough to define a solid routine interface. If the basic structure is not stable, then perhaps these rules are not a good choice for procedural migration.

XSEL's strategy of discriminating between parts based on comparisons of their features was an accepted model and had been used for a few years. We thought that it could continue to meet user needs for the foreseeable future.

2. *The functionality of the targeted rules should not still be growing.* It is important to define what portions of the solution have potential for being enhanced by the work of a rule writer. If it is likely that some functionality will increase in scope, then those rules should stay in OPS5, or the interface with the procedural code should be written so that a group of rules can be written to intervene in the results of a procedure, based on new knowledge.

   In the `further-specify` module, some functionality was suited to procedural code and some was more suited to rules. Knowledge about the relevant features of a set of parts, about the default responses that should be provided with questions to the user, and about the best way to proceed through the discrimination questions was kept in OPS5 rules, since this knowledge was most likely to require frequent change. The actual comparison of the features that the user specified, the set of candidate parts, and the pruning of the candidate set were delegated to external routines.

3. *The functionality should be modular.* A section of rules that perform a rather isolated task with a narrow and well-defined interface to the rest of the system is easier to prune out than is a less clearly delineated section. For example, if the task of the rules targeted for migration is to maintain a complex set of relations that is accessed throughout the rest of the system, then it will be more difficult to define an external-routine interface if those relations are moved out into external-routine data structures. In contrast, rule groups that view a limited set of WMEs and make minimal changes are easier to reimplement as external routines. This distinction is important, since it is difficult for OPS5 rules and external routines to use each other's data; OPS5 rules cannot directly access data structures of an external routine, and external routines cannot directly access OPS5 WMEs.

   XSEL's `further-specify` module had a simple interface with the rest of the system. It had one input and one output; it was given an underspecified part name and it returned the fully specified name. Unfortunately, because of the previously mentioned knowledge-engineering requirements, the entire module could not be migrated out of OPS5. A more complex call interface was designed that allowed the major portion of the knowledge to remain in OPS5.

Design and Implement the Migration

Once the rule-based requirements are determined, an interface between the rules and the external routines must be designed carefully.

A good interface design minimizes the changes that have to be made to procedural code. The OPS5 rules retain the ability to do the problem-solving work; the procedures are simply tools that the rules use in applying their knowledge. Procedures should be delegated computational and not knowledge-intensive work. Minimizing the control power of procedures increases system flexibility, since the rules can be modified easily and procedure-call arguments can change, whereas the procedures can remain relatively stable. It is especially important to maintain autonomy of the rules from the external procedures in dynamic-domain systems, where rule-set structure is likely to change often. A good interface protects the more rigid external routines from the instability of the rules.

A good interface design is not necessarily a simple one. A carefully designed interface can often entail a sophisticated set of external routines called from the rule set. For example, if a set of WMEs is being transformed into external-routine data structures, you may need both LHS and RHS routines to access, make, modify, and remove parts of the data structures.

It is important to devote to the task of designing the interface between rules and external procedure someone who is an experienced OPS5 programmer, who is knowledgeable about the system, and who is also experienced in procedural programming languages. The developer needs to bring together all these skills to design a maintainable combination of OPS5 rules and procedural code.

When the interface between rules and procedural code has been designed, its implementation is usually straightforward. Carefully designed procedural migration does not change the structure of the whole system. Rather, it solidifies those parts that are stable and procedural.

In designing the procedural component and its connection to rules in the `further-specify` discrimination module in XSEL, a set of external routine interfaces was used to handle the pruning of the candidate components generated from the partial part name given by the user. From this partial name, OPS5 rules chose a prototype part that was used to provide default responses to questions the system posed. The external routine was then handed a feature and a default value derived from the prototype part. For example, a rule might send the attribute-value pair `^color green`, indicating a green phosphor tube for a terminal. The external routine would make a WME that contained the number of candidates left, the number of unique values for the attribute `color` among the candidates, and a list of those values, headed by the given default value, if that value is present in one of the candidates for the given attribute. The rules would next obtain the preferred value from that set of choices, either by inferring the value or by asking the user. Finally, a call to an external routine would prune those candidates that did not have the required value. This process would repeat until only one part was left in the set of candidates, or until a part had to be chosen randomly from the remaining parts.

This redesign in XSEL vastly improved response time, allowing candidate sets completely out of reach in the previous implementation. Various enhancements have been made to the rules, yet the external-routine interface remained largely unchanged for a 5 year period after its implementation.

12.1.4 Alternative Architectures

Up to this point, we have been discussing systems that are written mostly in OPS5. The "main program," as well as most of the peripheral tasks, is performed by the rules. As an OPS5 system matures, more procedural functionality may be migrated to other languages. This process *distills* knowledge in the rules such that, if the process continues for long enough, the only task remaining in the rules is the decision making. OPS5 programs that make extensive use of procedural code are called *hybrid systems*.

Hybrid systems do not have to be designed with OPS5 at the center. OPS5 rules also serve well as subroutines in largely procedural applications where knowledge-intensive decision making is required. In LISP-based OPS5 implementations, an OPS5 module may be invoked by a LISP program that needs the rule-based paradigm for only a small part of the problem. VAX OPS5 also allows the creation of an OPS5 rule module that may be called as a subroutine by modules written in other languages that conform to the VMS calling standard. Check your OPS5 documentation to see how or whether you can call OPS5 modules as subroutines.

The next step beyond hybrid systems is distributed expert systems. These are expert systems comprising independent expert modules, on a common machine or spread over a network, cooperating with one another to do problem solving. Each expert module acts both as a server, accepting requests from other modules, and as a client, sending requests to other modules when necessary. Together, the modules form a type of *knowledge network* [Lynch 1986].

Distributed expert systems have several desirable features. The delivery environment can be distributed over a network of machines, and each module can have multiple instances. Module redundancy can help to distribute computer resources and to minimize the effects of hardware failure. Although mechanisms are available for building such distributed expert systems, the difficulty lies in the design of each module and of its asynchronous interaction with the others—a topic beyond the scope of this text.

12.2 Organization of Development Teams

One way to combat the growing complexity of a large OPS5 system is to form specialized development teams. *Rule-writing teams* can each concentrate on a major feature or area of expertise in the system. A *support team* can take responsibility for all non-OPS5 procedural programming, including interfaces to traditional databases and systems. This specialization is inevitable once the system becomes too complex for everyone to be equally competent in all areas of the system.

In smaller development groups, the same people often perform both rule-writing and support activities, and the team distinctions may not be practical. Nonetheless, it may be useful to view the team's tasks as separate activities.

12.2.1 Rule-Writing Teams

Rule-writing teams are responsible for the OPS5 rules of the system. They add expertise to the system by extending and adding rules. They also provide the support team with functional specifications of the external routines that they need. Rule writers must have good interviewing and interpersonal skills, since they interact directly with the domain experts and users. Rule writers also must understand the underlying model on which the system's design is based, or at least the model involved in their specialty. The senior rule writers are responsible for the overall design of the system. In many environments, rule writers are called *knowledge engineers.*

There is a danger that members of a rule-writing team will become over-specialized if they concentrate too heavily on only one area of functionality. Without cross-team cooperation during enhancement or development projects, a rule writer's efforts may be too isolated from the development of the system as a whole, or so specialized that the writer's specific knowledge of the system is not reproducible or replaceable.

12.2.2 Support Team

Development of large OPS5 systems involves much more than just the development and maintenance of the rules. There are many tasks that are similar to those addressed by traditional programming teams. These tasks are different from those of the rule writers, especially when the system becomes complex. A separate group of developers, that we call the support team, can be assigned all the responsibilities for system development outside of the rule base.

The support team is responsible for the following areas, to the extent applicable:

- *Development environment*, including the coordination of concurrent development and testing
- *User interface code*, for both the development and delivery environments
- *External, procedural routines*, as requested by the rule writers
- *Database design and maintenance*, as needed by the particular application

- *Integration* with existing systems and *coordination* with the corresponding development groups
- *Delivery environment and architecture*, such as machine tuning, file structures required, and prerequisite software
- *Installation procedures*, for end-user installations
- *Problem-reporting and problem-tracking systems*, especially if the users are directly involved in setting project direction

12.3 Maintenance Tools

This section describes tools that are valuable for rule-writing teams that are developing large systems in OPS5. The tools required for a development effort vary from project to project. We provide an overview of those tools we found most important. These tools are targeted at the development of the OPS5 rules only. Other tools that are used with procedural code—such as problem reporting and project management—although certainly valuable, are beyond the scope of this book.

12.3.1 Interactive Source-code Control

Traditional source-code management tools do not usually provide adequate support for the level of granularity, update activity, and relationships needed in a large OPS5 program.

Rule Level Granularity

Good OPS5 programming minimizes rule dependencies. Each rule is viewed as an independent agent. Rule independence implies that source code must be managed at the level of individual rules. Large applications with thousands of rules require thousands of independently stored and accessed source-code modules, each with an automated edit history.

Rule Access

In addition to high-level browsing of the rule base, rule writers also need fast and direct access to individual rules. The user interface to the source-code management tool should provide a convenient way to browse through the source code and quickly to access individual rules by unambiguous abbreviations.

Hierarchical Relationships

OPS5 source code should be managed as a hierarchy. Rules combine to form subtasks. Subtasks form modules, and modules form programs. Access, reservations, versions, and modification histories may be required at each level.

Sharing Source Code

In larger development groups, there may be several OPS5 systems under development that share source code. Two related systems may share code for one or more subtasks. Perhaps the shared code is WME class declarations, high-level control rules, or some application-specific module. The source-code management tool should be tightly coupled with a system build process to keep track of which systems include a particular module and therefore know that when changes are made to that module, which systems need to be partially or completely rebuilt. Source-code sharing also emphasizes the need for locking at the rule, subtask, and module levels.

The XCON development group at DEC has built and uses an OPS5 source-code database that incorporates many of these features, and that can be accessed remotely from individual developer workstations.

12.3.2 Concurrent Module Development

Each rule in an OPS5 program has unrestricted access to any WME in the system. The OPS5 language does not provide any locality mechanism for WMEs—each WME is stored in a global database, where it can be modified or removed by any rule that matches it. This allows subtasks to be written to take full advantage of program state in deciding what rules to fire.

Because of the global nature of working memory, in many OPS5 applications, particularly in those that experience rapid growth, it is difficult to express precisely program state before and after a subtask executes. In these applications, subtasks cannot be adequately tested separate from the entire system. Subtask testing must take place as part of an entire program execution. When a subtask is tested, errors may not be detected until much later in the run, most likely in another subtask.

For OPS5 applications in which subtasks cannot be tested independently, concurrent development on a centralized version of an OPS5 program is necessary. In this environment, the developers work on a central version where their modifications become immediately available to all other developers.* Concurrent development is possible because OPS5 programs are fairly resilient to many rule errors (see Chapter 6, *Debugging an OPS5 Program*).

Problems of centralized development are exaggerated in a large OPS5 development group by the number of rule writers independently adding to or modifying the rule base. The system continually changes, and tools are needed to manage the compilation of developer modules into the central version.

Concurrent, centralized development requires both source-code management and automated compilation management. Developers need an environment in which they can reserve a subtask or individual rules, make changes,

*Usually, source code that is shared in a central version becomes accessible only when that code has met minimal acceptance criteria defined by the development group.

compile and test these rules in the context of the rest of the system, and perform these tasks concurrently with all other rule developers in the group.

In addition to a source-code database, the XCON development group has developed and uses a tool for managing the compilation of OPS5 code modules for a centralized development environment. Rule writers reserve rules from the rule base, make modifications, and then submit the modifications for compilation. Compilation requests from all the developers are queued to a batch job dedicated to recompiling and linking parts of the system. Compilation messages and errors are relayed back to the appropriate developers. When a major run-time error occurs, a developer can identify the problem rules and queue the previous, working version of those rules for compilation. Then, the other developers can continue their work while the problem is investigated.

12.3.3 Source-Code Analysis

When there are too many rule writers to maintain an accurate and up-to-date picture of the system, more sophisticated tools may be necessary. These tools analyze source code and associated databases to help the senior rule writers know when portions of the design are aging, how well redesign efforts are working, or when standards and conventions are not being followed. Some designs may also allow for specialized tools that look for inconsistencies and incompleteness in logic, and for potential control problems.

The XCON development group has a small set of analysis tools that provide a high-level snapshot of the system. These tools are used not only for checking the current design of the system, but also for facilitating training of new knowledge engineers in the group.

One tool maps the control paths in the system. It figures out what the subtasks are and where and how they are invoked. Output from this tool can be in the form of a graph, a spanning tree, or a cross-reference listing. From the graphical output, a developer can glean information about the depth of subtask activation, the overall program flow, and the relationships among specific subtasks.

Another tool used by the XCON group monitors the use of attribute's values in an associated external parts database. It knows the relationships between attributes of various elements and ensures that constraints are not violated. This tool, written in OPS5, maintains a degree of integrity within the XCON parts database, which contains over 30 thousand part descriptions.

Another useful tool, especially for training new developers, analyzes the rule base and outputs descriptions of the use of element classes and associated attributes in the system. It does not enforce type checking, but rather derives descriptions of an attribute based on observing the attribute's use in the system. For example, it may report that certain attributes hold only numeric values greater than 0. It also prepares a list of all the values that have been used with an attribute by rules in the system.

The XCON group also benefits from a tool that checks that rules obey the group's established OPS5 programming conventions. For example, rules are checked for variable-naming conventions, attribute usage, and conformance to certain semantic restrictions. This tool can be used interactively or can be integrated with the concurrent compilation manager or the source-code database to filter out errors before they become part of the central development version.

12.3.4 Intelligent Rule-base Editor

To help ensure standard coding practice and to minimize syntax errors, an intelligent editor is vital. This is especially true if the group is working on a central development system with no rule-checking filters, in which syntax errors during compilation may waste the whole group's time rather than just that of a single developer.

A straightforward approach to an intelligent rule-based editor is to program a customizable editor such as Emacs or VAX TPU™, or to use a language sensitive editor specific to OPS5. A customized editor is probably the best tool to use, since it can include both language syntax and the group's standards and conventions.

It is also important that the editor have an interface to the rule base. XCON developers do most of their development work on individual VAX stations™, with an experimental window-oriented VAX OPS5 environment, complete with a customized editor that communicates transparently to a remote centralized rule base.

12.3.5 On-Line Attribute Dictionary

As a system grows in size, so does its representation. The element class declarations become too numerous to keep track of manually, and the precise meaning of an attribute is easily lost. Semantic consistency in the purpose of attributes may be lost among many developers.

Attribute semantics should be documented explicitly and consistently. It is preferable to keep the documentation on-line, so that it is always readily available to developers. All element classes and their attributes should be liberally (and correctly) commented and kept up-to-date.

12.4 System Testing

Testing is clearly an important step in building any system. Testing ensures that users and management have confidence that the system does the task it is supposed to do, and that it passes the user's formal or informal acceptance criteria. Satisfaction of these criteria should result in a useable system that is perceived as being of good quality.

Unfortunately, software testing is particularly troublesome in many OPS5 applications. The problem is due both to the nature of the tasks commonly solved by OPS5 applications, and to the nature of the OPS5 language itself. These tasks are usually difficult to specify exactly, and the results are hard to label as simply right or wrong. The data-driven nature of the language complicates the analysis of the behavior of the rule base.

In this section, we discuss the problems of testing OPS5 applications and suggest some alternative techniques to traditional software testing. We make the assumption that OPS5 is being used for domains that are ill-structured and knowledge-intensive and for which programming begins before the domain task is completely specified. Without this assumption, some traditional testing methodologies would work, although the nature of the OPS5 language also contributes to testing difficulties. Our primary focus in this section is successful testing of OPS5 rules despite the use of an iterative, prototyping methodology.

Each OPS5 application presents its own testing difficulties based on how OPS5 is used and on what the application domain is. There are no magic, generally applicable solutions. The techniques presented in this section have been used effectively in industrial knowledge-based systems, and provide a starting point from which you can develop your own testing strategy.

12.4.1 The Difficulty of Testing

The first step in avoiding testing difficulties is to understand *why* it is difficult to test. There are three reasons:

- Without a functional specification, it is hard to know what to test
- Traditional techniques are not sufficient
- Evaluating test results after testing is complicated and costly

Lack of Functional Specification

Software testing usually relies on an explicit, detailed functional specification of the system. The functional specification, written before programming begins, determines exactly what the application is and is not supposed to do, and forms the basis of correctness and completeness testing.

For most OPS5 domains, however, it is futile to try to produce a detailed specification prior to programming. Exploration of the implementation of domain concepts can happen concurrently with the exploration of the domain. If a document of system functionality is necessary, it must be sufficiently abstract about the system's capabilities that maintaining the document is not as large a job as is maintaining the program. The more abstract the specification, the less useful it is as the basis of testing criteria.

Domains that evolve differently will differ in how amenable they are to being documented by a functional specification. The functionality of dynamic domains must continue to change to keep up with changes in the real world. A functional specification of such a system may never be worth the amount of effort required to keep it accurate. The system itself with the documentation of the code is a *living specification* of what the system can do at any point in time.

Static domains, although slightly more amenable to specification, still present problems. Static domains eventually reach a point at which their *functionality* is bounded and can be documented. The *knowledge* used to accomplish this functionality, however, still grows over time. A functional specification can be written, but it requires constant maintenance to reflect accurately the ability of the executing system.

Without a functional specification, there is no reference or standard against which to test. When there is no specific agreement as to what the system's task is, it is difficult to develop the test cases that demonstrate that functionality. It is extremely difficult to know whether testing is complete.

Interactive systems suffer even more from the lack of a specification than do noninteractive systems. When the knowledge in a system is constantly changing, the system responds to user interactions in changing and—as it may appear to the user—unpredictable ways. The testing process is then complicated because two functions must be evaluated simultaneously: the interactions with the user and the final result of the execution. Users tend to be critical and subjective in evaluating a user interface, and it is difficult to get users, experts, and developers to agree on acceptable interactions, particularly when no functional specification is available.

Difficulty of Using Traditional Testing Techniques

Software engineering has provided software developers with many techniques for effectively developing and testing complex software. Although we cannot examine all these techniques, we can evaluate the usefulness of applying some common testing techniques to OPS5 programs. In this section, we consider the use of

- Regression testing
- Complexity measures to determine testable unit size
- Unit testing

These techniques fail for reasons that are similar to the reasons why all traditional testing techniques are less effective when used on OPS5 programs.

Regression testing is a general technique for ensuring that new development work has not inadvertently corrupted previous functionality. An initial base test set is created that exercises the first capabilities of the prototype. Whenever the prototype is extended, new test cases are added to the base test set, forming an extended test set. The results of running the base test set and of running the expanded test set are compared. The only differences should be the results of the new test cases; the results of all tests shared by both test sets should be the same. After the results are compared and any differences are resolved, the base test set is discarded and the extended one becomes the new base test set.

The utility of using regression-testing techniques for OPS5 applications depends on the dynamics of the domain. Regression testing is easier to apply to stable domains than it is to dynamic ones. The knowledge in a static-domain application can be tested incrementally as it is added to the system; the results of the test set should remain stable as well. In a dynamic domain, however, it is not possible, and it is usually not desirable, for the results of a current test set to match the results of an earlier one; the system is *expected* to produce different results. Evaluating the new results of the test set becomes very difficult. Each disparity between the original test results and new ones must be evaluated. Is the new result the correct handling of a new problem? The correct handling of an old problem but with new knowledge? Is it an error? If so, why? Because the test case should have produced different results in the new system (knowledge has become obsolete)? Because the system has incorrect knowledge? Because knowledge is missing? The maintenance of the test set becomes a project in itself; a substantial commitment of time and resources is necessary for regression testing to play a significant role in testing a dynamic-domain application.

Complexity measures determine the relative complexity of source-code modules. A development team can agree on a maximum complexity number for all modules, so that each module is of limited enough complexity to be adequately tested.

One measure of the complexity of a source-code module is an enumeration of the number of unique control paths that can be exercised in that module. A control path is the set of branches that can be taken through an executing program. Each branch of a conditional statement in a sequential program, for example, represents a different control path. Modules that contain more conditional statements are more complex than are those with fewer conditionals. Although it is impractical to test every control path in a complex application, it is usually possible to bound the complexity by defining modules with a small set of control paths, and to develop tests that exercise the most important ones.

Independently testing program modules before integrating them together is called *unit testing*. For unit testing to be successful, the behavior of these modules must be completely specified; both input and output specifications must exist.

Unfortunately, complexity measures and unit testing are problematic when used with OPS5. First, complexity measures determined by the control paths through an OPS5 program show that it is difficult or impossible to identify modular, testable units. Whereas it is possible to divide a typical sequential application into modules based on a few conditional statements, comparably-sized OPS5 applications cannot be divided easily (Figure 12.2). Each rule in an OPS5 program is a decision point. An *N*-rule application can take *N* control paths at each rule firing. The rule clustering of the control techniques introduced in Chapter 5 limits the number of control paths somewhat, but it is

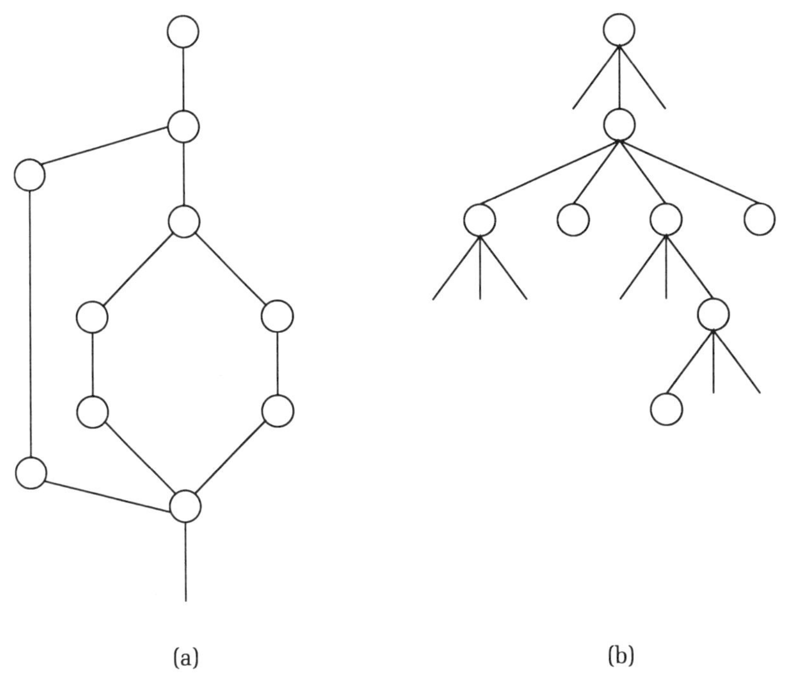

Figure 12.2 Typical control paths in (a) sequential applications and in (b) OPS5 applications.

still infeasible to devise tests that execute every control path within each rule module.

Unit testing of OPS5 applications may also be problematic because it requires that modules have completely specified input and output. Since OPS5 rules have access to all WMEs at all times, and can change working memory freely, it is rare to be able to specify the working memory states that exist when the rules are invoked and exited.

The specifications necessary to do unit testing also impose limitations on how rapidly the rule base can change. When a set of rules meets the specifications of unit testing—that is, there is a stable set of rules with definable input and output—this often indicates that the set is a good candidate for procedural migration out of OPS5 rules (see Section 12.1.3).

Section 12.3.2 discussed these problems of unit testing in the context of subtask testing.

The Difficulty of Evaluating Test Results

Suppose that, despite the difficulties of applying traditional testing techniques, we have defined a set of tests and a testing strategy for our application. Our testing plan is not complete, however, until we also define how the test results are evaluated, and what actions may be taken in response to that evaluation.

A fundamental requirement for evaluating test results is that one can distinquish between correct and incorrect behavior. An OPS5 application often cannot meet that requirement. Without a functional specification, and especially within a dynamic domain, there is no a standard or set of reference cases against which to verify the software.

The result of an OPS5 program is likely to fall into the category of "satisfactory" rather than "optimal." There is usually more than one satisfactory solution, and it is not usually practical to enumerate all satisfactory solutions in advance. Determining whether a solution is satisfactory therefore may require the judgment of someone knowledgeable of the domain.

Unfortunately, not even an expert may be able to determine whether a solution is definitively correct; sometimes experts disagree. One expert may judge the result to be satisfactory, whereas another may think that a modified solution would have been better. Experts may disagree on which result they prefer, even if the results produced are all acceptable to all of them.

If a solution is judged to be satisfactory, it may also be necessary to determine whether the solution was concluded for the right reasons. The reasoning used to derive a result may be just as important as the result itself, particularly if a criterion for the system's success is that users understand why an answer is correct. In addition, despite correct results in one case, faulty reasoning can cause unsatisfactory results in other cases. Problems with the reasoning used to derive a result can easily go unnoticed if the testing strategy concentrates on only the application's final result. An explanation capability helps the programmer to uncover this type of error, and is essential in systems in which the user requires additional support for a conclusion.

If a solution is determined to be *un*satisfactory, it is often necessary to know *why* the result is rejected. Is it "incorrect" because the test case exercised functionality that was not yet in the program? Was this missing knowledge, or knowledge that should be considered in only a later enhancement, or a "wish list" item that is beyond the scope of the project?

In any single test of a complex system, there may be many components of a single result. The final output can contain many interrelated details, each of which needs verification; some will turn out to be correct, and others will not. In systems such as these, there is no clear division between satisfactory and unsatisfactory. Instead, it is necessary to establish a "grading" of the application, and to determine the cutoff between an acceptable and unacceptable grade.

In a configuration system, for example, many components are interdependent. Although the system may never configure all the components properly, it may reliably configure some percentage of the components. But where is the line between "acceptable" and "unacceptable"? If there are 100 components on the output, is the run acceptable when 90 pieces are judged satisfactory? When 50 are satisfactory? Clearly not all pieces of output can be weighted equally. Some errors are more important than are others. Is the system acceptable when the five most important components are configured correctly, even if the majority of the other 95 are not? How do you determine what an important component is? Do you consider component cost? These are the types of questions the programmer, users, and domain specialists have to answer if they are to understand the grading of the application.

When it is difficult to determine the validity of a test result, it is necessary for the evaluator to have a thorough knowledge of the domain. The evaluation of complex system results can therefore be quite costly. High evaluation costs require decisions that limit the amount of testing to produce only what can be evaluated realistically. It is senseless to generate and run 1000 tests if you can evaluate only 100 test results.

This section should have convinced you that testing OPS5 applications of knowledge-intensive, dynamic domains is problematic. Without detailed specifications, it is difficult to determine what to test for, and conventional testing practices—such as regression testing and unit testing—are of limited use. Finally, once a testing strategy is developed, it does not solve the problem of how to evaluate difficult test results that are not clearly right or wrong.

12.4.2 Successful Testing Techniques

The difficulties of testing an OPS5 application all point to the need for some innovative testing methodologies. Perhaps the most important element in the methodology is an established standard against which to grade the application's results. Everyone involved in an OPS5 application—the developers, the users, the domain specialists, and management—must be involved in deciding how the system is to be graded and judged.

Establishing Testing Goals and Criteria

Although we have emphasized the difficulty of producing and maintaining a functional specification of most OPS5 applications, it is important that there be a document that reflects the expectations of all people involved with an application. This document probably will not be generated before the program is developed, but, like the program, will be constructed iteratively. Decisions on what functionality the program will and will not incorporate, how a system will be graded, and what the definition of an acceptable grade is are best specified in writing. A desired result of testing, or the standard, should be established.

It is important for everyone involved to agree on how tests will be evaluated. As early as possible, the developers, users, and domain specialists should agree on specific evaluation criteria that are as objective and reasonable as possible.

These criteria should focus on the usability of the system, not on detailed perfection. Remember, the goal is for overall performance to be satisfactory, not optimal, since optimal performance may not be attainable. Involve everyone concerned with the system in the decision about evaluation criteria. The risk of misunderstandings later in system development is minimized when more people are involved early in the development of the application.

Once an evaluation method is established, the group can begin to define acceptance requirements. Decide on a grading strategy that puts more weight on correctness in the important cases than in the unusual and infrequent situations. Distinguish between fundamental and trivial errors. Factor in the different costs of different types of errors. Try to determine the value of results that include an error. Make sure the group answers detailed, difficult questions such as the following. How should a result be evaluated if, during processing, the system said that it was "unsure" of something? If there is an obvious run-time error, under what conditions is the output still useable? If there is one unuseable portion and there are 99 useable portions in the output, has the application met your acceptance criteria?

An important aspect of test evaluation is setting expectations of users and other people about what the system will and will not be able to do. Unrealistic publicity about rule-based systems and their capabilities may make people's expectations about your application impossible to satisfy. Therefore, set early and realistic acceptance requirements, and be specific. Imprecision in these requirements can cause misunderstandings later. Regular progress reports to management and to users as the prototype is developed may help to maintain accurate expectations.

Generating and Maintaining Test Cases

It is helpful to devise tests that are representative of the volume of actual cases. Two good sources of test cases are:

1. *Historical cases.* These are test cases and results saved from a previous problem-solving approach. Sometimes, these cases need modification to fit the capabilities of the system.

2. *Test cases currently being solved by some other method.* If the problem is currently being solved by some other method, whether completely or partially manual, the OPS5 system can try to solve the problems concurrently with the other method. The results of the two methods can be compared.

Because of the time and effort involved in managing a test set for these applications, you should strive to keep the test-set size small. Reviewing test results, pruning and combining tests, and removing obsolete tests, cannot be done carefully if the test set grows too large.

Take the time to review the test set periodically, combining similar tests and pruning the less important ones. Try to manage the regression test cases along with the code. You can identify tests with rules or modules by comments in the software, so that, when the software changes, the developer will become accustomed to modifying tests along with the software.

Using Traditional Testing Techniques

Despite the associated problems, a testing strategy should make the best possible use of traditional testing methods.

Regression testing can be used to the extent that the set of test cases can be maintained and the results carefully evaluated. Some of the maintenance of the test cases can be automated. An effective test-management system simplifies the task of creating tests, scheduling test runs, executing test cases, detecting when output changes occur, and distributing results to the appropriate developers. In addition, tools may be written to analyze rule-firing trace files to ensure that the base regression test set is exercising the entire rule base.

In applications where independent unit testing is impractical, subtasks must be individually tested within the context of the entire application. A test input is then a working-memory state prepared by interaction with the parts of the system that execute before the subtask being tested. Test results are determined largely by the behavior of the code executing after the subtask being tested. This modified form of unit testing is called *integrated unit testing.*

Because integrated unit testing depends on other parts of the application to produce test cases, it is preferable to perform the testing in a concurrent development environment (see Section 12.3.2). Concurrent integrated unit testing would normally be impractical due to the instability of each unit. However, as discussed in Chapter 6, because an error in an OPS5 rule may simply cause the program to take another path through the system rather than to halt, the benefits of concurrent integrated unit testing seem to outweigh potential instability. Since some errors affect working memory in ways that do not affect the unit being tested, there is no way to know whether working memory has been corrupted except to run the unit test within an entire application run.

Testing External Routines and Routine Interfaces

External routines written in procedural languages can and should be tested in a conventional manner. This includes testing the interfaces between the rule base and the routine, as well as performing unit testing on fully specified code modules.

Interactive Testing

Users are especially important for testing interactive programs. A group of "naive" users—people who do not know what to expect the system to be able to do—can exercise many of the paths through the system, both anticipated and unanticipated. Provide these users with an on-line commenting facility through which they can communicate problems and suggestions to developers at any time while they are using the system. Have this commenting facility thoroughly log the user's problem and the state of the system at the time of the report, so that developers can re-create the situation and resolve the problem. Some applications may require that the entire interactive session be saved when the commenting facility is used to report a problem.

Automating Testing Tasks

In addition to managing regression testing and getting feedback from users, there are a number of software solutions to testing and to quality maintenance.

For some domains, it is possible to write rules that recognize cases that are at the limits of the system's reliable expertise. In these cases, the system either can decline to provide an answer, or at least can warn the user of the likelihood of errors from that point. These messages accomplish two purposes. First, they assure the user that the system acts "rationally" even in cases on the fringes of its expertise rather than just halting or producing an ignorant result without warning. Second, these messages also help the developers to focus their efforts on improving the system for the more common problems, while depending on the system itself to tell the user when the unusual case arises.

Assumption-checking rules (see Chapter 6) can be included to check for internal consistency in working memory. These rules are typically demon scouts that look for problems, and invoke specific subtasks to rectify those problems. We have had the most success with assumption-checking rules in applications that depended on real-time data or asynchronous interrupts, where session logs were not adequate to reproduce the problem. In some cases, rules can be written to be diagnostic, even to the point of detecting the inconsistency and correcting it. For example, a demon rule can match to inconsistent values in working memory, and can delete one of these values before the corruption spreads in working memory.

Explanation facilities may also play an important role in ensuring system quality. If a system can give an explanation of the reasoning it used to arrive at a decision, it is easier for developers or users to pinpoint faults in that reasoning.

Summary

- Significant expert systems have unique development needs driven by the complexity of the system's expertise, its design, and its development environment.

- It is important to determine the stability of the domain (static versus dynamic), to help plan system development efforts.
- Large OPS5 applications undergo an evolutionary process in which procedural rules are rewritten as external routines written in procedural languages.
- Beyond procedural migration, OPS5 modules may be used in hybrid systems and in distributed expert systems.
- The distinction between rule-writing and support-development tasks highlights the range of skills required by an effective development team.
- Rule-writing teams benefit from specialized tools to support OPS5 development, such as those that perform interactive source-code control, concurrent module development, and source-code analysis, as well as editors and attribute dictionaries specific to OPS5 and to the application.
- Testing is performed to ensure that the system does the task it is supposed to do, does the task correctly, and passes the criteria for useability.
- Software testing can be particularly difficult in OPS5 applications written in a prototyping development environment because of the lack of a functional specification, of problems with using traditional testing techniques, and of the difficulty of evaluating test results.
- One of the most important aspects of developing a testing strategy is to include everyone involved in the application in decisions concerning system functionality, evaluation and grading criteria, and a definition of acceptable results.
- A successful testing strategy encompasses an appropriate mix of traditional testing techniques, an integrated commenting facility, and the use of rules in the system itself to provide explanations of its reasoning and to monitor decision making and internal consistency.

APPENDIX A

Comparison of VAX OPS5 with a Public-Domain OPS5

SINCE THE PUBLICATION OF *The OPS5 User's Manual* by Charles Forgy in 1981, [Forgy 1981] many implementations of OPS5 have become available. Although there is no official language standard, Forgy's document has become the de facto standard description of the OPS5 language. The FRANZ LISP version* described in that manual, and various translations of it into other LISP dialects, are available and in the public domain. In addition to the public-domain (PD) implementations, application developers can also purchase OPS5 products offered by various vendors. These products boast advantages over PD OPS5 implementations, such as higher execution speed, less memory, sophisticated development environments, and the ability to run on a variety of machines from PCs to mainframes.

Our experience in developing large OPS5 applications has been primarily with DEC's VAX OPS5 product. Several of our applications began in a LISP-based PD OPS5 implementation before DEC had an OPS5 product. As the applications continued to grow, execution speed, memory requirements, and support became serious concerns. The current VAX OPS5 product compiles rules into VAX-native object code, eliminating the memory and execution time overhead of the LISP environment required for the PD OPS5.

---

*In this appendix, we refer to this version as PD OPS5.

In this appendix, we briefly compare and contrast VAX OPS5 V2.1 with the PD OPS5 defined in Forgy's 1981 user manual. Our discussion also allows you to compare VAX OPS5 with other familiar implementations. Most OPS5 products include a comparison with Forgy's manual. It is outside the scope of this book to attempt a comparison of all OPS5 products currently available.

Following is a simplified BNF description of the syntax of both PD OPS5 and VAX OPS5 V2.1. A plus (+) indicates that the preceding symbol may appear one or more times. An asterisk (*) indicates that the preceding symbol may appear zero or more times. A vertical bar (|) separates disjunctive clauses. Features that are specific to VAX OPS5 are shown in italics. Following the BNF are brief descriptions of the major differences between VAX OPS5 and PD OPS5. You can find a complete description of the VAX OPS5 product in the associated product documentation.

program ::= language-construct+
language-construct ::= (p symbolic-atom lhs --> rhs)
  | (external symbolic-atom+)
  | (initialization symbolic-atom)
  | (literal literal-pair+)
  | (literalize symbolic-atom+)
  | (vector-attribute symbolic-atom+)
  | (catch *symbolic-atom rhs*)
  | (startup *startup-action+*)
literal-pair ::= symbolic-atom = number
startup-action ::= action
  | (@ filespec)
  | (disable message-class)
  | (enable message-class)
  | (run optional-number)
  | (strategy strategy-type)
  | (watch number)
  | (watch)
message-class ::= warning | halt | back | timing
strategy-type ::= lex | mea
lhs ::= pos-ce condition*
condition ::= pos-ce | neg-ce
pos-ce ::= ce | { ce-var ce } | { ce ce-var }
neg-ce ::= -ce
ce-var ::= variable
ce ::= (lhs-term+)
lhs-term ::= ^non-float-constant lhs-test | lhs-test
lhs-test ::= lhs-value-test | conjunction
lhs-value-test ::= disjunction
  | predicate lhs-value
  | lhs-value

```
lhs-value           ::= atom | lhs-function
conjunction         ::= { lhs-value-test* }
disjunction         ::= << atom+ >>
lhs-function        ::= (compute expression) | user-defined-function
predicate           ::= < | <= | <=> | = | <> | >= | >
atom                ::= numeric-atom | symbolic-atom | variable
                              | constant
numeric-atom        ::= integer-atom | float-atom
non-float-constant  ::= symbolic-atom | integer-atom
constant            ::= symbolic-atom | numeric-atom | float-atom
rhs                 ::= action*
action              ::= (bind variable rhs-term*)
                              | (build rhs-term+)
                              | (call symbolic-atom rhs-term+)
                              | (cbind variable)
                              | (closefile file-id+)
                              | (default file-id default-mode)
                              | (halt)
                              | (make rhs-term+)
                              | (modify rhs-ce-var rhs-term+)
                              | (openfile file-id filespec file-mode)
                              | (remove rhs-ce-var+)
                              | (write rhs-term+)
                              | (addstate filespec)
                              | (restorestate filespec)
                              | (savestate filespec)
                              | (after numeric-atom symbolic-atom)
rhs-ce-var          ::= variable | integer-atom
rhs-term            ::= rhs-value | ^positional-atom rhs-value
rhs-value           ::= rhs-function | atom
rhs-function        ::= (accept)
                              | (accept file-id)
                              | (acceptline atom*)
                              | (compute expression)
                              | (crlf)
                              | (genatom)
                              | (litval positional-atom)
                              | (rjust positional-atom)
                              | (substr rhs-ce-var positional-atom end-atom)
                              | (tabto positional-atom)
                              | user-defined-function
expression          ::= numeric-atom | variable
                              | expression operator expression
                              | (expression)
operator            ::= + | - | * | // | \\
```

```
user-defined-function ::= (symbolic-atom atom*)
positional-atom       ::= symbolic-atom | integer-atom | variable
end-atom              ::= positional-atom | inf
file-id               ::= symbolic-atom | variable
filespec              ::= symbolic-atom | variable
file-mode             ::= in | out
default-mode          ::= accept | trace | write
```

A.1 Resource Requirements

Because VAX OPS5 is not embedded in a LISP environment, it does not require the overhead normally associated with a LISP-based OPS5. Rather than compiling rules into an interpreted data structure, VAX OPS5 compiles rules into directly executable code, which, when first introduced, executed between 20 and 100 times faster than its LISP-based predecessor. More recent versions have compiler and run-time optimizations that make applications run faster still.

The increased speed and decreased memory required make viable many problems that would not be attempted in many LISP-based implementations.

A.2 LHS Functions

Chapter 8, *External Routines*, described the use of built-in and user-written functions used in the matching process. This feature is included in VAX OPS5 but not in PD OPS5.

A.3 Initialization

VAX OPS5 provides the `startup` statement that contains interpreter commands that initialize an application when that application is executed. This is necessary, since an application written in VAX OPS5 can be run as a standalone program, where working memory must be initialized before rules can fire. Chapter 4, *Program Development*, discusses the use of the `startup` statement to initialize working memory.

A.4 Rule Firing Limits

To control rule firings, VAX OPS5 provides the `catch` statement and `after` action. The `after` action specifies that a named catcher is to be executed after a specific number of rule firings. The `catch` statement contains actions to be taken at that time. For example, knowing that your application typically executes 1000 to 2000 firings in a run, you can use an `after` action to invoke a catcher after 10,000 firings. This catcher may make a WME that would invoke a subtask to deal with a possible infinite loop and to take some appropriate action.

A.5 Saving and Restoring State

To aid in the development process, VAX OPS5 offers interpreter commands and actions that save, restore, or add to working memory and the conflict set. `savestate` saves the current state of the application into a file. `restorestate` restores a stored state in a later session of the same program. `addstate` merges the stored state into the current state. See Chapter 6, *Debugging an OPS5 Program*, for a description of how you can use `savestate` and `restorestate` to help you to debug an OPS5 application.

A.6 Differences in the Build Action

Rules added by the `build` action in PD OPS5 are instantiated by only those WMEs made *after* the rule is built. VAX OPS5 immediately matches a newly built rule with all WMEs in working memory at the time that rule is built. The VAX OPS5 `build` action is discussed in Chapter 6, *Debugging an OPS5 Program*.

A.7 Interpreter Environment

Another difference between VAX OPS5 and PD OPS5 lies in the user interface. The developer accesses PD OPS5 features through the use of top-level LISP functions. These functions can be invoked interactively or by a high-level LISP program. Compilation is obtained by loading rule files into the environment, implicitly executing a function or macro named `p` for each rule. VAX OPS5 provides a separate compiler accessed by a standardized VMS DCL™ command. The compiled code can be linked to be called by another program or run as a standalone program. The compiler can include the OPS5 command interpreter for debugging purposes, or can leave it out to allow the immediate execution of the rules when the program is run.

The OPS5 command interpreter is discussed in more detail in Chapter 4, *Program Development*, and in Chapter 6, *Debugging an OPS5 Program*.

A.8 External-Routine Interface

VAX OPS5 provides a routine interface based on the routines defined in Forgy's 1981 manual [Forgy 1981]. This allows VAX OPS5 to call any language conforming to the VMS procedure-calling standard. See Chapter 8, *External Routines*, for more details about the external-routine interface in VAX OPS5 and PD OPS5.

A.9 Rule Timing Package

A rule timing package is provided by VAX OPS5 for finding relative costs of rules in an application run. Using this package, the developer can produce reports that, for each rule, list the firing frequency, time spent attempting to match, and time spent executing. This is an invaluable aid in optimizing applications for production use. See Chapter 10, *Efficiency*, for more details on using this tool to tune an application.

A.10 Processing Real-Time Events

Chapter 8, *External Routines*, also discusses a feature in VAX OPS5 that allows an application to receive and process notification of asynchronous events using VMS asynchronous system traps (ASTs).

APPENDIX B

OPS5 Coding Conventions

THE PURPOSE OF developing and adhering to a style of coding in an OPS5 program is to make the process of modifying, debugging, and maintaining a program more manageable. In projects with multiple developers, a uniform coding style is essential for writing readable and reuseable code.

This appendix contains descriptions and explanations of coding styles we have seen used most frequently in OPS5 projects. We emphasize the styles we chose to use in this book, and explain our reasons for using them. In judging coding styles, however, the most important criterion is that the style you choose be the clearest and most natural one to you; the style you develop may differ from that offered here. The important point is to develop, write down, and—most important—follow religiously a set of standards for coding styles.

B.1 Rule Files

Large OPS5 programs are usually partitioned into several files of rules.* A rule file usually contains a group of subtasks that are functionally related, forming a single rule module.

All element class (`literalize`), vector (`vector-attribute`), and external-routine (`external`) declarations should be grouped into a single file that contains no rules. There are two reasons for keeping declarations separate from

*Not all implementations of OPS5 allow a single program to reside in more than one file.

executable code. First, by keeping all declarations in one place, developers are encouraged to maintain consistency in the naming and use of element classes. There is less chance of developers using the same attribute name for different purposes, or assigning identical names to element classes, vector attributes, or external routines. Second, keeping declarations separate from rules facilitates the use of automated system-building tools, such as DEC/MMS™. If any changes are made to the declarations file, the entire rule base must be recompiled. If the declarations file contained rules, an automated system-building tool that depended on file creation dates could not determine whether a new version of this file required a complete recompile of the rule base.

Demon rules are also often grouped into a single file. Since demons can fire at any time during program execution, developers must check how all new rules and new demons affect the existing demons. If demons are scattered throughout the program, it is less likely that developers will carefully check all rule and demon interactions.

Assumption-checking rules* must also be maintained in a separate file. These rules are compiled with the program during development, but they may be removed altogether from the user's version.

There should be a standard for the documentation required at the head of each rule file. This documentation often includes a one-line description of the rule file on the first line of the file and then a more detailed paragraph of description, any fragments of subtasks that are for some reason included in this file, a list of the subtask names, a list of the external routines referenced, a list of the authors, and the modification history of the module.

B.2 Declarations

As mentioned in the previous section, the attribute, vector-attribute, and external-routine declarations are held in a single file, or, if there is only one rule file, are grouped at the head of a single file program.

Careful documentation of declarations not only makes those declarations readable, but also is a method of enforcing the correct naming and use of attributes. Above or to the right of each element-class name should be a description of the purpose of the element class, or of the entity to which the attributes refer. Each attribute is documented with the characteristic that it names, and, if appropriate, the values it can hold. The values may be from a range (as in 1–100), or from a set of possible values. A shorthand notation for specifying a set of values is to use the OPS5 disjunction braces. Figure B.1 is an example of a documented element class.

Developers can use the documentation of the declarations as a reference to the purpose for which attributes were intended. When new code is written, attributes that are intended for one purpose, but are named ambiguously enough

---

*See Chapter 6.

```
;; Represents an item on an order
(literalize line-item
        line-number      ; The number (integer) of the line for this
                         ;   line item.
        price            ; Floating-point number
        part-name        ; Symbolic name of part from catalog
        request-date     ; Date the item has been requested to be sent
        schedule-date    ; Date the part is actually scheduled
        schedule-status); << NIL PENDING SCHEDULED >>
```

Figure B.1 Documenting declarations.

to be used for another dissimilar purpose, should not be "borrowed" for the occasion. A new attribute should be created.

If an existing attribute does seem appropriate for a new situation, its new values or use should be added to its documentation. When the comment after that attribute holds many values or uses, so it would be difficult to tell to what use the developer intended out of so many possibilities, it is time to create a new attribute, perhaps by splitting the old attribute into two new ones.

B.3 The Control Structure

The rules that drive the control of an OPS5 program should be clearly demarcated in the code, usually before all other domain rules. If a group of subtasks has a special control mechanism, this mechanism should be highlighted at the start of that group of subtasks.

The creation of control WMEs should also be given emphasis by these WMEs' placement or comments. This is especially true of the creation of subtasks that start the program.

B.4 Subtasks

The subtasks are the basic functional units of a program and can be documented with the thoroughness of a procedure or function of a sequential language. Introductory comments at the head of the subtask can include

- *Functional description*—the purpose of the subtask, the heuristics that are used, and the side effects of the subtask.
- *Assumptions*—the assumptions that the rules in this subtask make, certain values the subtask expects in working memory, certain values it expects will not be in working memory, or the state of problem solving expected when the task is invoked. Assumption-checking rules may be created directly from these comments.

- *Exit conditions*—when the subtask should exit correctly, and the reasons for any abnormal exits from the subtask.
- *Side effects*—the other subtasks, WMEs, and rules that could be affected by rules firing in this subtask.
- *Modification history*—the people who changed rules in the subtask, when, and for what purposes.

B.5 Rules

The coding styles of rules have three components: the rule name, the spacing within the rule, and the documentation.

B.5.1 Rule Names

Rule names should represent the rule's intended function as accurately as possible. There is a tradeoff between the length and clarity of a rule name; clearly, given a long enough string, the action of the rule can be expressed fully. In most systems, however, the brevity of a rule name is also important, since the full name has to be typed during debugging. Some tolerable compromise must be established.

It is helpful to start each rule name with the name of the subtask of which the rule is a part. (If the rule is a demon, its name can begin with "`demon.`") Use of the subtask name as a rule-name prefix makes rule traces easier to read. As the list of firing rules scrolls during a trace, the repetition of the subtask name for a group of rules firing within the same task forms a pattern that can be easily tracked when viewed on a video terminal. When the subtask changes, the change in the pattern is obvious.

The subtask name is usually followed by a special character, such as an exclamation point, followed by a phrase that characterizes that rule's role in the subtask. These phrases should have a construction similar to that of rules with similar purposes. (Some OPS5 development groups include a number in the rule name that indicates the approximate position of this rule relative to other rules in the same subtask.)

```
schedule!line-item-unschedulable
schedule!line-item-scheduled-in-month-requested
```

B.5.2 Rule Formatting

There are several basic variations to the formatting of an OPS5 rule. A formatting convention is usually one of the earliest conventions to emerge in a project, and, probably because the pattern is repeated so many times during program development, it is usually followed strictly and upheld vehemently.

```
(p  subtask!explanation
;
; Rule comments...
;
   { <Element-variable-of-any-length>
      (ce ^attribute val ...
          ^attributeN valN) }
      - (negated condition element...)
   -->
      (action)
      .
      .)
```

Figure B.2 Formatting an OPS5 rule.

The rule-formatting scheme used in this book, illustrated in Figure B.2, is as follows:

- The *opening parenthesis* and p for the rule are separated by two spaces from the *rule name.* This spacing helps to highlight the rule name.
- The left parenthesis on *condition elements* and *actions* appears on a common column (six spaces from the left margin). This format allows you to scan for a particular condition element or action by following a straight vertical line, rather than requiring that you do a horizontal search on each line as well as a vertical one.
- The *element variable* is on its own line preceding its condition element, and begins on an earlier column than that for the condition elements and actions. Putting the element variable on a separate line leaves room for it to be as long or short as needed without interfering with the formatting of the condition element. The element variables also begin on a common column for scanning purposes (three spaces); they sit to the left of the starting column for condition elements because element variables are actually the "labels" for the condition elements and they stand out more prominently in that position. Element variables are always capitalized to distinguish them visually from value variables.
- The formatting of condition elements that contain several attributes follows three basic schemes. The first, used in this book, places attributes and their values on the same line. If the condition element is longer than a single line, the break is made at an attribute name, which is indented to just under the first attribute on the previous line:

```
(class-name ^attribute1 short ^att2 longer-value
            ^attribute3 short ^att4 and-the-longest-value)
```

A second scheme places only one attribute on a line, and aligns all the attributes in a condition element on top of one another:

```
(class-name ^attribute1 short
            ^att2 longer-value
            ^attribute3 short
            ^att4 and-the-longest-value)
```

Although this format makes it easy to find each attribute, the beginning of the attribute's value is still difficult to pick out. For that reason, a third scheme aligns each value to a column further to the right:

```
(class-name ^attribute1      short
            ^att2            longer-value
            ^attribute3      short
            ^att4            and-the-longest-value)
```

If the column for the values is too far to the right, however, it is sometimes difficult to draw the invisible line that associates an attribute with the correct value on the right. This scheme is also more difficult to maintain, since the spacing between attributes and values is based on the longest attribute name used in the condition element.

Text editors customized for indenting LISP expressions make either of the first two schemes easy to adopt.

- The negation of a *negated condition element* is placed at the column for the condition elements, followed by a space and the left parenthesis. Offsetting the left parenthesis of the negated condition element makes it less likely that the hyphen will be missed by the reader; whenever a condition element is offset two columns, it means that it must be a negated condition element, whether or not the negation is visible.
- The arrow (`-->`) separating the LHS from the RHS begins at the same column as the element variables do (three spaces).

B.5.3 Rule Documentation

The most important guideline for documenting rules is to make the comments useful and to avoid redundancy with the rule itself. The lack of obscure OPS5 syntax makes rules English-like to read; the comment on a rule does not have to paraphrase the conditions and actions in the rule. Instead, the comment should point out the function of the rule in the broader context of the subtask of which that rule is a part. The comment should include any assumptions the rule makes about working memory or any effects the rule will have on working memory that are particularly important to another rule or subtask. Any "tricks" or "cleverness" the rule uses should be confessed and explained.

B.6 Element Class and Attribute Names

The naming of element classes is an art; some people can find just the right names that clearly express purpose. As in naming rules, there is a trade-off between length and clarity, with both extremes undesirable. There is no reason to abbreviate a word if it is difficult to remember the abbreviation; the mistakes in guessing the abbreviation incorrectly will take much more time to sort out than would typing the full word. For example, it is usually not worth abbreviating an attribute such as `capacity`, because there is no standard abbreviation. Would it be `cap`? `capty`? `cpacty`? Long element-class and attribute names, on the other hand, are tedious to retype, particularly if they are used frequently.

OPS5 allows the use of one attribute name in more than one element class. It is good practice to avoid using the same attribute name in more than one class unless it is defined with precisely the same meaning in each one. For example, the attribute named `student-id` may be appropriate to repeat in more than one element class for computational reasons; the name is specific enough that there would be no confusion as to the use of that name in one element class versus another. On the other hand, the attribute `name` in the element classes `student` and `class` is very ambiguous—does `name` refer to the name of the student taking the class, or to the name of the class?

There is another school of thought that says an attribute may be viewed as local to a WME class, so that there is no ambiguity when it appears in a rule. An attribute in a condition element or action is always used within the context of some WME class. For example, the use of `^name` in the `student` WME class is not related to the use of `^name` in a `class` WME. Furthermore, `student ^student-name` is much more awkward to read than is `student ^name`. The basis for this argument lies in conventions for the analogous problem of selecting names for record or structure types in other languages, where such naming restrictions do not normally exist.

Whichever convention you adopt, it should be understood and used consistently by all members of your development team.

Attribute names sometimes include a verb so that, when they are placed next to their value, they form a readable phrase. For example, rather than,

```
^price <too-much>
```

it may be more readable to write

```
^price-is <too-much>
```

This practice makes it easier to select meaningful variable names.

B.7 Variables and Values

As mentioned in Section B.6, values and variables should represent their meaning and use.

Value names should not be unnecessarily abstract. If you want to express the values true and false, you can use the symbols `true` and `false`, rather than `t` and `f`, or, worse, `1` and `0`. If the attribute name is one that suggests the values `yes` and `no`, perhaps you should use more meaningful values that can be understood even when they are not written adjacent to an attribute name. For example, if the attribute name is `employed?`, the values can be `employed` and `unemployed` rather than `yes` and `no`.

Variable names should describe the value to which they match. If the variable is used without ambiguity to represent that value later in the rule, its name can be the same as the attribute name. For example, the variable `<price>` is meaningful in the following context:

```
    (line-item ^price <price> ...
       :
-->
    (call (evaluate-price <price>) ...)
```

If a variable is used in comparison with others, however, it is more helpful to name the variable after the role it plays in the comparison. When the `<price>` variable is used in the following context, for example,

```
(line-item ^price <price> ^token <token>)
(line-item ^price >= <price> ^token <> <token>)
```

it is not as helpful a name as

```
(line-item ^price <lower-price> ^token <cheaper>)
(line-item ^price >= <lower-price> ^token <> <cheaper>)
```

If several rules share condition elements and matching values, it is helpful to use the same variable names in those rules.

APPENDIX C

Initial Rules for Order Scheduling

THE RULES IN THIS APPENDIX implement the first rules written for the order scheduling problem, as developed in Chapter 11, *Designing an OPS5 Application*. These rules ignore input, output, and control; they were developed using pseudo-rule refinement (see Section 11.4.1).

```
;; The number of line items manufactured in a given month.
(literalize allocation
    item            ; Name of the line item
    month           ; Month of manufacture
    available)      ; Quantity available this month

;; A component or group (bundle) of components on the order.
(literalize line-item
    order-id        ; Identifier of order that owns this
    name            ; Name of line item
    number          ; Line number
    quantity        ; Quantity ordered
    parent          ; Parent bundle, if any
    schedule-month  ; Month in which this line item has been
                    ;  scheduled
    month-offset)   ; Increment over the order schedule month
```

```
;; A list of line items, request month, and some information on the
;;  customer (header information) that specifies a sale.
(literalize order
    status          ; Initially CURRENT, then SCHEDULED,
                    ;  or PROBLEM
    id              ; Unique identifier of this order
    customer        ; Customer name
    address         ; City and state
    partials        ; YES if allowed, else NO
    request-month   ; Date when the customer requested the
                    ;  order
    schedule-month) ; Month when order is to be scheduled,
                    ;  initially = request-month

;;
;; Rules
;;

(p  schedule-line-item-on-request-month
;
;  1. If there are sufficient allocations,
;     then schedule a line item for its scheduled month.
;
        (order ^status current ^id <current>
               ^schedule-month <asked>)
   { <Line-item>
        (line-item ^order-id <current> ^name <item>
                   ^quantity <qty-desired>
                   ^month-offset <incr>
                   ^schedule-month nil) }
   { <Allocation>
        (allocation ^item <item>
                    ^month (compute <asked> + <incr>)
                    ^available { <left> >= <qty-desired> }) }
   -->
        (modify <Line-item>
               ^schedule-month (compute <asked> + <incr>))
        (modify <Allocation>
               ^available (compute <left> - <qty-desired>)))

(p  move-out-partialed-line-item
;
;  2a. If you cannot schedule a line item for the offset
;             schedule month,
;          and the order can be partialed,
```

```
;       then increment the line-item month offset by 1.
;
         (order ^status current ^id <current>
                ^schedule-month <asked> ^partials yes)
   { <Line-item>
         (line-item ^order-id <current> ^name <item>
                    ^quantity <qty-desired>
                    ^month-offset { <incr> <= 3 }
                    ^schedule-month nil) }
        - (allocation ^item <item>
                ^month (compute <asked> + <incr>)
                ^available >= <qty-desired>)
   -->
         (modify <Line-item> ^month-offset (compute <incr> + 1)))

(p  move-out-max-partialed-order
;
;  2b. If a line-item month offset is greater than 3,
;       then reset it to 0
;           and increment the order schedule month by 1.
;
   { <Line-item>
         (line-item ^month-offset > 3 ^order-id <current>) }
   { <Order>
         (order ^status current ^id <current>
                ^schedule-month <failed>) }
   -->
         (modify <Line-item> ^month-offset 0)
         (modify <Order> ^schedule-month (compute <failed> + 1)))

(p  unschedule-line-item
;
;  2c. If a line-item schedule month is less than the order
;           schedule month,
;       then unschedule that line item.
;
   { <Line-item>
         (line-item ^order-id <current> ^name <item>
                    ^quantity <allocated>
                    ^schedule-month { <scheduled> <> nil }) }
         (order ^status current ^id <current>
                ^schedule-month > <scheduled>)
   { <Allocation>
         (allocation ^item <item> ^month <scheduled>
                     ^available <left>) }
```

```
    -->
         (modify <Line-item> ^schedule-month nil ^month-offset 0)
         (modify <Allocation>
                ^available (compute <left> + <allocated>)))

(p  move-out-unpartialed-order
;
;   3a. If you cannot schedule a line item for its request
;           month, and the order cannot be partialed,
;       then increment the order schedule month by 1.
;
;   Note: month offset not needed here, since no partialing
;          allowed.
;
    { <Order>
         (order ^status current ^id <current>
                ^request-month <requested>
                ^schedule-month
                  { <asked> <= (compute <requested> + 3) }
                ^partials no) }
         (line-item ^order-id <current> ^name <item>
                    ^quantity <qty-desired>
                    ^schedule-month nil)
         - (allocation ^item <item> ^month <asked>
                ^available >= <qty-desired>)
    -->
       (modify <Order> ^schedule-month (compute <asked> + 1)))

(p  cannot-move-out-problem-order
;
;   3b. If an order schedule month is more than 3 months beyond
;           the request month,
;       then mark the order as a problem order and do not
;           schedule it.
;
    { <Order>
         (order ^status current ^request-month <requested>
                ^schedule-month > (compute <requested> + 3)) }
    -->
         (modify <Order> ^status problem))
```

References

[Barr 1981] Barr, A., Feigenbaum, E. A. (eds.), *The Handbook of Artificial Intelligence*. Vol. I. Reading, MA: Addison-Wesley, 1981.

[Brachman 1985] Brachman, R. J. and Levesque, H. J. (eds.), *Readings in Knowledge Representation*. San Mateo, CA: Morgan Kaufmann, 1985.

[Brownston 1985] Brownston, L., Farrell, R., Kant E., Martin N., *Programming Expert Systems in OPS5*. Reading, MA: Addison-Wesley, 1985.

[Buchanan 1984a] Buchanan, B. G. and Duda, R., "Principles of Rule-Based Expert Systems," Heuristic Programming Project Report HPP-82-14. Stanford, CA: Stanford University, 1982.

[Buchanan 1984b] Buchanan, B. G. and Shortliffe, E. H., *Rule-based Expert Systems: The MYCIN Experiments of the Stanford Heuristic Programming Project*. Reading, MA: Addison Wesley, 1984.

[Chomsky 1957] Chomsky, N., *Syntactic Structures*. The Hague: Mouton, 1957.

[Clancey] Clancey, W. J., "The Advantages of Abstract Control Knowledge in Expert System Design," *Proceedings of the National Conference on Artificial Intelligence,* Washington, DC, 1983. San Mateo, CA: Morgan Kaufmann, 1983, pp. 74–78.

[Davis] Davis, R. and Lenat, D. B., *Knowledge-Based Systems in AI.* New York: McGraw-Hill, 1982.

[DECZ500] Digital Equipment Corporation, "Introduction to VAX/VMS System Routines," *VAX/VMS V4.4.* Order # AA-Z500B-TE. Maynard, MA: Digital Equipment Corporation.

[Forgy 1981] Forgy, C. L., *OPS5 User's Manual,* CMU-CS-81-135. Pittsburgh, PA: Carnegie-Mellon University, 1981.

[Forgy 1982] Forgy, C. L., "RETE: A Fast Algorithm for the Many Pattern/Many Object Pattern Matching Problem," *Artificial Intelligence,* 19:17-37, 1982.

[Forgy 1984] Forgy, C. L., *The OPS83 Report System Version 2.* Production Systems Technologies, Inc. 1984.

[Forgy 1987] Forgy, C. L. and Shepard, S. J., "RETE: A Fast Match Algorithm," *AI EXPERT.* 1987.

[Gruber 1985] Gruber, T. R., *Guidelines for Knowledge Engineering in Rule-based Systems,* EKSL Report 86-1. Amherst, MA: University of Massachusetts, Department of Computer and Information Science, 1985.

[Gruber 1986] Gruber, T. R. and Cohen, P., "Knowledge Engineering Tools at the Architecture Level," *Proceedings of the Tenth International Joint Conference on Artificial Intelligence,* Milan, 1987. San Mateo, CA: Morgan Kaufmann, 1986, pp. 100–103.

[Gupta 1985] Gupta, A., *Parallelism in Production Systems.* Pittsburgh, PA: Carnegie-Mellon University, Department of Computer Science, 1985 (Ph.D. dissertation).

[Gupta] Gupta, A. and Forgy, C. L., *Measurements on Production Systems,* CMU-CS-83-167. Pittsburgh, PA: Carnegie-Mellon University, December 1983.

[Harmon 1985] Harmon, P. and King, D., *Expert Systems: Artificial Intelligence in Business.* New York: John Wiley, 1985.

[Harmon 1988] Harmon, P., Maus, R. and Morrissey, W., *Expert System Tools and Applications.* New York: John Wiley, 1988.

[Hayes-Roth 1983] Hayes-Roth, F., Waterman, D.A. and Lenat, D.B., *Building Expert Systems.* Reading, MA: Addison-Wesley, 1983.

[Hayes-Roth 1985] Hayes-Roth, F., "Rule-based Systems," *Communications of the ACM,* 29:921–932, 1985.

[Klahr] Klahr P. and Waterman, D. A., *Expert Systems: Techniques, Tools and Applications.* Reading, MA: Addison-Wesley, 1986.

[Lynch 1986] Lynch, F., Marshall, C., O'Connor, D. and Kiskiel, M., "AI in Manufacturing at Digital," *AI Magazine.* 7:5 53–57, 1986.

[Marcus 1988] Marcus, S. (ed.), *Automating Knowledge Acquisition for Expert Systems.* Boston, MA: Kluwer, 1988.

[Markov 1954] Markov A., *A Theory of Algorithms.* USSR: National Academy of the Sciences, 1954.

[McDermott 1978] McDermott, J. and Forgy C. L., "Production System Conflict Resolution Strategies," in Waterman, D., Hayes-Roth, D., and Lenat, D. (eds.), *Pattern-Directed Inference Systems.* New York: Academic Press, 1978.

[Minsky 1967] Minsky, M., *Computation: Finite and Infinite Machines.* Englewood Cliffs, NJ: Prentice Hall, 1967.

[Moskowitz] Moskowitz, L., "Rule-based Programming," *BYTE Magazine,* November 1986.

[Newell 1972] Newell, A. and Simon, H. A., *Human Problem Solving.* Englewood Cliffs, NJ: Prentice-Hall, 1972.

[Nilsson 1980] Nilsson, N. J., *Principles of Artificial Intelligence.* Palo Alto, CA: Tioga Publishing Company, 1980.

[O'Keefe] O'Keefe, R. M., Balci O. and Smith E. P., "Validating Expert System Performance," *IEEE EXPERT,* Vol II, no. 4 :81–89, 1987.

[Post 1943] Post, E., "Formal Reductions of the General Combinatorial Problem," *American Journal of Mathematics,* 65: 197–268.

[Rich] Rich, C. and Waters, R. C. (eds.), *Readings in Artificial Intelligence and Software Engineering.* San Mateo, CA: Morgan Kaufmann, 1986.

[Soloway 1987] Soloway, E., Bachant, J. and Jensen, K., "Assessing the Maintainability of XCON-in-RIME: Coping with the

Problems of a VERY Large Rule Base," *Proceedings of the Sixth National Conference on Artificial Intelligence,* Seattle, WA, 1987, pp. 824–829 San Mateo, CA: Morgan Kaufmann, 1987.

[van de Brug] van de Brug, A., Bachant, J. and McDermott, J., "Doing R1 with Style," *Proceedings of the Second Conference on AI Applications*, Miami, FL, 1985.

[Waterman 1978] Waterman, D. A. and Hayes-Roth, F., *Pattern Directed Inference Systems.* New York: Academic Press Inc., 1978.

[Waterman 1986] Waterman, D. A., *A Guide to Expert Systems.* Reading, MA: Addison-Wesley, 1986.

[Webber 1981] Webber, B. L. and Nilsson, N. J. (eds.), *Readings in Artificial Intelligence.* San Mateo, CA: Morgan Kaufmann, 1981.

[Winston 1984] Winston, P. H., *Artificial Intelligence.* Reading, MA: Addison Wesley, 1984.

Answers to Exercises

Chapter 1

1. a. Welder's assistant: backward-chaining problem solving. This is best viewed as a diagnostic problem. The explanation of the faulty welds are symptoms from which a hypothesis of the problem is formed. The rule base would attempt to substantiate the hypothesis or hypotheses using knowledge of the welding process.

   b. Pharmacist's assistant: forward-chaining problem solving. This problem is driven by the information on record about the customer. The rule base would contain information about harmful combinations. The number of goal states is too numerous to use backward chaining.

   c. Distribution manager: forward-chaining problem solving. The initial state is a set of goods at different locations and a set of trucks at different locations, and the goal state must be constructed using a set of constraints for minimizing the distance. It would be difficult to enumerate all goal states. Parts of the problem, however, such as suggesting why parts originating from a particular plant are often damaged, may be solved through backward chaining.

2. a. IF
      controller says GO
      and there is a space on the belt
      and I am not holding a bin
   THEN
      lift a bin from storage.

b. IF
   controller says GO
   and there is a space on the belt
   and I am holding a bin
   THEN
   place the bin on the belt.

c. IF
   controller says WAIT
   and there is a bin on the belt
   and I am not holding a bin
   THEN
   lift a bin from the belt.

d. IF
   controller says WAIT
   and I am holding a bin
   THEN
   place the bin in storage.

Chapter 2

1. Instead of using the `^vacancies` attribute, the students placed in the room can be counted, and this number can be checked against a maximum number of occupants:

```
(literalize room
        number
        max-in-room
        currently-in-room)
```

2. `(student ^placed-in <> nil)`

3. The WME looks like this:

1	2	3	4	5	6	7	8	9
room	1135	2	nil	nil	2	male	no	nil

   The values for the `^sexes-are` and `^smokers?` attributes have been overwritten, so they are not likely to match values tests on these attributes.

4. a. Matches a student that has been assigned to a room.

   b. The rule can fire only if there is no student that has not been placed in a room.

   c. The rule can fire if there is no student that has been assigned a room.

5. The make results in the WME

```
(ROOM ^NUMBER 302)
```

6. (write |There is a vacancy in room <room-no>|)
produces

```
There is a vacancy in room <room-no>
```

7. a. Place a student in a partially filled room.

```
(p  place-in-old-room
;
; Place the student in any compatible room with a vacancy.
;
   { <Homeless>
      (student ^name <who> ^placed-in nil
               ^sex-is <m/f> ^smoker? <preference>) }
   { <Room>
      (room ^number <room-no> ^vacancies { <openings> > 0 }
            ^sexes-are <m/f> ^smokers? <preference>) }
   -->
      (write (crlf) |Placing| <who> |in room| <room-no>
             |with| (substr <Room> occupants inf)
             (rjust 1) |.|)
      (modify <Homeless> ^placed-in <room-no>)
      (remove <Room>)
      (make (substr <Room> 1 occupants)
            ^vacancies (compute <openings> - 1)
            ^occupants <who> (substr <Room> occupants inf)))
```

b. Place a student in an empty room
See Figure 2.6.

c. Print an assigned student (use the formatting functions)
See the rule print-results-in-table *on page 38.*

8. Modify the class declarations as follows:

```
;; A Room for a group of students
(literalize room
     number       ; Unique room number
     type         ; For printout only:
                  ;  << SINGLE DOUBLE ... >>
     sexes-are    ; Gender of occupants << MALE FEMALE >>
     smokers?     ; Smoking preference << YES NO >>
     capacity     ; Maximum number of occupants: integer
     vacancies    ; Assignment openings for this room:
                  ;  integer
```

```
     assignments  ; Number of students already assigned:
                  ;  integer
     occupants)   ; Names of students assigned to this room

(vector-attribute occupants)

;; A student description
(literalize student
     name           ; Unique name
     placed-in      ; NIL or room number assigned
     sex-is         ; << MALE FEMALE >>
     smoker?)       ; << YES NO >>

;; Way to move groups of student assignments
(literalize group-placement
     students       ; Vector of student names to move
     placed-in)     ; New placement for these students

(vector-attribute students)
```

Then write the following rules to perform limited backtracking.

```
(p  condense-compatible-roommates
;
; If you can find two rooms of compatible students who
; could be put together in a room that currently has
; less students, do so and evict the other students.
; They will find another home.
;
 { <Small-room1>
    (room ^sexes-are <m/f> ^smokers? <preference>
          ^capacity <room1-size> ^number <room1>
          ^assignments { <in-room1> > 0 }
          ^type <type1>) }
 { <Small-room2>
    (room ^sexes-are <m/f> ^smokers? <preference>
          ^capacity <room2-size>
          ^number { <room2> <> <room1> }
          ^assignments { <in-room2> > 0 }
          ^type <type2>) }
 { <Big-room>
    (room ^number { <room3> <> <room1> <> <room2> }
          ^capacity { <room3-size>
                      >= (compute <in-room1> + <in-room2>) }
          ^assignments < (compute <in-room1> + <in-room2>)
          ^type <type3>) }
```

```
  -->
    (bind <merge-size> (compute <in-room1> + <in-room2>))
    (write (crlf) |Merging all| <merge-size> |folks from rooms|
        <room1> |and|
        <room2> |into the larger| (crlf) <type3> |room|
        <room3> (rjust 1) |.| (crlf) |  This kicks out|
        (substr <Big-room> occupants inf)
        |to find a new home.|)
    (make room ^number <room3> ^sexes-are <m/f>
        ^smokers? <preference>
        ^capacity <room3-size> ^type <type3>
        ^vacancies (compute <room3-size> - <merge-size>)
        ^assignments <merge-size>
        ^occupants (substr <Small-room1> occupants inf)
                   (substr <Small-room2> occupants inf))
    (make room ^number <room1> ^sexes-are nil ^smokers? nil
        ^type <type1> ^capacity <room1-size>
        ^vacancies <room1-size> ^assignments 0)
    (make room ^number <room2> ^sexes-are nil ^smokers? nil
        ^type <type2> ^capacity <room2-size>
        ^vacancies <room2-size> ^assignments 0)
    (make group-placement ^placed-in nil
        ^students (substr <Big-room> occupants inf))
    (make group-placement ^placed-in <room3>
        ^students (substr <Small-room1> occupants inf))
    (make group-placement ^placed-in <room3>
        ^students (substr <Small-room2> occupants inf))
    (remove <Small-room1> <Small-room2> <Big-room>))



(p  move-student
;
; Move a student to the specified room slot already
;  allocated for him.
;
   { <Directive>
      (group-placement ^placed-in <destination>
         ^students { <next> <> nil }) }
   { <Student>
      (student ^name <next>) }
   -->
      (modify <Student> ^placed-in <destination>)
      (bind <students-loc> (litval students))
      (bind <remaining> (compute <students-loc> + 1))
```

```
    (modify <Directive> ^students
                 (substr <Directive> <remaining> inf) nil))
(p  done-moving-groups
;
; Remove an empty group-placement.
;
   { <Empty-placement>
      (group-placement ^students nil) }
   -->
      (remove <Empty-placement>))
```

Chapter 3

1. There is only one instantiation formed. Although there are two rooms in which the student can be placed, only the largest passes the constraint imposed by the negated condition element

   PLACE-IN-LARGEST-PARTIALLY-FILLED-ROOM 4 9

2. a. QUERY-USER 84 10

   b. PLACE-STUDENT-IN-PARTIALLY-FILLED 6 4 9 12

   c. You cannot choose on the basis of recency. Two instantiations are equally recent:

      PLACE-STUDENT-IN-SINGLE 9 12 6
      PLACE-STUDENT-IN-DOUBLE 12 9 6

3. There are eight conditional tests in the rule.

Type of Test	Test	Number of Tests
Class name	task	1
Predicate with constant	= item-search	1
Class name	item	1
Each test in conjunction:		
Disjunction	{ << 30 40 50 >> }	1
Class name	item	1
Each test in conjunction:		
Predicate with bound variable	<> <item-type-1>	1
Each test in conjunction:		
Predicate with bound variable	<> <size1>	1
Predicate with constant	> 50	1
		8

4.

	LEX	MEA
a.	RULE-ONE	RULE-TWO
b.	RULE-FOUR	RULE-FOUR
c.	RULE-SIX	RULE-FIVE
d.	arbitrary	RULE-SEVEN

Chapter 4

1. a. A sample VAX OPS5 rule base:

```
;;;;;;;;;;;;;;;;;;;;;;;;;;;;;;;;;;;;;;;;;;;;;;;;;;;;;;;;;;;;;;;;;
;;; ROOM_ASSIGNMENT.OPS - Room-assignment demonstration rule base
;;;
;;; Abstract:
;;;        A sample solution for assigning students to rooms
;;;        on the bases of gender and smoking behavior.
;;;
;;; Modification History:
;;;
;;;

;;;;;;;;;;;;;;;;;;;;;;;;;;;;;;;;;;;;;;;;;;;;;;;;;;;;;;;;;;;;;;;;;
;; Declarations and initialization

;; A Room for a group of students
(literalize room
        number           ; Unique room number
        type             ; For printout only:
                         ;  << SINGLE DOUBLE ... >>
        sexes-are        ; Gender of occupants << MALE FEMALE >>
        smokers?         ; Smoking preference << YES NO >>
        capacity         ; Maximum number of occupants: integer
        vacancies        ; Assignment openings for this room:
                         ;  integer
        assignments      ; Number of students already assigned:
                         ;  integer
        occupants)       ; Names of students assigned to this room
(vector-attribute occupants)

;; A student description
(literalize student
        name             ; Unique name
        placed-in        ; NIL or room number assigned
```

```
        sex-is          ; << MALE FEMALE >>
        smoker?)        ; << YES NO >>


;; Way to move groups of student assignments
(literalize group-placement
        students        ; Vector of student names to move
        placed-in)      ; New placement for these students
(vector-attribute students)


(startup
      ; Load file of MAKE for initial students and rooms
      (@ room_assignment.wm)
)


;;;;;;;;;;;;;;;;;;;;;;;;;;;;;;;;;;;;;;;;;;;;;;;;;;;;;;;;;;;;;;;;;
;; Rules

;; Placement strategy is to try to fill the largest rooms first,
;;  so that, for example, we don't end up with a lot of smokers
;;  and only nonsmoking slots.


(p  placement!old-room
;
; Place the student in the largest-capacity room with a
;  vacancy.
;
   { <Homeless>
      (student ^placed-in nil ^sex-is <m/f>
               ^smoker? <preference> ^name <who>) }
   { <Room>
      (room ^vacancies { <openings> > 0 } ^capacity <max-size>
            ^sexes-are <m/f> ^smokers? <preference>
            ^number <room-no> ^type <room-type>
            ^assignments <sofar>) }
      - (room ^vacancies > 0 ^capacity > <max-size>
              ^sexes-are <m/f> ^smokers? <preference>)
  -->
      (write (crlf) |Placing| <who> |in the|
          <room-type> |numbered| <room-no> |with|
          (substr <Room> occupants inf) (rjust 1) |.|)
      (modify <Homeless> ^placed-in <room-no>)
      (modify <Room> ^vacancies (compute <openings> - 1)
          ^assignments (compute <sofar> + 1)
```

```
          ^occupants <who>
                     (substr <Room> occupants inf)))

(p  placement!new-room
;
; If there are no vacancies in partially filled rooms, put
; the student in the largest new room available.
;
   { <Homeless>
      (student ^placed-in nil ^sex-is <m/f> ^smoker? <preference>
               ^name <who>) }
      - (room ^vacancies { <vacancies> > 0 }
              ^capacity > <vacancies> ^sexes-are <m/f>
              ^smokers? <preference>)
   { <Room>
      (room ^capacity <max-size> ^sexes-are nil ^smokers? nil
            ^vacancies <openings> ^number <room-no>
            ^type <room-type>) }
      - (room ^capacity > <max-size> ^sexes-are nil ^smokers? nil)
   -->
      (write (crlf) <who> |will be the first one in the|
          <room-type> |room number| <room-no> (rjust 1) |.|)
      (modify <Homeless> ^placed-in <room-no>)
      (modify <Room> ^vacancies (compute <openings> - 1)
          ^occupants <who> ^sexes-are <m/f>
          ^smokers? <preference> ^assignments 1))

(p  placement!condense-compatible-roommates
;
; If you can find two rooms of compatible students who could be put
; together in a room that currently has less students, do so, and
; evict the other students.  They will find another home.
;
   { <Small-room1>
      (room ^sexes-are <m/f> ^smokers? <preference>
            ^capacity <room1-size>
            ^number <room1> ^assignments { <in-room1> > 0 }
            ^type <type1>) }
   { <Small-room2>
      (room ^sexes-are <m/f> ^smokers? <preference>
            ^capacity <room2-size>
            ^number { <room2> <> <room1> }
            ^assignments { <in-room2> > 0 }
            ^type <type2>) }
   { <Big-room>
      (room ^number { <room3> <> <room1> <> <room2> }
```

```
          ^capacity { <room3-size> >=
                    (compute <in-room1> + <in-room2>) }
          ^assignments < (compute <in-room1> + <in-room2>)
          ^type <type3>) }
  -->
    (bind <merge-size> (compute <in-room1> + <in-room2>))
    (write (crlf) |Merging all| <merge-size> |folks from rooms|
        <room1> |and| <room2> |into the larger|
        (crlf) <type3>|room| <room3> (rjust 1) |.|
        (crlf) |  This kicks out|
        (substr <Big-room> occupants inf)
        |to find a new home.|)
    (make room ^number <room3> ^sexes-are <m/f>
         ^smokers? <preference>
         ^capacity <room3-size> ^type <type3>
         ^vacancies (compute <room3-size> - <merge-size>)
         ^assignments <merge-size>
         ^occupants (substr <Small-room1> occupants inf)
                    (substr <Small-room2> occupants inf))
    (make room ^number <room1> ^sexes-are nil ^smokers? nil
         ^type <type1> ^capacity <room1-size>
         ^vacancies <room1-size> ^assignments 0)
    (make room ^number <room2> ^sexes-are nil ^smokers? nil
         ^type <type2> ^capacity <room2-size>
         ^vacancies <room2-size> ^assignments 0)
    (make group-placement ^placed-in nil
         ^students (substr <Big-room> occupants inf))
    (make group-placement ^placed-in <room3>
         ^students (substr <Small-room1> occupants inf))
    (make group-placement ^placed-in <room3>
         ^students (substr <Small-room2> occupants inf))
    (remove <Small-room1> <Small-room2> <Big-room>))


(p  placement!move-student
;
; Move a student to the specified room slot already allocated
;  for her.
;
   { <Directive>
     (group-placement
          ^placed-in <destination>
          ^students { <next> <> nil }) }
   { <Student>
     (student ^name <next>) }
```

```
   -->
      (modify <Student> ^placed-in <destination>)
      (bind <students-loc> (litval students))
      (bind <remaining> (compute <students-loc> + 1))
      (modify <Directive>
           ^students (substr <Directive> <remaining> inf) nil))

(p  placement!done-moving-groups
;
; Remove an empty group-placement.
;
   { <Empty-placement>
      (group-placement ^students nil) }
   -->
      (remove <Empty-placement>))
```

b. `$ ops5/exe room_assignment.ops`

c. A sample make file:

```
;; Students
(make student ^name fred ^sex-is male ^smoker? yes)
(make student ^name albert ^sex-is male ^smoker? yes)
(make student ^name mary ^sex-is female ^smoker? no)
(make student ^name penny ^sex-is female ^smoker? no)
(make student ^name michael ^sex-is male ^smoker? yes)
(make student ^name ted ^sex-is male ^smoker? yes)
(make student ^name nancy ^sex-is female ^smoker? no)
(make student ^name sue ^sex-is female ^smoker? no)
(make student ^name linda ^sex-is female ^smoker? yes)
(make student ^name cindy ^sex-is female ^smoker? no)
(make student ^name suzie ^sex-is female ^smoker? no)
(make student ^name george ^sex-is male ^smoker? yes)
(make student ^name lester ^sex-is male ^smoker? yes)
(make student ^name sarah ^sex-is female ^smoker? no)
(make student ^name wendy ^sex-is female ^smoker? yes)
(make student ^name joe ^sex-is male ^smoker? no)
(make student ^name tom ^sex-is male ^smoker? no)
(make student ^name alan ^sex-is male ^smoker? no)
(make student ^name andy ^sex-is male ^smoker? no)
(make student ^name lenny ^sex-is male ^smoker? no)

;; Rooms
(make room ^number H201 ^type single ^capacity 1 ^vacancies 1
   ^assignments 0)
```

```
(make room ^number H213 ^type triple ^capacity 3 ^vacancies 3
   ^assignments 0)
(make room ^number D12 ^type double ^capacity 2 ^vacancies 2
   ^assignments 0)
(make room ^number D101 ^type single ^capacity 1 ^vacancies 1
   ^assignments 0)
(make room ^number M313 ^type triple ^capacity 3 ^vacancies 3
   ^assignments 0)
(make room ^number M104 ^type quad ^capacity 4 ^vacancies 4
   ^assignments 0)
(make room ^number M122 ^type double ^capacity 2 ^vacancies 2
   ^assignments 0)
(make room ^number B104 ^type quad ^capacity 4 ^vacancies 4
^assignments 0)
```

d. Chose default LEX strategy.

e. Sample run:

```
LENNY will be the first one in the QUAD room number B104.
Placing ANDY in the QUAD numbered B104 with LENNY.
Placing ALAN in the QUAD numbered B104 with ANDY LENNY.
Placing TOM in the QUAD numbered B104 with ALAN ANDY LENNY.
JOE will be the first one in the QUAD room number M104.
WENDY will be the first one in the TRIPLE room number M313.
Placing LINDA in the TRIPLE numbered M313 with WENDY.
SARAH will be the first one in the TRIPLE room number H213.
Placing SUZIE in the TRIPLE numbered H213 with SARAH.
Placing CINDY in the TRIPLE numbered H213 with SUZIE SARAH.
LESTER will be the first one in the DOUBLE room number M122.
Placing GEORGE in the DOUBLE numbered M122 with LESTER.
SUE will be the first one in the DOUBLE room number D12.
Merging all 4 folks from rooms D12 and H213 into the larger
 QUAD room M104.
  This kicks out JOE to find a new home.
JOE will be the first one in the TRIPLE room number H213.
NANCY will be the first one in the DOUBLE room number D12.
Placing PENNY in the DOUBLE numbered D12 with NANCY.
TED will be the first one in the SINGLE room number D101.
Merging all 3 folks from rooms D101 and M122 into the larger
 TRIPLE room H213.
  This kicks out JOE to find a new home.
JOE will be the first one in the DOUBLE room number M122.
MICHAEL will be the first one in the SINGLE room number D101.
MARY will be the first one in the SINGLE room number H201.
Merging all 3 folks from rooms H201 and D12 into the larger
```

```
 TRIPLE room M313.
  This kicks out LINDA WENDY to find a new home.
WENDY will be the first one in the DOUBLE room number D12.
Placing LINDA in the DOUBLE numbered D12 with WENDY.
ALBERT will be the first one in the SINGLE room number H201.
Merging all 2 folks from rooms H201 and D101 into the larger
 DOUBLE room M122.
  This kicks out JOE to find a new home.
JOE will be the first one in the SINGLE room number D101.
FRED will be the first one in the SINGLE room number H201.
```

Chapter 5

1. There are at least two problems with representing clusters by a single atom rather than by a separate element class:

   - Readers of the program have no idea which WMEs represent control and which do not. This makes maintenance very difficult.

   - There is no way to manipulate control with a control rule that is general to all clusters; therefore, there is no way to centralize control.

2. The instantiations of the subtask fire first because their first condition element matches the most recent control WME (which is more specific than the `pop-subtask` rule and more recent than instantiations for the `pending-to-active` rule). When all instantiations of the subtask have fired, the `pop-subtask` rule fires because it is instantiated by the most recent control WME, and that is more recent than any control WME that has the value `pending` for the `^status` attribute. Once the most recent control WME is removed, however, the most recent instantiation of the `pending-to-active` rule fires, creating a new control WME with the value `active`, and probably instantiating new subtask rules.

3. - Define the main tasks in your program, and give a symbolic name to each of them.

   - Decide what your control element class will look like. Declare the new element class with a literalize declaration.

   - Add a condition element to each rule to match the control WME.

   - Write the control rules that switch from one task WME to the next.

   - Initialize the control WMEs, or decide where the control WMEs will be created.

   - Set the MEA strategy.

4. A second element class can be created for control that is called `pending` but is otherwise the same as the `subtask` element class:

```
(literalize pending
     name)
```

All control WMEs except the most recent can be created as a `pending` WME:

```
(make pending ^name post-mortem-report)
(make pending ^name execute-actions)
(make pending ^name consult-user)
(make subtask ^name plan-actions))
```

One rule could be used to modify the most recent `pending` WME to be a `subtask` WME:

```
(p  pending-wme-to-subtask-wme
   { <Next-subtask>
      (pending ^name <next-active>) }
   -->
      (make subtask ^name <next-active>)
      (remove <Next-subtask>))
```

5. The control rules would include (1) a rule that changed the subtask name—this rule would fire first during a subtask switch—

```
(p  next-subtask-from-agenda
   { <Control>
      (subtask ^agenda <next>) }
   -->
      (bind <next-task> (litval agenda))
      (bind <remaining> (compute <next-task> + 1))
      (modify <Control> ^name <next>
              ^agenda (substr <Control> <remaining> inf)
                       *expired*))
```

and (2) a rule to move to the next agenda (if there is more than one). This rule would fire only when all the subtask names in the agenda have been used.

```
(p  done-with-agenda
   { <Old-agenda>
      (subtask ^name *expired*) }
   -->
      (remove <Old-agenda>))
```

The `pop-subtask` rule is not used in this case, because the list of future subtask names is in the same WME as the active subtask name. If you "pop" the subtask name, you lose all future subtask names also.

The previous two rules handle both agenda sequencing and subtask popping.

6. You can make an agenda that contains all the subtasks in the cycle. Whenever the control rule that uses the agenda takes a name from the head of the agenda, it can place that name on the end of the vector instead of just deleting it:

```
(p  cycle-subtasks-in-agenda
   { <Control>
      (subtask ^agenda <next>) }
   -->
      (bind <next-task> (litval agenda))
      (bind <remaining> (compute <next-task> + 1))
      (modify <Control> ^name <next>
              ^agenda (substr <Control> <remaining> inf)
                      <next>))
```

The agenda can be made in the initialization subtask or `startup` statement.

7. No, there are still problems. Walk through the following case:

   A => B
   B => C, D, E
   C => F
   F => G

   In this case, when the subtask WME is created for **G**, **F** will be set to `pending` by `hide-interrupted-subtask`. When **G** is popped, **D** (and then **E**) will become active before **F** can continue. If `enable-new-subtask` does not exist, then, for example, **B** will continue right after **C** and before **D** and **E**.

   In general, it is not a good idea to mask interrupted subtasks by changing control WMEs for two reasons:

   - You lose the benefits of *refraction* in conflict resolution, since the control WME is changed.
   - The subtask rules must be rematched when the control WME is changed back from `pending` to `active`, which may be very expensive if these rules are doing expensive matching (see Chapter 10).

8. In this situation, the agenda control technique degenerates to the subtask-stack technique. All subtask elements are made, and will be instantiated in the reverse order from the original placement in the vector attribute. This is now a subtask stack without masking of inactive control WMEs.

9. No `nil`s: All subtasks would be processed, but the last subtask name would eventually be written over each value in the vector attribute and would continually call the last subtask in the vector.

   Two `nil`s: There would be no adverse effects on the execution of the system since the `compute` adds only 1 to `<first-position>`, causing the `substr` to shift the vector one position. The second `nil` in the `modify` is not needed in this case. See Section 2.3.3.

Chapter 6

1. a. The first condition element matches a number WME whose value for the ^value attribute is greater than the value bound to <x>. The second condition element matches a number WME whose value in its second position is the symbol value, and whose value in its third position is greater than the value bound to <x>.

   b. A condition element matching the first is

   ```
   (number ^value 15)
   ```
   A condition element matching the second is

   ```
   (number value 15)
   ```

2. a. Legal syntax.

   ```
   (number ^value 12)
   (number ^value -1)
   ```

   b. Legal syntax. Both left curly brackets are compiled as constant tests.

   ```
   (number ^value |}| 100 nil 1 |}|)
   (number ^value |}| nil 3.14 0 |}| nil)
   ```

   c. Legal syntax. Tests are made on the first three values at ^value.

   ```
   (number ^value anything not-100 17)
   (number ^value nil nil 10 nil)
   ```

   d. Legal syntax. Predicates are treated as constants within a disjunction.

   ```
   (number ^value 0)
   (number ^value |>|)
   ```

   e. Legal syntax. The predicate causes the << to be seen as a constant. And since a disjunction is not open, the >> is also seen as a constant test.

   ```
   (number ^value nil 0 100 |>>|)
   (number ^value not-<< 0 100 |>>| end)
   ```

3. a. In general, for every variable you use in a compute function, add a numeric same-type-as test where the variable is bound. Assuming we expect floating point, here is one solution*

   ```
   (clipboard ^estimate { <best-guess> <=> 1.0 }
              ^receipt > (compute <best-guess> * 1.10))
   ```

*If your OPS5 distinguishes between integer and floating-point atoms, then you would need to write two separate rules—one for integers and one for floating-point atoms.

b. Write an assumption-checking rule that complains if the value of the attribute ^estimate of a clipboard WME is ever a symbol.

```
(p  found-symbolic-estimate
      (clipboard ^estimate <=> symbol)
   -->
      (write |Found a symbolic estimate!|
           |Fix and run again.|)
           (halt))
```

4. a. ppwm—to look for WMEs relevant to the error symptom.

b. back—to back up to the source rule for the error WME. If the error is not in that rule, to continue backing up to the sources of WMEs that were matched.

c. run—to step incrementally through rule firings or to rerun up to a particular cycle.

d. pbreak and wbreak—to halt the recognize-act cycle when a particular rule is about to fire or when a WME enters working memory.

e. watch—to trace the execution of your program at several levels of detail.

f. cs and next—to examine the conflict set and dominating instantiation.

g. matches—to see how a particular rule matches or does not match working memory.

h. wm—to see the working memory elements associated with time tags displayed in output of other commands.

i. make, modify and remove—to effect changes to working memory to test a proposed bug fix.

j. excise—to remove rules from the current session to test a proposed bug fix.

Chapter 7

1. Primary roles played by the values in report!display-neighbor:

	Class	Info	Distinct	Assoc
subtask	X			
^status report		X		
region	X			
^name <what>			X	
^status display-neighbors		X		
neighbor	X			
^of <what>				X
^is <neighbor>				X
region	X			
^name <neighbor>			X	
^color <neighbor-color>		X		

2. a. It could never match. Since the negated input condition element matches every WME that the positive one does (because of the added =), there is a contradiction and no matches succeed.

   b. One solution is to replace the rule note-highest-priority with this one:

```
(p  note-highest-priority
;
; If you find an input with the highest priority
; and there is none at that priority already marked,
; then mark it as the highest priority input.
;
   { <Unmarked-maximum>
      (input ^status received ^priority <max>) }
      - (input ^status received ^priority > <max>)
      - (input ^status received ^priority <max>
               ^highest-priority yes)
   -->
      (modify <Unmarked-maximum>
          ^highest-priority yes))
```

3. The benefits of this technique are as follows:

   - They use refraction to avoid infinite looping.
   - Rules are relatively simple because they do not need extra attributes or conditions to inhibit them from uncontrolled looping.
   - Non-modifying iteration rules are relatively fast—especially if they make no changes to working memory.

- No reset pass is needed to iterate again—simply invoke the subtask again, and the new subtask element refreshes rule matching.

The drawbacks can be summarized as follows:

- To depend on refraction can be dangerous, since it assumes that no other rules modify particular WMEs while in the same subtask as the iteration rules.
- The program cannot enter a subtask using non-modifying iteration unless you want those rules to iterate again. That is, there is no record of the iteration.
- You have no control over the order of WME processing.

4. a. Attribute/value marker:

```
(p  report!display-region
;
; Match a region and report its color assignment.
;
      (subtask ^name report)
   { <Unprinted-region>
      (region ^name <region-name> ^color <assigned-color>
              ^printed <> yes) }
-->
      (write (crlf) <region-name> |is colored|
             <assigned-color>)
      (modify <Unprinted-region> ^printed yes))
```

Another rule would be needed to reset the value of `^printed` if regions were to be displayed more than once during the program's execution.

b. Marker WME:

```
(p  report!display-region
;
; Match a region and report its color assignment.
;
      (subtask ^name report)
      (region ^name <region-name> ^color <assigned-color>)
      - (marker ^reason region-printed ^region <region>)
   -->
      (write (crlf) <region-name> |is colored|
             <assigned-color>)
      (make marker ^reason region-printed ^region <region>))
```

Another rule would be needed to remove the marker if regions were to be displayed more than once during the program's execution.

c. Temporary set:

```
(p  report!initialize-printed-set
;
; Create a temporary set for regions that you print.
;
      (subtask ^name report)
   -->
      (make set ^identifier (genatom)
                ^membership printed-regions))

(p  report!display-region
;
; Match a region that is not a member of the set of
; printed regions, and report its color assignment,
; and make it a member of the printed set.
;
      (subtask ^name report)
      (set ^identifier <printed-set>
           ^membership printed-regions)
   { <Unprinted-region>
      (region ^name <region-name> ^color <assigned-color>
              ^member-of-set <> <printed-set>) }
   -->
      (write (crlf) <region-name> |is colored|
             <assigned-color>)
      (modify <Unprinted-region>
            ^member-of-set <printed-set>))

(p  report!remove-temporary-set
;
; In general, remove the printed temporary set.
; This is a general case of the above rule, so it
; will not fire until all regions are printed.
;
      (subtask ^name report)
   { <Completed-set>
      (set ^membership printed-regions) }
   -->
      (remove <Completed-set>))
```

d. One solution is to use the temporary set technique, which involves adding another attribute to the set WME for each color.

```
(p  report!initialize-printed-set
;
; Create a temporary set for each color used in
```

```
; coloring the regions.  Assumes that ^name is a
; distinguishing value for color, and that there is a
; color wme for each color of region, and that the
; color wmes are not modified in this subtask.
;
      (subtask ^name report)
      (color ^name <which>)
   -->
      (write (crlf) (crlf) |Regions colored| <which> |:|)
      (make set ^identifier (genatom)
         ^membership printed-regions
         ^characteristic <which>))


(p  report!display-region
;
; Match a region that is not a member of the set of
; printed regions, and report its color assignment,
; and make it a member of the printed set.
;
      (subtask ^name report)
      (set ^identifier <printed-set>
           ^membership printed-regions
           ^characteristic <assigned-color>)
   { <Unprinted-region>
      (region ^name <region-name> ^color <assigned-color>
            ^member-of-set <> <printed-set>) }
   -->
      (write (crlf) |   | <region-name>)
      (modify <Unprinted-region>
         ^member-of-set <printed-set>))


(p  report!remove-temporary-set
;
; In general, remove the printed temporary sets.
; This is a general case of the above rule, so it
; will not fire until all regions are printed for
; this set.
;
      (subtask ^name report)
   { <Completed-set>
      (set ^membership printed-regions) }
   -->
      (remove <Completed-set>))
```

5. Shadow the region's population attribute in the region. Write a rule that detects a change in population, and corrects the total in the `color` WME.

```
(p  detect-population-change
;
; When you detect a change in population, then subtract
; the old value from the total, and add the new value
; in to keep the total color-specific population up to date.
;
   { <Changing-region>
      (region ^population <new>
              ^old-population { <old> <> <new> }
              ^color <color-group>) }
   { <Color-totals>
      (color ^name <color-group>
             ^population-total <color-total>) }
   -->
      (modify <Color-totals>
         ^population-total
            (compute (<color-total> - <old>) + <new>))
      (modify <Changing-region>
         ^old-population <new>))
```

6. Define one instance of the data as the source. Then write rules for each copy of that datum that notices when the copy differs from the source, and updates the copy. Chapter 9 describes some techniques that may be used to ensure that consistency is maintained globally, and at a high priority.

7. The following `make` statements describe the map:

```
(make region ^name A)
(make neighbor ^of A ^is B)
(make neighbor ^of A ^is C)
(make neighbor ^of A ^is D)
(make neighbor ^of A ^is E)

(make region ^name B)
(make neighbor ^of B ^is A)
(make neighbor ^of B ^is C)
(make neighbor ^of B ^is E)

(make region ^name C)
(make neighbor ^of C ^is A)
(make neighbor ^of C ^is B)
(make neighbor ^of C ^is D)
```

```
(make neighbor ^of C ^is E)
(make neighbor ^of C ^is F)

(make region ^name D)
(make neighbor ^of D ^is A)
(make neighbor ^of D ^is C)
(make neighbor ^of D ^is E)
(make neighbor ^of D ^is F)

(make region ^name E)
(make neighbor ^of E ^is A)
(make neighbor ^of E ^is B)
(make neighbor ^of E ^is C)
(make neighbor ^of E ^is D)
(make neighbor ^of E ^is F)

(make region ^name F)
(make neighbor ^of F ^is C)
(make neighbor ^of F ^is D)
(make neighbor ^of F ^is E)
```

The following VAX OPS5 program solves the map-coloring problem. There are many other possible implementations. This program counts borders, and then assigns colors to regions in order of largest to smallest number of borders.

```
;; Declarations
(literalize color name)
(literalize region name color border-count)
(literalize neighbor of is color counted)

;; Startup
(startup
    (strategy mea)

    ; They say we only need 4 colors...
    (make color ^name red)
    (make color ^name green)
    (make color ^name blue)
    (make color ^name yellow)

    ; Make subtask wmes
    (make subtask ^name report)
    (make subtask ^name color-regions)
    (make subtask ^name initialize)
```

```
    ; Load in the map
    (@ map.wm))      ; contains regions and neighbors

(p  pop-subtask
;
; In general, pop any subtask that is done.
;
   { <Old-subtask>
      (subtask) }
   -->
      (remove <Old-subtask>))

;; Subtask initialize
;;  Prepare the map for color assignment

(p  initialize!init-border-count
;
; Set any nil border count to 0 so that we can
; begin counting.
;
      (subtask ^name initialize)
   { <Uninitialized-region>
      (region ^border-count nil) }
   -->
      (modify <Uninitialized-region> ^border-count 0))

(p  initialize!count-border
;
; Find an uncounted neighbor wme and count it as
; a border, marking the neighbor wme ^counted yes.
;
      (subtask ^name initialize)
   { <Uncounted-neighbor>
      (neighbor ^of <region> ^counted <> yes) }
   { <Associated-region>
      (region ^name <region>
              ^border-count { <sum> <=> 0 }) }
   -->
      (modify <Associated-region>
         ^border-count (compute <sum> + 1))
      (modify <Uncounted-neighbor> ^counted yes))

;; Subtask color-regions
;;  Color all regions, ordered by number of borders.

(p  color-regions!tell-neighbor-about-color-change
;
```

```
; Use attribute shadowing to propogate a region's
; color to all its neighbor links.
;
     (subtask ^name color-regions)
     (region ^name <changed> ^color <new>)
   { <Neighbor-link>
     (neighbor ^is <changed> ^color <> <new>) }
   -->
     (modify <Neighbor-link> ^color <new>))

(p  color-regions!assign-unused-color
;
; Find an un-colored region with the highest
; border count, and a color not used by any of
; its neighbors.  Use that color for this region.
;
     (subtask ^name color-regions)
   { <Region>
     (region ^color nil ^border-count <max>
             ^name <next-region>) }
     - (region ^color nil ^border-count > <max>)
     (color ^name <free>)
     - (neighbor ^of <next-region> ^color <free>)
   -->
     (modify <Region> ^color <free>))

;; Subtask report
;;   For each region, display the color assignment.

(p  report!display-region
;
; Match a region and report its color assignment.
;
     (subtask ^name report)
     (region ^name <region-name> ^color <assigned-color>)
   -->
     (write (crlf) <region-name> |is colored|
            <assigned-color>))
```

Chapter 8

1. The bind action also fills the result element with the arguments that appear after the variable name. Then it picks up only the first atom in the result element and binds that atom to the variable. This technique can be used to pick up only the first value from a routine which returns a vector of results,

and to discard the rest. For example, the following bind action binds the variable <answer> to the first value of input (the symbol yes if there is no input) and disregards all the other values.

```
(bind <answer> (acceptline yes))
```

2.
```
#include stdio
#include "ops$library:opsdef.h"

/* Convert the given atom to string representation.
 * Return its length.
 */
int atom_to_string (atm, atm_buffer)
int atm;            /* The VAX OPS5 atom */
char atm_buffer[];  /* A buffer large enough to hold the */
                    /*  largest OPS5 atom */
{
    int atm_size;

    if (OPS$INTEGER (atm))
        atm_size = sprintf (atm_buffer, "%d", OPS$CVAN (atm));
    else if (OPS$FLOATING (atm))
        atm_size = sprintf (atm_buffer, "%f", OPS$CVAF (atm));
    else if (OPS$SYMBOL (atm))
        {
        atm_size = OPS$PNAME (atm, atm_buffer, OPS_ATOM_SIZE);
        atm_buffer[atm_size] = '\0'; /* Complete the C string */
        }
    else
        atm_size = 0;

    return atm_size;
} /* atom_to_buffer */
```

3. The following is a solution in VAX PASCAL:

```
MODULE OPS_SQRT;

%INCLUDE 'ops$library:opsdef.pas'

(* OPS_SQRT is a VAX OPS5 RHS or LHS function that computes the
 *  square root of an integer or floating atom, and returns it as
 *  a floating atom.  Symbolic argument yields 0.0 without error.
 *  An argument less than 0 causes a Pascal run-time error in
 *  SQRT.
 *)
[GLOBAL] FUNCTION Ops_sqrt (VAR atom_by_value : INTEGER): INTEGER;
```

```
VAR     atm_arg : INTEGER;
        result : REAL;
        result_atm : INTEGER;
BEGIN
  (* Get the real atom, which VAX OPS passes by value,
   * and Pascal expected by reference.
   *)
  atm_arg := IADDRESS (atom_by_value);

  (* Type the atom and get the SQRT. *)
  IF (OPS$INTEGER (atm_arg))
     THEN result := SQRT (OPS$CVAN (atm_arg))
  ELSE IF (OPS$FLOATING (atm_arg))
     THEN result := SQRT (OPS$CVAF (atm_arg))
  ELSE
     result := 0.0;

  (* Use OPS$VALUE for RHS return mechanism, and also
   * return the floating atom result as the function value.
   *)
  result_atm := OPS$CVFA (result);
  OPS$VALUE (result_atm);
  Ops_sqrt := result_atm;
END;

END.
```

4. *Testing LHS functions.* You can write a rule with a single condition element that contains the call to the function, then create a WME that should match the return value of the function. The following is an example:

```
(p  test!match_wild!success
      (match_wild <pattern>
              { <symbol> <=> word
                (match_wild <pattern> <symbol>) })
   -->
      (write (crlf) Matched <pattern> <symbol> ! (crlf))
      (remove 1))

(p  test!match_wild!failure
      (match_wild <pattern> <symbol>)
   -->
      (write (crlf) <pattern> does not seem to match
                    <symbol> !)
      (remove 1))
```

Testing RHS functions. You can write a rule that contains the function call in the RHS, then create the WME that matches the rule. If the function call is embedded in the `write` action, the function result is printed.

```
(p  retrieve-field
      (get_field <item> <field>)
   -->
      (write (crlf) |(| get_field <item> <field> |)|
             returned: (get_field <item> <field>))
      (remove 1))
```

5. ```
   ;;  DEBUG-MSG facility

   (defvar *debug-detail-level* 0
     "Level of debug-msg detail to be allowed through.")

   (defun set-debug-detail-level ()
     "(CALL SET-DEBUG-DETAIL-LEVEL new-debug-detail-level)
      OPS5 subroutine that sets a new maximum detail value
      for printing debug messages."
     (setf *debug-detail-level* ($parameter 1)))

   (defun debug-msg ()
     "(CALL DEBUG-MSG detail-level atom...)
      An OPS5 subroutine that writes its parameters if the
      first parameter is <= *debug-detail-level*."
     (if (<= ($parameter 1) *debug-detail-level*)
         (let ((num-atoms ($parametercount)))
           (princ "DEBUG: ")
           (do ((position 2 (1+ position)))
               ((> position num-atoms) (terpri))
             (princ ($parameter position))
             (princ " ")))))
   ```

6. One possible solution is to put a description of an event on a queue when the event occurs. Then call the `OPS$COMPLETION` routine with the address of a routine that, when called in the cycle-interrupt window, calls `OPS$COMPLETION` with a 0 argument and creates one or more WMEs for each event description on the queue.

Chapter 9

1. Two distance WMEs are required because the program may need to match from the perspective of either piece.

2. Yes. However, rules that consume these resources must deposit a symbol such as `*empty*` or `nil` instead of using the `substr` function to pop the
   ```

resource vector, and the function `allocate_next` must then allocate only a single resource per call.

3. a. Besides efficiency considerations, subtask-scoped WMEs should be removed from working memory so that their values do not conflict with the same WMEs that are created when the same subtask is enabled again.

   b. The problem with removing all subtask-scoped WMEs while the subtask is still active is that, in some cases, the local is there to prevent a loop. For example, the following rule creates a local for other rules in the subtask to manipulate. If the local is removed before the subtask WME is, this rule will fire again and cause a loop. When the subtask element is removed first, the subtask is disabled before the local is removed, and a loop is avoided.

```
(p  object-entry!initialize-new-block-count
;
; If we do not yet have a new-block-count,
; create one and initialize it to 0.
;
      (subtask ^name object-entry)
      - (local ^content new-block-count)
   -->
      (make local ^content new-block-count ^value 0
          ^scope object-entry))
```

   c. Some possible ways to remove locals:

      i. Remove the subtask when you remove the local. This approach has several problems. For one, you want subtask rules to fire until they are exhausted. You may later add rules that may want to fire after the local is removed from working memory, and they will not get the chance if the subtask is removed at the same time. Also, in removing the subtask, you may be removing an agenda, if such a list is kept in the subtask element.

      ii. Remove the local after you return to the previous subtask. This makes the subtasks less modular, and is generally messy since every calling subtask would require an extra rule to remove the local.

      iii. Follow each invocation of `object-entry` with another containing rules to clean up working memory before returning. This approach would necessitate a companion subtask for each subtask creating local WMEs, and would complicate the control flow. This method has no real benefit over the demon solution.

4. a. Add a control WME to the end of the LHS.

```
(p  demon!unpriced-transmission
   { <Transmission>
      (transmission ^name <name> ^price nil) }
      (subtask ^name select-transmission)
   -->
      (write (crlf) |Oops - a| <name>
                    |has no price!  Enter price:|)
      (modify <Transmission> ^price (accept)))
```

   b. This rule will fire with priority over any rule in the subtask `select-transmission` for any transmission made while that subtask is active.

   c. Normally, under MEA, only those rules associated with the newest subtask are considered for execution during conflict resolution. However, this demon will be able to fire not only when the `select-transmission` subtask is the newest, but also when newer subtask WMEs exist.

   Suppose that, if `select-transmission` cannot find a particular transmission in an external database, it invokes two subtasks, one to design a custom transmission and the other to price it. We want our demon to wait until the program returns from the pricing subtask to `select-transmission` before it complains that the custom-designed transmission does not have a price.

5. Being the first action, the new `subtask` WMEs will have older time tags than will any other WME made through a `make` or `modify` in the same RHS. Thus, a demon that matches one of these WMEs with its first condition element is guaranteed to take precedence over the subtask rules.

Chapter 10

1. The three rules are compiled into a match network resembling the one shown in Figure C.1.
   Removing rule `color-regions!assign-new-color` would have little or no effect, since it shares all its two-input nodes with `color-regions!assign-unused-color`.

2. In the following tables, tokens are represented by WME time tags enclosed in square brackets.

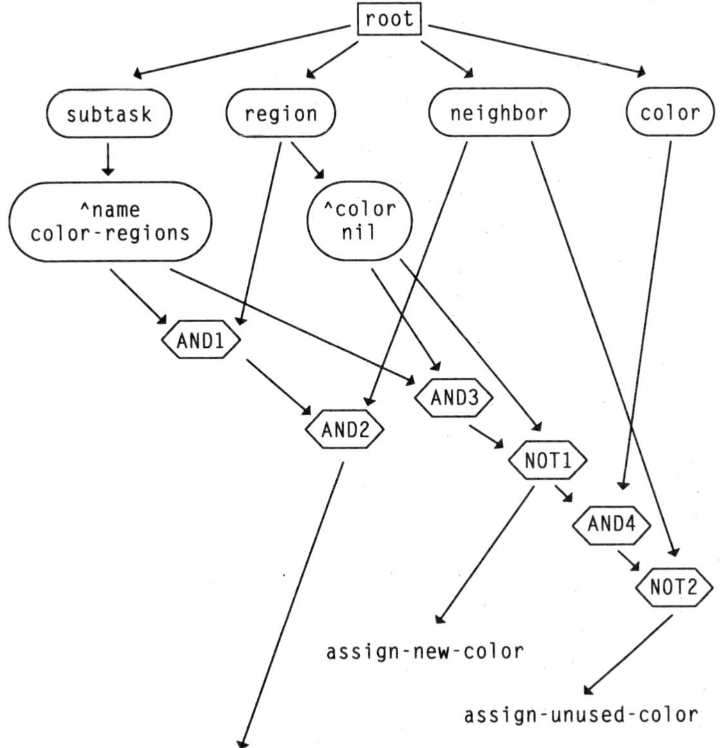

Figure C.1 Solution to Exercise 10.1.

a. Suppose the `make` action creates a `subtask` WME with time tag 1.

Node	Left Memory	Right Memory
AND1	[1]	
AND2		
AND3	[1]	
NOT1		
AND4		
NOT2		

Conflict set:

(empty)

b. Suppose the `make` action creates a `region` WME with time tag 2.

Node	Left Memory	Right Memory
AND1	[1]	[2]
AND2	[1 2]	
AND3	[1]	[2]
NOT1	[1 2]	[2]
AND4	[1 2]	
NOT2		

Conflict set:

```
color-regions!assign-new-color 1 2
```

c. Suppose the `make` action creates a `region` WME with time tag 3.

Node	Left Memory	Right Memory
AND1	[1]	[2] [3]
AND2	[1 2] [1 3]	
AND3	[1]	[2] [3]
NOT1	[1 2] [1 3]	[2] [3]
AND4	[1 3]	
NOT2		

Conflict set:

```
color-regions!assign-new-color 1 3
```

d. A `color` WME is created, time tag 4, and the "crowded" region (time tag 3) is given a color, changing the time tag to 5.

Node	Left Memory	Right Memory
AND1	[1]	[2] [5]
AND2	[1 2] [1 5]	
AND3	[1]	[2]
NOT1	[1 2]	[2]
AND4	[1 2]	[4]
NOT2	[1 2 4]	

Conflict set:

```
color-regions!assign-new-color 1 2
color-regions!assign-unused-color 1 2 4
```

e. This action removes the `subtask` WME, time tag 1, and clears out all left memories.

Node	Left Memory	Right Memory
AND1		[2] [5]
AND2		
AND3		[2]
NOT1		[2]
AND4		[4]
NOT2		

Conflict set:

(empty)

3. a. A RETE match network is shown in Figure C.2.

   b. Without node sharing, the seven shared one-input nodes and two shared two-input nodes would be duplicated in the network.

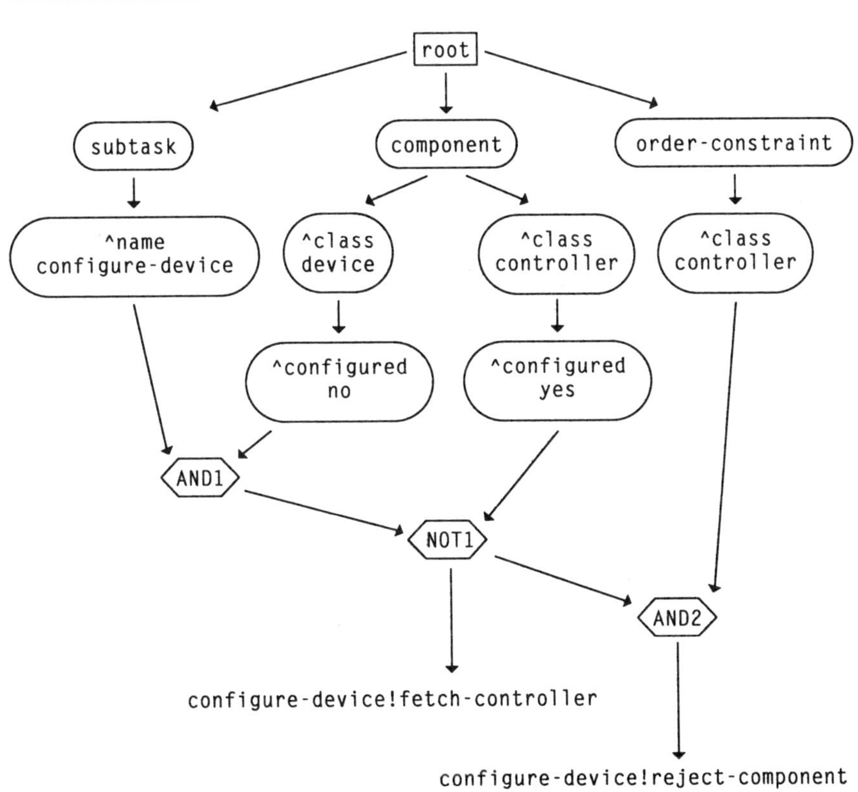

Figure C.2 Solution for Exercise 10.3.

c. Only one two-input node is added when the second rule is compiled.

4. A subtask agenda control strategy does not create a subtask until that subtask is to be executed. A control strategy in which sequencing is accomplished by creating subtask WMEs in reverse order causes unnecessary matching activity in the rules of the older subtask WMEs while the newest subtask is executing. When the subtask WME is kept out of working memory until absolutely necessary, two-input node action is limited.

5. Consider breaking out the `^status` attribute of a line item into another element class. The few rules that modify status may do so by matching and modifying the `line-status` class.

```
(p  schedule!done
;
; When the schedule date is set, mark the line item as
;   ^status scheduled.
;
      (subtask ^name schedule)
      (line-item ^part-name <finished>
                 ^schedule-date <> nil)
   { <Line-status>
      (line-status ^part-name <finished>
                   ^status <> scheduled) }
   -->
      (modify <Line-status> ^status scheduled))
```

Rules that do not depend on the value of the `^status` attribute will not be affected by changes to the `line-status` WME.

One drawback of this technique is the cost of an extra condition element to match status and other attributes of a line item. Another drawback of representing line-item status using two condition elements is the inability to represent attributes from both classes together in a negation.

6. A match network for the rule `area-schedule!temporarily-assign` is shown in Figure C.3.

   a. The sizes of the token memories for all two-input nodes are large, and these nodes are quite active due to the many `part` WMEs. There is significant two-input node action even if no line items are to be scheduled.

   b. Make it more efficient by moving the `line-item` condition element to the second position in the LHS. Now the token memories are all smaller, and they are often cut off by the lack of WMEs matching the more restrictive `line-item` and `build-area` WMEs.

7. First, look at the rule `evaluate-placement!illegal-placement`. Although this rule did not fire during this particular run, it has taken a substantial

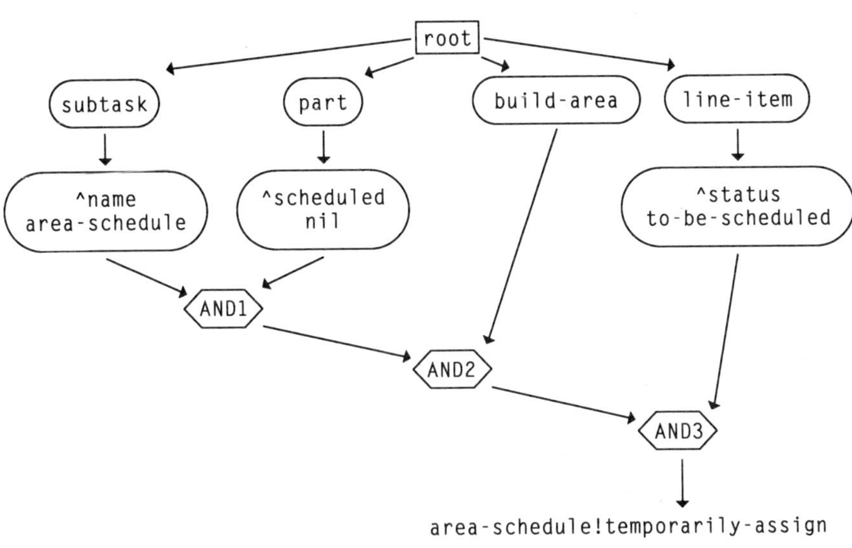

Figure C.3 Solution for Exercise 10.6.

amount of matching time. The rule should be reviewed to see whether it can be removed from the rule base.

If greater efficiency is required, look next at the rules that take the most LHS time. Perhaps the subtask `update-squares`, which accounts for most of the execution time, should be reviewed for improvement or redesign of rules or of representation.

Note that some rules are reported as having no LHS time. This means that either the time spent in two-input nodes was insignificant, or the rule had only a single condition element.

Index

A

D

E

R

U

V

W